Gender and History
Series Editors: Amanda Capern and Louella McCarthy
Gender, Mastery and Slavery
William Henry Foster

Gender, family and sexual relations defined human slavery from its classical origins in Europe to the rise and fall of race-based slavery in the Americas. *Gender, Mastery and Slavery* is one of the first books to explore the importance of men and women to slaveholding across these eras.

Foster argues that at the heart of the successive European institutions of slavery at home and in the New World was the volatile question of women's ability to exert mastery. Facing the challenge to play the 'good mother' in public and private, free women from Rome to Muslim North Africa, to the indigenous tribes of North America, to the antebellum plantations of the southern United States found themselves having to manage economically slaves, servants and captives. At the same time, they had to protect their reputations from various forms of attack and themselves from vilification on a number of fronts.

With the recurrent cultural wars over the maternal role within slavery touching the worlds of politics, warfare, religion, and colonial and imperial rivalries, this lively comparative survey is essential reading for anyone studying, or simply interested in, this key topic in global and gender history.

William Henry Foster is Fellow and Director of Studies in History at Homerton College, University of Cambridge. He is a former holder of the Keasbey Fellowship at Selwyn College, Cambridge, and has previously taught American History at Cornell University and the University of Pennsylvania.

Gender and History
Series editors: Amanda Capern and Louella McCarthy

Gender and History Series
Series Standing Order ISBN 978–14039–9374–8 hardback
(*outside North America only*)

You can receive future titles in this series as they are published by placing a standing order. Please contact your bookseller or, in case of difficulty, write to us at the address below with your name and address, the title of the series and the ISBN quoted above.

Customer Services Department, Macmillan Distribution Ltd

Gender, Mastery and Slavery

From European to Atlantic World Frontiers

William Henry Foster

First published 2010 by
PALGRAVE MACMILLAN

Palgrave Macmillan in the UK is an imprint of Macmillan Publishers Limited,
registered in England, company number 785998, of Houndmills, Basingstoke,
Hampshire RG21 6XS.

Palgrave Macmillan in the US is a division of St Martin's Press LLC,
175 Fifth Avenue, New York, NY 10010.

Palgrave Macmillan is the global academic imprint of the above companies
and has companies and representatives throughout the world.

Palgrave® and Macmillan® are registered trademarks in the United States,
the United Kingdom, Europe and other countries.

ISBN 978–1–4039–8707–5   hardback
ISBN 978–1–4039–8708–2   paperback

This book is printed on paper suitable for recycling and made from fully
managed and sustained forest sources. Logging, pulping and manufacturing
processes are expected to conform to the environmental regulations of the
country of origin.

A catalogue record for this book is available from the British Library.

A catalog record for this book is available from the Library of Congress.

10 9 8 7 6 5 4 3 2 1
19 18 17 16 15 14 13 12 11 10

Printed and bound in Great Britain by
CPI Antony Rowe, Chippenham and Eastbourne

Rose gratias

Contents

Acknowledgements

Two former students made substantial contributions to this book. Rose Grey's extraordinary critical insight is here embroidered throughout. I thank as well Siân Pooley for the idea to start. Terka Acton and Sonya Barker patiently guided the project at Palgrave, and special appreciation is due to Jim Sandos and John Morrill for their unfailing encouragement of my research. Sue Foster helpfully read the final form of the manuscript. My thanks to the faculty of the University of Redlands, California, for the research prize that aided the book's completion. The Principal and Fellows of Homerton College, as well as the Cambridge University Faculty of History, provided the best kind of academic support. Final thanks to Sue and Maddie Foster, Lydia Johansen, Richard Aplenc, John Vigna, David Smith, Michael Robson, and the Greys of Hampshire Cottage – for kindnesses small and large.

An earlier version of portions of the introduction herein appeared in W. H. Foster, 'Women slave owners face their historians: versions of maternalism in Atlantic World slavery', in *Patterns of Prejudice*, volume 41, number 3, (2007): 303–320. Reproduced with permission of the Taylor and Francis Group.

W. H. Foster
Hills Road, Cambridge
18 July, 2009

Introduction: The Problem of Gender, Mastery and Slavery

On the eve of the American Civil War, the wife of a prominent Georgia slave owner wrote of white women affected by their husbands' sexual abuse of enslaved women, asserting in her diary that 'southern women are ... all at heart abolitionists.'[1]

In an 1838 edition of an abolitionist journal called 'The Emancipator,' a recently escaped black slave related how white women would socialise their female children to enforce the slave regime. His mistress regularly sent her daughter out to watch the gangs of slaves working independently and report any laxity. He wrote of the girl that it 'pleased her mightily to have us whipped.'[2]

Another ex-slave testified as to the pragmatism of his female owner. 'Miss never allowed no mistreating of the slaves, 'cause they was raising slaves for the market, and it wouldn't be good business to mistreat 'em.'[3]

Yet another former slave claimed that 'the women are always beat worse than the men,' by their masters. Held in a prison for the correction of refractory slaves in the Carolinas, he witnesses slave women on their knees, begging white men to 'forgive me this time, and I will serve massa well.' Master would say 'you bitch, you've got the devil in you, and I'll get it out.'[4]

In Charleston, South Carolina in June of 1838, a free 'coloured' woman named Patience McKenzie filed a lawsuit against another free 'coloured' woman, Eliza Mackey, for the ownership of a 'mulatto' slave called Joe. Patience had employed Joe for some time, and claimed in court she had paid Eliza for full title and ownership of the man. Eliza claimed that to the contrary, she had been paid by Patience only for Joe's labour. In court, Patience also claimed Joe as her husband.[5]

Men, women and mastery

Gender has always defined human slavery. This book is a survey and an exploration of how women and men – *as women and men* – experienced and represented systems of slavery they made together. It is a story that begins in the deep origins of Europe, Africa, and the Americas – and culminates in the destruction of race-based New World slavery in the nineteenth century.

1

Generations of free women and men defined their relationships with slavery and servitude through *mastery*. Mastery at its simplest level describes the command of servants and slaves as authorised by law or custom. Yet mastery was also something used by the free, the marginal, and even the enslaved themselves in the attempt to shape as much as they could of their physical, spiritual, and intellectual worlds. Mastery was always more dynamic than simple 'authority'. Authority describes the officially prescribed, one-way path of power from the mind of the master to the body of the slave. Mastery, by contrast, describes often conflicting and ambiguous *environments* of power accessed by a variety of people in order to control others, themselves, their immediate surroundings, or their entire cultures. Beyond individuals, mastery defined how whole slave-holding societies understood themselves. Thoughts and controversies about the nature of mastery prompted evolving styles of writing, drama and political propaganda in countless times and places. Thoughts about mastery could define one's land, empire or nation – or defame one's enemy. And the challenges of mastering others showed free men and women, as well as those who aspired to be free, what they should value in themselves or despise in others.

Mastery, men, and women made a volatile mix. The very intensity of the gender dynamics of human slavery riveted the attention of virtually every slaveholding society. To begin to assess the place of gender within mastery and slavery, it is useful to begin with how mastery itself has been described in masculine terms. Theorist of slavery Orlando Patterson has written:

> [w]hat a captive or condemned person lost was the master's gain. The real sweetness of mastery for the slaveholder lay not immediately in profit, but in a lightening of the soul that comes with the realization that at one's feet is another human creature who lives and breathes only for one's self, as a surrogate for one's power, as a living embodiment of one's manhood and honor. Every slavemaster must, in his heart of hearts, have agreed with Nietzsche's celebrated declaration: 'What is good? Everything that heightens the feeling of power in man, the will to power, power itself. What is bad? Everything that is born of weakness. What is happiness? The feeling that power is growing, that resistance is overcome.'[6]

Yet slavery is not always best viewed according to these abstract physical and psychological extremes of authority – of simple domination and subordination. The relationships among men and women against the backdrop of slavery forces the consideration of more dimensions to mastery – those made by complex networks of human relationships in which power was changeable, multi-directional, and often quite subtle. Slaveholding might confirm manhood. But it could challenge, compromise, or defeat manhood as well. And there was also *female* mastery defining slavery as well. Could a female master experience a definition of her *womanhood* through mastery?

The next step of this exploration is to move beyond simple opposition of male and female when discussing sex (biological difference) or gender (how sexual difference was defined, represented and experienced). It is crucial to observe that human slavery was in its essence a *family* institution. Family dynamics created by a mother, father, and children were typically the fundamental points of reference in which slavery was understood and lived. This is not to say that *domestic* slavery was always the dominant setting in the past. Even large groups of agricultural, public or military slaves could assume the ideological status of children in their societies. Relations of slave and master were universally seen as metaphorical relationships between public and private mothers and fathers on one hand, and their children/slaves on the other. Slaves (and associated coerced labourers such as indentured or convict servants) constituted whole categories of people deemed incapable of adulthood, and in need of supervision by their metaphorical or 'fictive' parents. Mastery, like slavery, was a family dynamic. Beyond simple relationships of the powerful and the powerless, family-based mastery meant that subordination could be infused with allegiance or the need for protection and aid. In other words, societal-scale bondage and family bonds were inextricably linked.

The family-centred aspects of slavery have been discussed most often by historians in the context of 'paternalism'. This idea places the slaves as metaphorical children under the guiding hand of the father/master. Much less evident in the writings around slavery are the beliefs and actions surrounding the female master, something that might be termed *maternalism*. Maternalism is in several respects the historical key to understanding the intersection of gender, mastery and slavery. The maternal role was often the only one authorised by custom to give free women legitimate authority over slaves. Those who were not actual high-status mothers made concerted efforts to be considered nevertheless to inhabit a respected maternal role, lest they be under social suspicion of betraying womanhood with tyranny, sexual depravity, or some combination of both. Should this happen, these women would then be unable to contribute to the economic success of herself, her family, and community. Yet maternalism was not what some have termed "exceptional power" – the wielding in mastery in a man's absence. It has its own, separate history. Over the centuries, western slavery placed free women in an almost paradoxical position. Their management skills were encouraged because they were greatly needed economically, yet at the same time her proximity to enslaved people made her powerful – and thus culturally dangerous. Slaveholding societies both depended on and were profoundly troubled by women's mastery.

Of course, others who were neither metaphorical fathers nor mothers contributed to the mastery that supported slavery. Older sons and daughters (the latter especially important for domestic management) grew into their mastery typically starting at a young age. Skilled slaves for their part might transcend the usual abjection of their status. Such people as nurses, business managers, land stewards, foremen, tutors, highly skilled artisans, and child-minders existed passively as slaves carrying out the will of others. Yet these ancillaries also acted with their own circumscribed agency, helping their own masters grow in freedom and authority. For their part, slaves and other kinds of bondservants sometimes chose willingly, if partially, to define themselves by the character and attributes of the owner family. Of course, even the most privileged of slaves served the interests of a free family at the expense of their own. Serving 'fictive' fathers and mothers came at the cost of their own potential to act as fathers, mothers, and siblings and children. One fundamental pain of servitude for women and men was their inability to define their own family life, location, social role, and sexual expression.

Traditionally, studies of slavery have presented 'men' and 'women' as separate and mutually opposed camps. Accordingly, four major questions have preoccupied historians of gender and slavery. First, did slavery exaggerate and ultimately expand the private and public power of an elite patriarch – accelerating male prerogative? Second, were the wives and daughters of these men, so-called 'free' women, merely the most privileged 'slaves'? Third, was the condition of bondage in its various forms harder to bear for men, whose manhood was necessarily assaulted in the process of enduring servitude, or, was it worse for women, whose identities relative to work, family, and personal and bodily integrity were constantly besieged? Fourth, who was able to forge relationships with whom legitimately across slave/free boundaries?

A rigorous overview of mastery exercised by men and women separately and together can help illuminate these older questions as well as help define new ones. To begin, historians and social theorists of gender and slavery have traditionally taken their cue from an archetypical antebellum American plantation mistress and diarist, Mary Boykin Chesnut, who wrote on the eve of the American Civil War that 'there is no slave, after all like a wife ... all married women, all children and girls who live in their father's house, are slaves.'[7]

Early studies of women and slavery virtually precluded the possibility of female mastery as separate from the authority of the master. One pioneer in this field, Gerda Lerner, outlined a link between women and slavery using evidence from ancient Mesopotamia, arguing that human slavery only became possible with the fundamental and general subordination of women in complex societies. In this model, there might have been little apparent or functional difference between matrimony and concubinage.[8] Wives and female slaves were therefore variants of the same basic commodity, subject to transfer and use by networks of men. By implication, whatever power a free woman possessed served as a guided instrument of some version of father-rule known generically and imprecisely as 'patriarchy'. Following this were a multitude of specific studies placing free woman clearly among the categories of dependency and domestic enslavement. The extreme hierarchies of slavery in turn gave their husbands and fathers extraordinary authority in the context of their times. In his description of the Germanic tribes of the Middle Ages, for example, J. Thorsten Sellin vividly recounts that their wives, like slaves, could be stripped and flogged through the streets for the crime of infidelity. Like slaves, the former wife's ability to marry would then be circumscribed.[9] Wealthy widows, noblewomen, or others who by chance and character exercised the quality of authority typical of a man are frequently considered of relatively marginal historical importance by virtue of accidental circumstances.[10]

By contrast, local studies of household management began to allow for the possibility of a separate, yet not independent, mastery among free women by emphasising the sheer scale on which women's household management of slaves could be carried out. Works on the Roman household for example have shown imperial women in direct charge of vast households where they would supervise an array of slaves in different tasks (most of them men). Crucial to understanding female mastery is first to understand that it could exist even in reference to a woman who was dependent on men, her family, and a whole array of social connections and obligations. Second, it credits supervision as power. One did not need to be the highest ranking member of the household to wield a separate mastery. However, imperial Roman matrons however certainly fit the descriptions of exceptional in terms of a general population.[11]

Important studies on sexuality within slavery expanded these perspectives. These scholars emphasised sexual dominance as a function of exerting violent control, both over women and conquered, lower-ranking men. Ruth Mazzo Karras, for example, writing of medieval Scandinavia, has observed that across time and space, free men's sexual access to women of all statuses was rarely seriously impeded and was 'about power and not simply about sexual desire or release of sexual energy. The men of any one group dominate the women of their own group; they also dominate the lower groups, in part through the appropriation of the others women.'[12] The domination of female victims then also helped conquerors exert mastery over other men, and the possibility of free women's mastery is eliminated entirely (signified by their own lack of sexual access to those same subordinated men).

The study of sexual contact between free men and male slaves, however, complicated the view. For example, Richard Trexler has amplified Karras's argument while challenging Lerner on the question of who was the target of male mastery. Trexler considered the situation in which a free man placed himself in a role of sexual dominance over an enslaved male. Beginning with the lessons of antiquity, he proposed that in Athens and on into the later history of Western Europe, reciprocal and hierarchical relationships with other men defined masculine social identity more than any other factor.[13] Male sexual dominance of other men accomplished this directly. Yet even male sexual exploitation of females from a conquered or dishonoured rival group was an act reinforcing the conquest of other men – the fathers, husbands, and brothers of the female victims. The ultimate target of sexual conquest then was not women themselves, as Lerner might have it, but instead the political mastery that came from bodily sovereignty over those who had previously run the vanquished society. Trexler cites one Greek writer, Xenophon, who claims that even the sexual violation of captive women could be in preparation for the true objective, the conquest of male concubines who they had either brought with them or captured on a campaign.[14]

However, it is the American historiographical tradition that has tended to be extremely influential on gender and slavery studies more generally. For example, historians who have explored connections between women and slavery in pre-1865 America have often concluded that intricate relationships existed among race, sexual license and gender roles in plantation economies. These developed over time and created situations in which free, white women were increasingly socially marginalised from pragmatic influence even as they rose in theoretical status. In one such schema forged by Kathleen Brown, planter-husbands manipulated the levers of public law, social thought, and coercive force to accomplish the simultaneous subjugation of white women as well as non-whites of both sexes.[15] From the point of view of female mastery, this is a model of decline over time, at least in its most visible aspects.

In addition to the confluence of race and gender, the violence endemic in American slavery has also been seen to define the possibility for female mastery. One study by eminent historian Drew Gilpin Faust surveyed the slaveholding women of the American Civil War south (1861–5) and found a tendency for profound discomfort with the prospect of directing physical control and violence against a restive wartime slave population. Slavery confronted Victorian-era women with what they perceived to be their physical and emotional limitations in their husband's houses and fields.[16]

A subsequent and equally useful study, this one by Kirsten Wood, changed the conditions of this experiment. Rather than surveying the distorting effects of wartime, the exceptional condition was widowhood in the decades leading up to the war. Through the loss of a husband a troubled history of what Wood calls 'fictive mastery' was derived. A widow's mastery might be 'fictive' because her authority over her own slaves was placed within a web of male authority from which she could never escape: indirect oversight by relatives, employed overseers who would not listen to their female employers, and neighbours who could withhold access to local economic networks. All these applied social pressure to women wishing to behave acceptably as women, and even slaves who doubted a woman could physically enforce her regime.[17]

These relationships were not uncomplicated. In another innovative study that examined how men could define female mastery, mistresses in colonial Virginia who were victimised by actual and threatened violence from their own indentured servants or slaves were most likely to be supported in their authority by their own husbands and local authorities who upheld the principle (and the economic benefits) of female mastery. The author of the study, Terri L. Snyder, also showed though how subordinate males proved remarkably willing to resist practical female mastery – leaving the women in ambivalent and precarious positions.[18]

All these works represent laudable innovations. Yet in addition to the evolution of thought about these relationships within, the historian needs to be constantly aware of the outsized influence that case studies concerning American slavery have tended to exert on the study of the rest of the world. The specific associations among gender, race and violence in the American past cannot be universally applied without due rigour or problems can result. One study, for example, has plausibly speculated that free Catholic Italian women during the Renaissance 'might prefer to take on the challenge of directing female rather than male slaves', because 'female workers were considered more tractable than male' – citing previous work on the American antebellum south.[19] Clearly there is a need for more comprehensive models.

Thinking about female mastery in terms of legitimate authority is one way reliance on a single national example has been transcended. The crucial link was that established between mastery and motherhood. The idea was that wives and female slaves were not often interchangeable because a wife and mother as an *authority* figure might be socially necessary – to the point of being indispensable. Marriage often meant subordination to one man only – while granting authority over family members and workers of both sexes. It is necessary to be sensitive to the reality that these women learned to reconcile the roles of subordinate and manager each day of their lives.

Margaret Sommerville, a historian of gender and authority in early modern Europe, has worked out two essential ideas applicable to female mastery

in the context of motherhood. She observed first the seemingly obvio
often overlooked reality that mistresses were as common as masters – imply...
that while mistresses collectively were subordinate to masters, they were also
a social force when the sum of their individual activities are considered. Sommerville also reminds us that the only household member with a higher status
than the mistress was the master – with servants and slaves joining children in
owing allegiance and obedience to both fictive parents.[20] One did not need to
inhabit an imperial household to hold authority. Ordinary relative social status
granted licence to the mother that could transcend the disabilities of 'women'.
This is not to say there were never conflicts between the role of mother and
woman. Indeed the conflict produced many fundamental controversies over
female mastery and the nature of social authority itself.

The association, then, of mastery and motherhood is broadly useful, but
potentially treacherous. What, after all, is the character of motherhood? Historians, again taking their cues from the nineteenth-century southern United
States, have associated female slaveholding and management with maternal
benevolence. Indeed, some southern women wrote that they understood their
role as caretaking, thus presenting a kinder, gentler version of the master's face.
It would be a mistake, however, to generally assume that the maternal role in
slavery was something consistent, universally understood and uncontested.
Nor was it always or even often intended, as some have argued, to smooth the
rough and cruel edges of slavery. Even where the maternal role was accepted
by free and slave alike, it could be capable of carrying out calculating, rational
plans and enforcing rigorous, even cruel, slave regimes. Defining 'maternalism'
is no less involved than defining the closely related concept of 'female mastery'.

Another complication of seeing mastery clearly is that free men and free
women have not received equal and balanced portrayals. The male master is frequently considered from both an economic and cultural perspective; he is shown
trading and exploiting labour to produce commodities while at the same time
envisioning himself as the metaphorical father to all his dependants – servants,
slaves, wife and children. Free women by contrast are most often seen as con-
ductors and mediators of the cultural, household-based family relationships created by slavery. Yet, with a few recent and notable exceptions, the economic
importance of maternal management within slavery is not usually considered to
the point where it can be evaluated meaningfully.

One of the main purposes of this book is to further develop female mastery
and maternalism in order that a fuller picture of gender and slavery may come
into focus. Tested here is the hypothesis that free women, with remarkable
consistency, tended to approach slavery and servitude with as much rationality (as well as irrationality) as did their husbands, fathers and sons. But there is
the question as well of shared versus separate goals. Did women act with men
conservatively as masters to combat the radical uncertainties of their worlds –
seeking to reinforce and protect the economic and social hierarchies that included
slavery? Or, did women and men use their mastery together to create altogether
new worlds of status relationships in public and private?

It is plain over the sweep of world history that free women did not always,
or even often, act in lockstep with their male counterparts. Master and

mistress did not often occupy the same status or perform the same roles. Female mastery is best defined within the larger context of battles at the *mid-levels* of authority. These mid-levels were inhabited by free women, overseers and managers of both sexes, freedpersons and older children. In other words, authority hierarchies were in constant flux, surrounded by whole societies in motion. They were being defined by struggles among people who were neither the most nor the least powerful.

Which brings us full circle back to the history of the family. This study of the mid-levels of power does not seek to replace a more exclusive focus on patriarchy and paternalism so much as establish a broader context. Family mastery has been underappreciated for its crucial role in public discourse and propaganda in which a society was judged. A female master was not simply a flesh-and-blood woman. She was also part of a collective symbol prompting always controversial and sometimes explosive meanings. A long view of gender and slavery is necessary to see recurring patterns, leading to the inescapable conclusion that gendered assumptions of New World slavery did not simply emerge from nothing. They were the end result of a long heritage centuries in the making on all sides of the Atlantic.

The final objective here is to present the individual intimacies of the relations among all categories of the free and unfree. Rightly or wrongly, historians of slavery have tended to treat slavery as an exceptional, exotic human condition. This partly originates in the fact that most written records emerge from an age when abolition was an internationally potent force. But it cannot be the complete story. There was a whole other reality to slavery that is far more elusive for the historian to recapture. This is the routine, unremarkable aspects of slavery – the degree to which coerced labour was incorporated and absorbed into ordinary life. As such, slavery was defined by all the complex unpredictability of day-to-day interactions at all possible levels. Looking at slavery from the vantage point of modernity (and postmodernity), it is essential to focus on emotion and visibility. Who was 'invisible' to their masters? Who was entitled to 'see' and legitimately 'look upon' another across lines of social hierarchy, was extraordinarily complex in the smaller-scale communities that existed before the nineteenth century. Whether guided by love, hate or some complex mix of emotions, servants, slaves and masters acted interdependently, using intimate, exclusive forms of communication. Most important, these interactions among masters, servants and slaves did not always produce the expected, shared values of a certain single race, ethnicity, age or sex. The remarkably flexible and adaptable calculations of gendered mastery produced unexpected alliances and rivalries.

The examination of gendered mastery – the subject of this book – then leads directly to a new set of questions. First, were the mastery practised by men, and the mastery practised by women, fundamentally different? Did men and women act together to build unfree labour systems? Did they challenge one another for supremacy? Or did they simply pursue separate goals? How were these versions of mastery perceived differently by others – servants and slaves as well as judges, priests and social observers? Does mastery let us link slavery to other forms of servitude: practices of indentured servitude, convict labour and race-based slavery so often assumed to be mutually exclusive? And finally, as just discussed, how did mastery of men and women expose the inner structures of family, social hierarchy, and honour and shame within any of these societies?

Purpose and outline of the book

This book is a synthesis. It links many previously unrelated works of scholarship from around the world and across key time periods, culminating in the abolition of slavery in the Americas. It is also an extended essay using documentary sources to argue for the fundamental relationship of gender and slavery through mastery – identifying the patterns emerging over time in the Christian west, its borderlands and diasporas. It is hoped this approach will prove useful to students and scholars approaching the subject with a variety of interests – whether the focus is on slavery generally as a human institution, or on a particular time and place. Within each chapter, the American experience is related to how predecessor societies dealt with the same problems and complications in ways similar and dissimilar. In one sense this is a comparative history. However, the societies examined here often influenced and affected the practices of others, directly or indirectly. While there might seem for example to be a great distance between ancient Hebrews or classical Rome and nineteenth-century America, slaveholders in the latter frequently used biblical and classical texts to justify, explain and design their actions. Similarly, the architects and beneficiaries of the Atlantic slave trade – a vast 'slave frontier' – were influenced by the other slave frontier of the time, that of mutual enslavement separating (and binding together) Christian Europe and Muslim North Africa.

In a book of wide scope and introductory length, the evidence presented herein is necessarily selective. The case studies and developments described here are not meant to be comprehensive or definitive, but instead to provoke questions. Above all, it is hoped that these examples might serve as a central point of departure for both broader and more specific work on the vast and intimate interrelationships of gender and slavery.

This book will explore gender and slavery according to four thematic categories, each corresponding to a chapter of the book: the birth of maternalism, conquest, empire and nation. Each is briefly introduced here:

The birth of maternalism: Christian, Muslim, and Hebrew traditions

In spite of the rivalries and animosities that set them apart, Islam, Judaism and Christianity possessed aspects of remarkable consistency on questions of maternalism and paternalism. Each faith possessed founding texts in which the new (or renewed) faith was invested closely in the figure of the virtuous male slave. These stories portrayed masculine, religious virtue coming of age in the process of overcoming the maternal but faithless figure of the female slaveholder. Foundational cultural stories abounded of Christian men finding virtue by defeating the pleasure-addicted pagan women who held them. Likewise, male slaves of unbeliever women used the transformative experience of transcending fictive childhood to prove themselves stalwart, virile followers of the prophet Mohammad. In finding faith they broke free of the metaphorical mothers who held them. Jewish tradition alone resisted the idea of this kind of redemption, with men who languished under always-suspect female Jewish mastery being dishonoured outcasts. Nevertheless, the juxtapostion of motherhood and slave ownership was an important metaphor for Hebrew writers and religious commentators. Tight controls on free female behaviour were used to police and question the honour of Jewish women, who for their part often pursued their own agendas outside of rabbinical dictates. Accordingly, each group of faith-oriented societies, behind the rhetoric, adapted practical customs for the real maternal authority on which they were all dependent. And women for themselves developed their own maternal mastery for practical governance – separate if not often independent. Also remarkably constant among these foundational peoples was the virtually unlimited paternal and patriarchal mastery that could be attained. Yet male mastery was rarely if ever unlimited to the point that it was free of public sanction. Particularly monstrous behaviour could be curbed for the sake of public piety and order, both formally and informally.

We see in the origins of these three traditions very private battles becoming not only public, but iconic and religiously vital. The far-flung, and internally varied, religious-cultural systems had to equip themselves to weather all kinds of reversals, disorder and instability. Situations of masters serving former slaves and masters fallen through their own actions acquired special piquancy and explosiveness when they involved reversals, inversions or distortions of established gender roles. For women to rule men was not only a feared and shameful reality (if male writers are a reliable guide) but an immensely powerful social metaphor. War, stress, pestilence, decay or hubris could radically upset or sustain gender norms, and when the society featured slavery, it was naturally drawn into the discourse. The Christian tradition tested men against female sexuality, communalism, and the necessity for men to refrain from crime and violence against honourable women. Muslims, Jews and Christians who overcame temptations laid by slavery – mastering mastery – could inform and reassure individuals, families and peoples of their own virtue and civic honour, expressed by sure masculine control. The dynamics of gender and slavery provided a cultural language for countless societies and peoples to turn temporary defeats and setbacks into ultimate cultural victories. In all of these struggles, ideas about what should be restricted in a devout slaveholding family clashed with practical realities about what had to be done to sustain its economic productivity. All of these patterns would remain in the diasporas of these founding peoples.

Europeans, Native Americans and the Muslim world

The private battles of the maternal and paternal ultimately extended to define whole frontiers, colonial enterprises and the empires that supported them. This represents the ultimate extension of a principle outlined above – that the health and or depravity of a foreign people could be determined by their perceived conduct as enslavers and the enslaved.

Related to gendered conquest is the question of gendered frontier. The-orists of frontier history have argued that for many times and places it is more useful to think of a frontier as a nebulous zone of cultural interpenetration rather than a strict line of demarcation separating one people from another.[21] The two major, long-enduring frontiers examined in the second chapter, the Mediterranean frontier separating the Muslim and Christian worlds and the European/Native American frontier, each included mutual enslavement as one among many types of cultural interaction. Gender was at the core of the exchange. From the prevailing Christian view, Muslim male and female masters each possessed distinctive characteristics of their land and faith, to be derided as well as feared. Male and female Muslim slaves in Europe showed the vulner-ability of their people and faith as a whole. A parallel, revealing dynamic was seen contemporaneously in frontier America. The enslavement and defeat of Native American men imparted in one sense evidence of European prowess, but also undercut alliances that some Europeans felt needed to be built with the indigenous peoples.

Yet it was Europeans in peril from Muslim women and men, as well as Native American men and women, that proved the most resonant to Europeans. Sodomy discourse condemned Muslim and Native male mastery, providing met-aphors for the imagined defective manhood of Christendom's rivals. Enslaved boys in this literature who appeared as victims of their masters served to shame the Christian authorities who had failed to protect them. The far-flung fron-tiers also made European men both heroic and dangerous. Stories of encounters with Muslim and Native American societies reconstituted the older, three-faith tradition of overcoming the maternal (and paternal) mastery of their captors. Religious, cultural and even sexual enticements, though, could induce captured and enslaved European men to turn the tables on their countrymen and become destructive renegades, converting to the faith and lifestyle of their Muslim ene-mies. To do so was a powerful rebuke to home societies, which internal critics seize upon to highlight weaknesses at home. Men could become illegitimately masterful through the rebirth of apostasy, but so could women. Special venom was reserved for white female captives who derived a new savage mastery from their Muslim and Native husbands and lovers, and wielded it over their less fortunate former countrymen – now their slaves.

Of course, the experience was not one-sided. Muslim and Native American peoples used the honour and shame of mastery and subordination for their own purposes as weapons in cultural and physical warfare, which came to influence the behaviours of the Europeans in turn. Although Christian propa-gandists made much of the enslavement practices of Muslims and to a differ-ent and lesser degree Native Americans, the captors had their own intensions that intentionally fed these fears. European fears of powerful women proved congruent for example with Muslim family management practices in which a woman could supervise slaves, 'unveiled, in the privacy of their homes'. Native American practices, even from pre-contact times, had been used to humili-ate captive warriors by treating them as women. The thread of feminisation of men, and their efforts to overcome the loss of mastery, defined both these frontiers.

Empire and white servitude

Questions of frontier immediately lead to questions of empire. When powerful European empires projected out into the New World they dramatically reinvented the mastery – and the gendered mastery – within their own social structures. In different ways and for varied lengths of time according to their needs, these powers subjected their own people to servitude in indentured and convict systems that preceded or supplemented race-based slavery.

Traditionally in slavery studies, non-permanent statuses of servitude have been excluded or marginalised, especially where multi-generational slavery has been based on race. There are good reasons for this separation when economic and social history are concerned. Yet indentured and convict systems had certain crucial qualities in common with true slavery, in much the same manner as intercultural captivity and frontier slavery inform one another. When white indentured or convict servants referred to themselves in writing as being treated as 'slaves', we cannot wholly dismiss the sentiment as a flight of dramatic complaint. When seen through the framework of gendered mastery, the cultural understandings of slavery and other forms of servitude are closely related.

The first factor was deprivation of family in favour of a free family to serve. As a rule, male and female bondservants were forbidden from starting families, and indeed barred from sexual expression. If a servant had a family, forced separation was the norm. Historians often argue that eventual freedom was the most important long-term difference separating a bondservant mentally and emotionally from a slave, but understandably, short and medium-term deprivations weighed very heavily on white servants (especially since survival to the end of a term was uncertain, and terms could be extended as punishment). The problem was not so much the pains of sexual frustration (court records reveal plenty of illicit opportunities taken), but that the fundamental definition of manhood and womanhood for western Europeans was the realisation of procreation. Servitude destroyed at least for a time a full sense of themselves as gendered as well as sexual beings. This proved especially painful for those who had lived as free adults.

The tension surrounding gender and status in imperial environments brought up traditional struggles which are now long familiar to those in the Christian west. Critics of the colonies and their people saw in vengeful American mistresses what critics of paganism had perceived 1,500 years before. The New World bore the potential to turn virtuous mothers into monsters, and what better way to illustrate this than to describe violent or unnatural treatment of servants. And in certain colonies experiencing a demographic shortage of women, the sudden promotion of socially marginal white women to mistresses of property might undermine their legitimacy (and raised the resentment of male servants who enjoyed no such pathway).

For their part, male masters accused of turning to shameful, unmanly sexual violence against helpless white female servants were also asserting a new form of patriarchalism. For the male masters at least, assertion of mastery was precisely the objective of sexual violence and domination. Their expansion of the authoritarian role courtesy of bonded servitude, and later slavery, became central to the larger frameworks of political organization in the British North American colonies.[22] Yet in the face of criticism, masters might remain defensive about their colonies when criticised by their European cousins. The New World, it seemed, could turn men as well as women into monsters.

Also defining white servitude were individual relationships. Those masters and servants sharing a cultural heritage had ways of communicating with one another that proved far more complex and ambiguous than their absolute statuses would suggest. For men and women of all ranks, servitude proved an intimate, personal struggle of the body and the mind. As was the case with some permanent slaves, indentured and convict servants could acculturate to the values of their masters, although the failed promise of upward mobility for many fed social unrest. Even emotional attachments between servant and free might fulfil the needs of the individuals involved – but at the cost of creating innumerable problems to accepted social orders.

Finally, white servitude built new alliances and communities in the American setting. Though the promotion of marginal females to high status and the depravity of men both high and low-born might have led some to think of America as a topsy-turvy world thanks to its servitude systems, the meeting of various peoples across statuses gave birth to an informal frontier within the colonies. Beyond its ideological challenges white servitude put marginal peoples of different races and origins into close enough proximity to one another to create uniquely American communities and relationships which questioned the European, African, and indigenous Native American traditions that were brought together.

Race and nation

The book concludes with a fourth chapter, exploring the legacies of gender and mastery in the United States of America. While race is justifiably thought of as having been the master determiner of status there, the intricacies of gender relations within enslaved and free American families complicated the picture substantially. And in a pattern reminiscent of previous chapters, private family struggles over slavery became profoundly significant as symbols or order, disorder, legitimacy and depravity to a wider American, and international, public.

Two phenomena dominated the American past in the eyes of the people who made it and later chronicled it as historians: white male paternalism and sexual violence against enslaved black women. Paternalism in this context consisted of the benevolent stance of control that a master assumed over his fictive, enslaved 'children'. Whether or not this was a sincerely held belief and persona among masters, or merely an exercise in self-deception, is debatable and doubtless varied between individuals. Yet this paternalism came to have vital political import in defending slavery from its critics and attackers within and outside the United States. Slavery was beneficial, this line of reasoning went, because slaves, as inferior beings, needed the father figure to fulfil the limited potential of their lives, which meant performing work in exchange for basic care and (eventually) religious instruction. Slavery, the justification continued, was more benevolent than even industrial capitalism because unlike the northern free states and Britain, which disposed of workers who had ceased to be useful, slavery looked after the vulnerable from cradle to grave. Their critics were not impressed. The graves, of course, would have been unmarked, and the paternalism model was simplistic to a ludicrous extent.

The second prominent American feature, sexual violence, alone negated this argument entirely. An enslaved woman targeted for rape was obviously not a conscientiously, spiritually cared-for dependant and fictive child.

In other ways, the American experience with race and slavery pertaining to gender was at once exceptional and typical of long-established patterns. In terms of the exceptional, race did produce a social structure that eliminated much of the fear and flexibility of upward and downward mobility which had so characterized the history of world slavery. Although reversals (such as sensationalistic stories of helpless 'white slave' children) were sometimes employed in fiction and political propaganda to serve abolitionist purposes, free and the slave could not realistically change places with one another in a racialised system. This racial hierarchy would seem to allow for the white southern patriarchs in question to be in unusually and utterly secure positions. But in fact, American slavery is also the story of paternalism under siege. Here we see the old patterns. Tyrannical plantation mistresses, supposedly given alternately to violence and sexual debauchery, became the living symbol of the evils of the institution. Paternalists by contrast went to pains to portray their wives and daughters as creatures of exceptional refinement and gentility, maternal when necessary but ultimately separate from the unpleasantness of managing slaves. As their ancestors had done, slaveholding women themselves negotiated a minefield of assigned identities and sought competence and pragmatism in their managerial roles.

The great public and private complications of slavery, then still originated in the mid-levels of authority. That those interactions were often hidden beneath the extremes of master and slave only added to their potential power to disrupt a family or society. And it was unpredictable – power striking out in every direction, then back on itself. Mastery, as ever, was like lightning: it was difficult to catch in any bottle.

1

Gender, Mastery and Maternalism: Christian, Muslim and Hebrew Traditions

Maternalism

When attention is focused on free families in slaveholding societies, the emphasis naturally falls upon the authority of the father. Countless eyewitness testimonies and historians' works have developed an image of the universal male household head, receiving his legitimate authority from the fountainhead of a masculine god, clergy or political leadership. Public and private authority were often two ends of the same conduit of power. This chapter is designed to add to and complicate that model by exploring an alternative, additional force at the centre of mastery: maternalism – a female equivalent of father-rule. Sometimes the maternal added to the gravitational centre of the paternal. Sometimes the gravity of mother-rule pulled in a direction entirely its own. It was always socially vital.

Maternalism reflects the importance of the role of the mother, giving it centre-stage in the disputes over free women's roles and behaviour within slavery. As mentioned in the introduction, the central irony of this conflict was that men who constructed negative portraits of female mastery often depended economically, directly or indirectly, upon the managerial and practical skills of real, flesh-and-blood women. For these women themselves, maternal status was often the only means available to fully establish their legitimate use of authority and, by extension, their complex forms of mastery. It was generally in the interest of unattached women without dependants, be they younger daughters or older widows, to access the mantle of the mother. This maximised their chances of being taken seriously by their families, neighbours, male clerical and secular authorities – and by their servants and slaves. But it was often a narrow, treacherous path. Deviations from the maternal could place women in danger of being used in negative cultural or religious propaganda or being attacked themselves.

There was a symmetry with which maternalism and slavery created one another in the realms of family, sexuality, law, propaganda and culture. Christian, Muslim and Jewish traditions across Europe, the Mediterranean and the Near

East would serve as antecedents to later European and Euro-American slavery systems.

Hebrew origins

Some patterns of Jewish gender and mastery are laid down in the Old Testament and later developed in the Talmud and rabbinical literature. These examples are important for understanding the culture of one of the three principal faiths giving rise to Mediterranean and ultimately European civilisation.

One of the archetypical stories appears as early as Genesis, its contours to be iconic and endlessly reinvented through the ages. Joseph in Egyptian bondage is appointed by his master Potiphar to manage his affairs. But he quickly lands in peril:

> And it came to pass after these things, that his master's wife cast her eyes upon Joseph; and she said, Lie with me.[1]

Joseph refused, asserting to his mistress that he outranked her in the household. She would not be dissuaded:

> And she caught him by his garment, saying Lie with me: and he left his garment in her hand, and fled, and got him out.[2]

This resulted in a predictable cascade of events, with the wife using the cast-off garment as evidence of his attack against her, prompting Potiphar to order Joseph's indefinite imprisonment. Within this short, devastating tale are the fundamental elements of the struggle over gendered mastery. Who would prevail, the master's wife; or a trusted male slave? Who was virtuous, who was depraved? Could a woman of influence hope to refuse the opportunity for carnal and moral corruption granted by slavery? The crucial detail of course was that Potiphar's wife was a foreigner, a non-Hebrew, an Egyptian. Her debauchery was a cultural and religious attack. Yet as the history of the Hebrews unfolded, they would also be concerned with the virtue of their own mothers and daughters.

Hebrew female mastery was also a powerful social metaphor in the Old Testament. Deborah, of the Book of Judges, lived a life suggesting to some that only an errant people would be fit for – or choose – the governance of a corrective mother:

> And the children of Israel again did evil in the sight of the Lord .... And the Lord sold them into the hand of Jabin king of Canaan .... And Deborah, a prophetess, the wife of Lapidoth, she judged Israel at that time ... and the children of Israel came up to her for judgement.[3]

One line of interpretation suggests that Deborah's very position shamed these men who failed to govern themselves. It had become lamentably necessary for them to become dependent boys again.[4] The idea of the dishonour of the errant son would haunt institutions of slavery for thousands of years.

In accordance with this passage from Judges, for ancient, medieval and early modern Jews, slavery was intimately bound up in the relationships among honour, shame and the struggle for male privilege. In the Torah itself, Leviticus provides for the self-sale of a Jewish man fallen on hard times.[5] Under this law however the custom essentially functions as a social safety net, as Hebrew masters could only hold their co-religionists for six years and could not treat them harshly. In fact, Hebrew slaves themselves were known to take full advantage of their status as insiders, to the point that one commentator claimed that 'whoever buys a Hebrew servant buys a master for itself'.[6]

The biblical portrait of Hebrew slavery, the model that continued to inform early modern peoples, elaborated on this benevolent, paternalist model of male mastery. The emphasis was placed on the reciprocal obligations between a master and his wards. Foreign as well as Hebrew slaves were to be treated as family dependants rather than as animal-like property.[7] There would be ramifications if a master killed or maimed a slave, raped a female slave, or otherwise took sexual advantage of a woman captive who was married or betrothed.[8] The portrait that emerges from the Torah is the paterfamilias whose human domain happened to include some in formal bondage. Fathers could arrange for the marriage of female captives to their sons, as long as the woman in question was allowed a month for mourning and assimilation (thus presumably establishing the legitimacy of any offspring).[9]

Women slaves seemed to enjoy at least a possibility of pursuing the avenue of marrying into freedom not enjoyed by their male counterparts. Under the dictates of Exodus and Deuteronomy, a former female slave who had suffered as a neglected or abandoned wife was always to remain a free woman.[10] The situation for men was more ambiguous. Ideally a master would have his male slave circumcised and accept conversion to Judaism in order that the slave might take part in rituals bringing him closer to the free members of the household. However, Rabbi Akiba ben Yossef's second-century Talmudic ruling warned that this did not necessarily mean that a converted, newly Jewish male slave could or should be manumitted according to Leviticus.[11]

Suffused within the relevant Hebrew texts was a message that mastery was transcendent – paternalist authority being deeply symbolic of a liberated, free people. A nation or people in bondage was one in which paternal authority had been stolen, replaced and perverted (shades of the rule of Deborah as well as Potiphar's wife). Likewise on a smaller scale, men truly enslaved were stripped of their privilege to direct children and female members of their household and were denied their duty to protect them. The collective memory of this loss of privilege seems to have stung Jewish ideologues and lawmakers with particular strength, prompting the creation of elaborate legal structures designed to restore masculine prerogatives.

The power of the Hebrew master was indeed jealously guarded, as reflected in the Yad ha-Hazakah of Rabbi Maimonides of the twelfth century, which urged that a Hebrew man should not sell himself as a slave to a Hebrew woman. Jewish women in this conception were legally equated with the status of converts to Judaism or Gentiles – the two other categories of individual unsuitable to own an adult Jewish male. For a Hebrew man, self-sale to a woman meant something beyond simple loss of status. It conveyed a loss of honour of the kind reserved for submission to socially marginal converts or outright Gentiles. However, this admonition against this kind of self-sale was wishful thinking – something that could hardly be prevented in reality. Maimonides affirmed that a Jewish woman's purchase of a previously free Jewish man fallen onto hard times or into social or criminal disgrace was nevertheless as legally valid as would be her purchase of a Gentile or convert.[12] Regardless, it remains an open question whether these female purchasers felt at any point in the process they were 'buying their own masters.'

Opprobrium also fell on free women. The conflicting sources clearly illustrate the content of rabbinical dispute on the topic of female honour and shame. The Sculchan Aruch makes it clear that:

> there should be no steward in the house, so that he might not seduce the women. A scholar is not allowed to live in a house with a widow. A woman is not permitted to keep male slaves, even if they are children. An unmarried male shall not be a teacher, because mothers come to pick up their children.[13]

The Masoretic text [MT] of the Hebrew Bible had already qualified this by allowing for women to at least own male children up to the age of nine.[14] The clear motive here was to police the presumed unrestrained sexual impulses of dependent men and free women. Whether the primary target was the supposedly depraved sexuality of the free female living without adequate male supervision, or the depraved sexuality of the enslaved but opportunistic male living under dangerously unstable female supervision, became a legal and rhetorical battleground.

At stake here were cultural dynamics far more complex than simply curbing female authority. Maternalism, honour and shame came into play as well. This is reflected in the emphatic statement in the Tractate Baba Mezi'a of the Babylonian Talmud making clear that prospective Jewish female slave buyers might only purchase and keep a male slave who is Gentile ('Canaanite') – leaving the prohibition on the acquisition of Jewish men in place. The reasoning in the document is almost certainly unique in the annals of gender and slavery – yet in its substance would be recreated in hundreds of variations in the centuries to come. The key factors were the actions and honour of the chattel himself. The provision was that the Jewish woman may not buy a Jewish man because 'he has a feeling of shame and regard for appearances. Therefore she [the female master] may be emboldened to an illicit relationship, in the certainty that he may not disclose the fact: hence she may not purchase him.' However, the Gentile man is portrayed as 'feeling no shame therein; therefore she [the female master] fears intimacy with him, lest he boast thereof, and so may buy him.'[15]

Although we have no way of knowing how seriously these edicts governed actual circumstances, the attitudes are revealing. The central assumption here is that the free woman was by nature undisciplined, and would have felt a natural impulse to enter into a sexual relationship with her slave. The rabbi, as a father figure making pronouncements to his metaphorical daughters, feels he must govern these circumstances because the women in question cannot be trusted to govern themselves. The female's honour is something she cannot be trusted to uphold herself in the face of temptation. From the point of view of honour this makes a Jewish mistress (and mother) distinctly deficient as compared to her Jewish male slave. Such a man, even one fallen so low as to be the potential slave of a woman, always retained his inherent dignity as a Jew. Even if he could not resist the advances of a sexually aggressive mistress, his silence was assured. (Or, alternatively, a man of honour feeling the shame of his status might also be inclined not to draw attention to this.) If the free woman therefore thought that an affair with him would never be discovered, it posed a sexual danger to societal order. A Gentile man, by contrast, felt no shame and thus lived in a state of permanent, unchanging dishonour, making it likely that such a slave who would in due course broadcast the 'conquest' of his mistress no matter what were the exact circumstances of the encounter. (And, having no honour he might not even be aware of the shame of living under a woman's perpetual direction.) Somewhat ironically the Jewish woman was allowed to purchase, own and direct 'shameless' non-Jewish men who supposedly would have no compunctions about defiling their mistresses – a circumstance which might clearly have posed a real personal and bodily threat to them. Even in this circumstance, the female masters were not credited with the ability to maintain honour because they were Jews. Such a woman's ability to maintain order would only arise out of her fear of exposure.

Thus under suspicion, the household mistress and mother bore a significant burden in maintaining appearances. Another example concerned the honour and shame of the unfaithful wife, who upon conviction was to be stripped of her clothing, reinforcing as punishment the loss of status she had brought upon herself. The woman was then allowed to reclothe herself but in a shoddy or unattractive way, with the people of the congregation then invited to view the dishonoured woman in accordance with the exhortation from Ezekiel 'that all women may be taught not to do after your lewdness'. The only ones apparently barred from this ritualistic viewing of the dishonoured body of the mistress were the 'menservants and maidservants, because she felt superior to them and so would have been humiliated in front of them'.[16] The special if suspect status of the female slave owner is thus pragmatically acknowledged and her honour and dignity are protected, even as her behaviour as wife and mother is being held up to public scrutiny and ridicule.

Jewish tradition also introduced the problem of how the practical necessity of work is reconciled with pronounced cultural fears. Although many writers bowed to inevitability and provided for Jewish women to manage Gentile and sometimes Jewish men, writers and rabbis did not separate the supervision of work from sexual seduction as easily as (we shall see) many of their Muslim counterparts. Thus another rabbinical stipulation asserted that a free woman could supervise two or more men at once, but not one man working alone.[17] Presumably this was to avoid a one-to-one private assignation, but obviously this arrangement was hardly likely to achieve this – if it were even practically possible. The idea that a woman was permitted to oversee men only arranged in pairs or groups is also interesting in light of the later claims regarding societies as varied as Renaissance Italy and the antebellum United States mentioned in the introduction, that women could shy away from managing men because of concerns about physical control. By implication the Hebrew authors of this prescription did not feel a single woman was physically incapable of supervising multiple men. The woman's own latent immorality evidently posed a greater risk to her than potential resentment or rebellion from those men collectively.

Nor was the male master spared the ultimate responsibility for ensuring an orderly domestic establishment. A mistress who went 'out with her hair loose, going out with her shoulders uncovered, shameless in the presence of her male slaves, shameless in the presence of her female slaves' reflected badly on the husband and his ability to control his household. Such behaviour amounted to 'a commandment to divorce her.'[18]

A final vital factor introduced at least obliquely in the rabbinical literature is a central theme in Muslim and Christian tradition as well – slavery as a test of manhood. Could a slave, like a free young man, grow to overcome the mother/mistress's authority? The Babylonian Talmud accordingly uses slavery to ridicule both men and women involved in inverted relationships. The writer of the Tractate Gittin portion of the Babylonion Talmud (Gemara, fourth century) asserted that a number of common activities – eating, drinking and engaging in sexual intercourse – might be potentially fatal if performed when an individual was standing upright. The text describes a woman named Me'orath who had subjected her male slave to all three of these standing ordeals – after which the poor man died. The mocking is directed mostly at the unfortunate slave. The writer offers the caustic comment that the dead man had been a 'weakling' – implying that a virile man could have survived this experience (and in any case a free man would, it was implied, naturally choose his own sexual position as well as that of his female partner). The woman Me'orath, as a slave-owner, is not completely spared from the implied ridicule. The mere fact that she had chosen the sexual positions for herself and her man clearly violated the Talmudic imperative that females adopt the typical submissive and receptive bodily posture (that is, remain supine) during lovemaking. However, the main point of the story in its original context is public health, not slavery or even gender relations. And as with other texts, female mastery is held up as an example of private disorder, immorality, and even the ridiculousness to which individuals exerting unnatural power might stoop.[19] Yet the other aspect of meaning is a far more intimate version of the Deborah story in the Book of Judges applying to all of Israel. Shamed men might end up directed by a female, but the men in question, to find redemption, must be willing and ultimately able to overcome her inconstant, female maternal authority and reclaim the paternal privilege.

In the Ottoman era, the sources let us go well beyond the rabbinic literature. Historian Yaron Ben-Naeh points out that while prescriptive rabbis were prone to write of male slaves, the early modern Ottoman Empire court records and associated documents he studied primarily concern Jewish ownership of female slaves – all of whom in these documents were white and of mostly Slavic, Hungarian, Germanic or Circassian origin.[20] Ben Naeh describes an environment in which many official and religious edits from Muslim and Jewish authorities were widely ignored or only capriciously applied in time of crisis. Despite official prohibitions, non-Muslims, including Jews, did in fact own slaves in most areas, times and places. Most of these slaves were Christians, but that Jews might even own Muslims indicates that another important theoretical Ottoman prohibition could easily be broken.[21]

The Ottoman Jewish community also seemed to have ignored some rabbinical literature, such as that issued by Maimonides to the effect that when a master had indulged in sexual contact with his female slave he must either free and marry her or send the woman away. The evidence points instead to the practice of widespread concubinage without manumission, something that was a concern to Jewish religious authorities which proved largely powerless to stop it. Slavery then became one way that Muslim and Jewish families came to resemble one another, at least in this respect. One Jewish master by way of justification offered the boast that he 'lay with [his slave] whenever he wished, and no one could tell him what to do because he had bought her with his own money'.[22] There was not always a great deal of difference between the duties and activities of the free women of the household and the female slaves, so manumission, or continued concubinage, might not have mattered tremendously to many within the household, especially if a slave woman was herself Jewish and had given birth to her master's child.

As in Muslim Ottoman households, slavery also provided the opportunity for pragmatic and economically useful activity for free Jewish women in the early modern era. Some, like 'Sara – daughter of Avraham – the Jewess, known as the slave trader' dealt in white women as their business. Ben-Naeh's data seems to suggest that Jewish families might have had a preference for female domestic slaves even over and above the proportion that was usual in the Muslim world around them.[23] Yet even in the early modern Ottoman Empire, the ancient debate over male slaves and female owners was still very much alive and laden with public symbolism. Male Jewish critics condemned the practice of their fellow Jewish women in Ottoman Cairo of sexually exploiting their male slaves, presumably of Christian, Jewish and Muslim origin alike.[24] All tended to agree that the maternal was sacred and should remain legitimate in slave holding society.

Overcoming the maternal: the birth of Islam

Traditions of maternalism are found at the beginnings of the Muslim faith – the Prophet Mohammed's youngest wife Aisha in eighth-century Arabia reportedly independently owned both male and female slaves.[25] This reflects the assumption of some early Islamic texts, with no further commentary needed, that a female could manage and own slaves even within marriage. Female mastery also developed from simple authority to encompass the management of men as well as women. The Prophet himself reputedly remarked to an assembled group of Meccan women that if any of them owned a man who was aspiring to free himself she should begin covering herself before him.[26] The appeal to modesty did not question their authority, and in fact confirmed that enslavement rendered the slaves something less than human.

Female mastery, defined by early Muslim men, was an issue far more important than the simple definition of appropriate authority. Its maternal aspects could represent the old, pre-Mohammad order that Islamic civilisation replaced. Overcoming female mastery in the form of maternal authority came then to represent the advent of Islam itself, and how standing fast in the faith against false mothers could make true men. By the same token, adherence to the new faith also demonstrated how the men who remained under a form of female rule were unworthy to be Muslim.

Foundational texts of the religion established a common theme: a man would be found serving a woman as a slave, and due to his virtue and natural piety he was noticed, acquired, and freed by either the Prophet himself or one of his (male) followers. The ex-slave then became fully able to exert his manhood in the service of a righteous cause. One such influential tale concerned a boy named Khabbab, who, according to traditions, was an Arab youth from the Tamu Tamim tribe taken as a slave to Mecca, where he was bought by a woman called Umm Anmaar of the rival Arab Khuza group. As Khabbab grew into full adulthood, he worked for his mistress as an artisan, eventually becoming an acolyte of Mohammad who was a regular visitor to the workshop. Umm Anmaar vigorously resisted Khabbab's new allegiance, and ordered him to be tortured repeatedly. The woman in time received the wisdom in the new faith when a terminal illness impelled her to turn to the Prophet as well. Mistress and slave, now united in purpose, next followed Mohammad to Medina where Khabbab in time became a warrior at the side of his new master in the faith.

The story of Salman the Persian is similar – with a few pedagogical differences. Salman was born a Zoroastrian who as an adult had converted to Christianity. Told by a monk to seek the location where the last Prophet of God would emerge, he travelled to Arabia where he was captured by bandits and sold in the marketplace of Medina. He was bought there by a Jewish woman and put to demeaning domestic service. The 'Jewess' of the story proved a cruel and capricious mistress, and the suffering of the virtuous Salman was only lifted when he was purchased and freed by Mohammad himself (whom Salman had previously recognised as the Prophet of New Testament scripture). Salman's spiritual strength and fortitude in battle led him eventually to be considered one of the four pillars of the Muslim faith. Salman the Persian came to represent Mohammad's call beyond Arabia to a wider world and to many faiths.[27]

Both men though had to pass through the common experience of female ownership as a trial of spiritual manhood before each could truly be considered a convert. It was the test of the potentially worthy boy growing out of his mother's purview. Mother and mistress were one.

Still, in addition to their metaphorical value, these and other conversion stories indirectly assume that their listeners will be familiar with the ubiquity of female ownership. Accordingly, a multitude of different sources inform us that the tests of faith and manhood casting fictive motherhood into a negative light did not prevent the full integration of Muslim women's slaveholding into the fabric of day-to-day life in the early, medieval and early modern Muslim worlds. However, the Muslim cases tend to be distinctive in that orchestrated slavery, generally speaking, allowed more latitude to mistresses/mothers in the day-to-day management of slaves of both sexes than was generally countenanced in the Jewish and Christian worlds at parallel times. As we shall see in the second chapter, the differences affected the frontier interactions among the three faiths sharing the Mediterranean frontier.

While across great distances of time and space both mainstream Muslim and traditional Jewish thinking registered strenuous objections to free women's sexual involvement with slave men, they each made concessions to the pragmatics of slave management. In Islam, the *mahram* principle granted a wife-manager the latitude to oversee a household without having to don cumbersome dress in front of slaves. This is a key but essential detail often missed by historians but well known by infidel slaves in Muslim lands, who found that they had assumed the status of a legal child inhabiting the body of an adult (officially Muslims could not own other Muslims, but this precept was sometimes locally violated). According to some (but not all) writers in the traditional *hadith* literature (non-Koranic narratives and commentaries on the life of Mohammed), male slaves could join female slaves as being considered *mahram* – a conceptual category of the household in which they became, like children, legally invisible – especially in a sexual sense. Carnal relations with these slaves would be considered incestuous. Thus a slave, as part of an extended family, was by definition sexually unthreatening. The aim was partially practical. Typical is this observation of one Iranian cleric: 'Since the male slaves work within the house and [free women] covering before them would cause great difficulty, [the slaves] are *mahram*. There are a great many traditions to this effect.'[28] Thus adult male slaves, like their female counterparts became fictive children legally, religiously and practically.

Much later, after Christian slaves were no longer held in Muslim lands, 'orientalist' art in Europe would correctly surmise that slavery in Islam was intimately tied to 'gaze' – who may look upon or interact with whom in a given circumstance. But the orientalists took no account of those Muslim contests over who or what the free female might and might not gaze upon. To understand how this tended to work practically, men and women were not necessarily interchangeable as slaves or as masters. Male slaves were degendered but not necessarily desexualised – a distinction with obvious implications for Muslim female mastery. At issue was sexual licence. Free women could arrange workers in their household, but sexual power over slaves would according to most (but not all) sources violate the incest taboo that extended to all slaves and children in the family. At issue were always two sets of 'gazes'. How the mistress appeared to the gaze of her slaves was, as we have seen from Mohammed's own admonition to the women of Mecca, immaterial – so long as the man remained a slave. Just as the very young child may look upon his mother, the slave could look upon his mistress. Such practices are reflected far enough to cause one early modern historian to comment on the 'remarkable freedom with which Christian slaves were permitted to mix with and look upon Muslim women, unveiled, in the privacy of their homes'.[29]

In this respect, the seemingly far-fetched stories of female mastery within Islam must be approached far more carefully than as the products of European cultural propaganda or orientalist European male fantasy. As Algerian anthropologist Marnia Lasreg has described the early modern circumstances:

> [Algerian] [w]omen used male European captives to help them clean their houses, run errands, care for animals and carry their paraphernalia to the Turkish

baths. Women did not veil themselves before these captives. The idea behind this practice, which remained in force during the colonial era, was that no Muslim woman could be interested in a Christian captive. Some women believed these men 'could not see'.[30]

Indeed, one of the seventeenth-century captives, Emanuel d'Aranda, commented directly on this question of gaze. When their female masters were 'at home, they are not so shy of the Christian slaves; for they say that the Christians are blind; but if a Mohametan should see there faces uncovered, 'twere a great sin.'[31] Lazreg claims that actual sexual liaisons and love affairs between Muslim female owners and their Christian slaves would have been extremely difficult 'given the extended nature of the Algerian family'.[32] But d'Aranda's shrewd reading of his own situation proved quite congruent with the *mahram* principle. If the Christian commentators are at all reliable, there seem to have been a multitude of violent retributions against Muslim women who subjected themselves to the indignity of a real rather than imagined relationship with a slave, including one affronted man who killed all four of his wives when the youngest had sought out one of his Jewish bondsmen.[33]

As will be further discussed in the next chapter, when the Muslim world encountered their Christian and Jewish rivals, clashing over matters of gender and slavery, a profusion of competing narratives emerged. To an extent greater than the rabbinical literature permitted of Jewish women, female mastery among many Muslims of the premodern centuries seemed the rest on a reinforcing combination of the practical need to supervise domestic work and cultural and religious chauvinism. Treating adult European Christian (and Jewish) men as fictive children however raised social fears among Muslim masters. Christian subordinates for their part expressed some combination of romantic fantasy and opprobrium of their mistresses' tyranny. Violence ended some of these actual interpersonal conflicts. The slave of a man, as the traditional Persian proverb has it, lives for a hundred years, while the slave of a woman dies in six months. But the public war of worlds over female mastery would remain.

Maternalism in Christian European tradition

The one who raised me sold me to a certain Rhoda at Rome. Many years later I became re-acquainted with her and began to love her as a sister. After some time, as she was bathing in the river Tiber, I saw her, gave her my hand, and brought her out of the river. Seeing her beauty I thought in my heart: 'How happy I would be if I had such a wife, both in regard to beauty and manner.' I wanted only this, nothing more. After some time, after I was on my way to the countryside … . I began to pray to the Lord to confess my sins. As I was praying, heaven opened, and I saw that woman upon whom I had set my heart, greeting me from heaven with: 'Hello, Hermas!' Looking up at her I said, 'Lady, what are you doing here?' But she answered: 'I was taken up in order to reproach you for your sins before the Lord.' … I answered her: 'Have I sinned against you? How? Or when did I say a shameful thing to you? Have I not always considered you a goddess? Have I not always honoured you as a sister? Why do you malign me, woman, with these evil and unclean charges?' Laughing she said to me, 'The

evil desire arose in your heart. Do you not think it is an evil thing if an evil de
arises in the heart of a just man ...?'[34]

In historian Carolyn Osiek's compelling analysis of this exceedingly complex,
multi-origin third-century AD narrative, the sin of the man Hermas refers to
two potential transgressions of social status. The first is sexual. Hermas's stated
desire to marry his former mistress and owner Rhoda is problematic because
such a sexual union, even within marriage, with a freedman would have been
frowned upon for a Roman free woman of the time. The second is that desire to
marry Rhoda also reflects Hermas's desire to raise himself in status and wealth,
offending the humility at once expected of a Christian man and one of his station.[35] The social difference that makes Hermas's goals illicit is apparently one
that, according to the original authors, the Christian god absolutely recognised.

The early history of Christian maternalism possesses many contradictory
facets. Another related way to interpret Hermas's vision of Rhoda is the inherent sinfulness seen in envisioning her transition from a mother/mistress figure to that of a wife, with all the connotations of sexual subordination. Osiek
points to the classical pagan references implicit in the scene, often involving
mortal man's surprising of bathing goddesses.[36] These are explicitly erotic
visions that the original audiences probably could not have failed to understand in that light. That Hermas actually refers to Rhoda as a 'goddess' and
that she is literally in heaven as he addresses her, makes it clear that the boundary between them is far too vast ever to be legitimately crossed. The disap-
pointed Hermas is later consoled by another vision, this of an older woman
sitting in a chair of snow-white wool. She reassures him of his essential virtue,
but also reminds him that Rhoda herself was a kind of test of that virtue: 'It is
an evil and terrible intention against a distinguished and tested spirit for someone to lust after an evil deed, especially Hermas the continent, who abstains
from all evil desires and is filled with simplicity and great innocence.'[37]

In stark contrast, many Christian men found their own wives far less than
goddess-like, and far more corruptible, when near slaves and slavery. When list-
ing the requirements a typical wife would have of her surroundings, St Jerome
sarcastically listed 'a eunuch who ministers to the safe indulgence of her lust'.
Such everyday hazards undercut the rule of husbands and fathers in the household – and by extension the society at large. With the advent of Christianity, such
undisciplined female behaviour became smeared as the hallmark of paganism,
just as it had for the pre-Islamic peoples of Arabia. Clement of Alexandria,
a Greek patristic father and third-century convert to Christianity, saw female
mastery as being intimately associated with sexual outrages – the hallmark of
the pagan. Clement wrote:

The baths are open to men and women alike, there they strip for the sake of lust ....
Those whose sense of modesty keeps them from such excess exclude men not
of their own household, but they will bathe with their servants, and strip naked
before their men-slaves. In fact, they even have themselves massaged by them,
giving them full freedom of touch, when the slaves are already afraid of giving
free rein to their lust.[38]

The central cultural message transmitted was that female action, given excessive licence by the institution of slavery, had to be curbed in the process of making good men and women into Christians. In this sense Clement and the author[s] of Hermas are in complete agreement – a Christian woman needed to remove herself from the baths (or river) and install herself above the run of humanity, in the metaphorical heavens. Family disorder could rapidly rot a society at its core – the unnatural mother revealing herself in the attributes of the vengeful, monstrous mistress holding more authority than she could responsibly handle. Such monsters were thought to be in their element when they made it their business to make miserable the lives of virtuous slaves. Slavery itself seemed to be the religious test by which female as well as male virtue was examined. According to one pedantic hagiographer, a tenth-century Byzantine noblewoman later canonised as St Mary the Younger did not consider:

> her male and female servants ... as slaves, but rather took care of them as if they were a part of her own body, wisely discerning all that comes from God, taking into account that we are all equal by nature and also that we use slaves as we do our hands and feet, and frequently we accomplish the hardest and basest services through them, while we ourselves take our ease. For these reasons she did not like to beat them, but was eager to feed and comfort them.[39]

Yet like the Jewish and Muslim parallels, it was still unbridled female sexuality that provided the opportunity for men to overcome and transcend the threat of the demeaning feminine. In this way accounts of challenging the unnatural mother might assist in the making of strong 'sons', albeit ironically. So goes the story of Aetius, the fourth-century founder of a Christian sect of Arianism, who had been impoverished as a child by the death of his father in one of the first cities of Christianity, Antioch (in present-day Turkey). The destitute orphan was sold into slavery and grew up in the personal service of a local woman named Ampelis, who compelled the young man to win his freedom by proving himself sexually 'in some disgraceful manner'.[40] Here is the polar opposite of behaviour of the virtuous Roman Rhoda, yet in both cases Christian men are forged.

This variety of stories took root alongside the main vein of prescribed social engineering reflecting the reality of the times. To that end Pope Callistus, writing in the same century that Clement had penned his screed, pronounced that Christian slaves could legitimately marry free women. This constructed a pathway for socially suppressed Christian men, effectively reversing their roles with free women after marriage under the legal precepts of father-rule. The goal was the legitimation of the Christian man through matrimony, achieving domestic and social stability by placing female mastery safely under the care of a proper and pious master. The potentially troublesome social upward mobility of slave marrying free clearly mattered less than the upset of gender norms that had so obsessed pagan Romans seeking to protect their free communities and lineages. The reality imposed by the early papacy, together with the febrile imaginings of Father Clement, promoted the establishment of moral and ethical models of God's kingdom on earth. This required in many circumstances that male acquiescence to female mastery be abandoned. In this way of thinking, social and spiritual disorder had been made a possibility when men had allowed themselves to stray from their responsibilities as masters. This had to be discouraged and stopped.

Beyond the confines of the late Roman world, similar kinds of social and cultural struggles began to manifest themselves with the dawn of Christianity. In one case from early medieval England it was suggested that enslavement to a woman, and a widow specifically, could be a rite of passage to manful leadership (in the same way as it was then serving for early Muslim leaders). Simeon of Durham, for example, told the legend of one Abbott of Carlisle who had a vision to the effect that a widow's slave named Guthfrith should be sought out and ransomed from his mistress. After being freed, Guthfrith became the King of Northumbria.[41]

Spiritual power for men could also accrue through resistance of female authority, which represented an eternal spiritual corruption within Christianity. The remarkable tale of Moisej the Hungarian, an eleventh-century attendant to a prince from Kiev (Ukraine), is one such case in point. Captured and taken to Poland after the assassination of his prince and patron, Moisej was confined in 'fetters' for a number of years by a Polish ruler Prince Boleshaw. Moisej, physically striking and venerably pious, caught the eye of an unnamed noblewoman described as 'young, beautiful, and possessing great wealth and power'. The smitten young widow offered to the captive the chance to become her 'master' and the ruler of the dominions that she recently inherited. Moisej, however, alarmed that her desire for him was obviously carnal, and that the precondition of his future mastery was that he 'submit' to her, resisted with the invocation of biblical examples of many godly men led astray by such submission. Adam's fall, as he describes it, was the result of submission to Eve. Samson, Solomon and Herod were similarly evoked. Blocked in her initial strategy, the noblewoman next purchased Moisej outright so that their formal relationship will now be one of mistress to slave, 'drag[ging] him off forcibly and shamelessly to unseemly activity'. Treated well and clothed richly, however, the Hungarian-born Kievan slave continued to resist his Polish owner, to the disbelief of those around him who noted the extraordinary wealth and power he was refusing.

At this point, Moisej's monastic future was presaged when he began to describe the incompatibility of serving Christ and serving a woman: '[h]e that is married careth how he may please his wife, but he that is unmarried careth how he may please God'. When further offers of wealth continued to be refused, the noblewoman resorted to violence, causing Moisej to be brutally tortured and starved. During this time, Moisej was visited by 'a certain monk from the Holy Mountain', who instructed the young slave on how not to turn his back on the enemy, and escape from this 'lecherous woman'. Others were also troubled by the unexpected resistance of this slave. The Polish ruler, Prince Boleshaw, issued an ultimatum to the noblewoman, telling her 'none of the prisoners ransomed [i.e. enslaved] by you are to be set free. But do as you wish, like a mistress to a slave, so that the others will not disobey their masters.' The woman's first new tactic was overtly sexual – she forced 'him to lie with her on her bed, kissing him and embracing him'. Refusing her yet again, Moisej nevertheless took time to assure his mistress of his sexual potence so as to emphasise that it was only 'for the love of God I shun you as an unclean woman'. In exasperation, she finally ordered his castration, which he barely survived. The dismemberment of Moisej, however, served as his liberation and empowerment. When his mistress (and Prince Boleshaw) were killed in a popular uprising, Moisej at long last made his escape east and fulfilled his charge when he joined the Kievan Caves Monastery.[42]

Moisej's castrated status became in this context a source of godly masculine power and strength. He advised other monks to 'never speak to a woman throughout your life'. When a young monk came to him, troubled by thoughts of sexual desire, Moisej struck the man in the breast with a stick, making his private parts permanently numb – solving the difficulty. The inverted symbolics of castration are crucial here. The ultimate act of unmanning serves as not only a liberation and transcendence of corrupting masculine desire but as reminder of how deathly serious is the challenge of unrestrained and ungodly womanhood. Also invoked in the tale is of course the Old Testament Genesis story of Joseph and Potiphar's wife. Moisej's story, like the one in Genesis, suggested that a woman will tend to ignore virtue for the sake of the flesh, even at the expense of her place and maternal identity. A woman with power over others was an especial danger – the female master of virtuous subordinates being an exaggerated metaphor for feminine prerogative taken to its logical extreme. The mistress is ultimately then a helpless slave to her own passions, a metanarrative that Christian men, with only minor variations, had in common with their Jewish and Muslim counterparts.

Maternalism and communal female mastery

A virtuous mother was obviously first defined by the relationship with her husband the father as well as with her children and other dependants. Another potential betrayal of the maternal role could be women living or acting communally.

One central example linking classical with early modern Europe was the elusive Amazons. These mythological independent female figures – often described as warriors and always as barbarous – were typically to be found on the peripheries of civilisations if not well beyond them. Writers designed how they would image the exotic topsy-turvy life at the edge of the familiar world according to what lessons, satires and prescriptions might be needed. In most places and times the reader or listener was asked to conjure up a group of women who were self-sufficient in economy, politics and war. They were at best indifferent to men, and at worst prone to emasculating them by death or enslavement. Whatever the content of the commentary might have been, the perennial use of Amazons to deliver urgent cultural messages speaks to the combination of the responses it apparently caused in men – evoking some mix of ridicule of the absurd, genuine horror and erotised fascination.

The Amazonian idea is relevant to maternalism because it speaks to actual, rather than metaphorical, slavery. Among all the cultural uses of the exotic and the mythological, what remains relatively unexamined is the message the idea of imaginary Amazons conveyed to past peoples about real slavery.[43] Amazons, like ordinary invading armies, bandits and kidnappers, were agents of sudden capture, the counter-reality in which master became slave. The fear of actual enslavement existed virtually everywhere Amazons were seriously imagined. In these settings, carefully assembled hierarchies could be suddenly wiped away and replaced by the utterly unpredictable – where civilisation and refinement would from then be subject to the brute, animalistic, and purely physical. As put by the fifth-century Gallic poet and cleric Orentius on the fall of Roman Gaul to barbarians: '[t]he unlucky mother fell with her child and husband, the master underwent servitude with his slave'.[44] According to Gibbon, when the eastern Roman (Byzantine) empire fell, 'senators were linked with their slaves ... in this common captivity, the ranks of society were confounded'.[45] Senators and other elites, coming from a ruined society, were unlikely ever to have been redeemed as there was no one left to redeem them. Amazons then became the imaginary agents of a distilled, gender-focused variation of slavery as the topsy-turvy world. Amazons, like any savage barbarians, might be drawn from anywhere. They could be stray, marginal, unprotected women who looked not to their male elders but to one another for strength.

That Amazons were specifically female was also crucial to the fears of slavery expressed in the myths. The opposite of slavery in these stories was not so much abstract 'freedom' as it was the preservation of male virtue. Being reduced by slavers to mere physical bodies rebuked any former master's refinement, intellectual culture, laws, customs and religion – and the fact of his enslavement by his strong metaphorical daughters highlighted the decay of his physical prowess as well as his moral weakness. The tension exposed was that between the masculine need for civilisation and for martial strength. Amazonian-like women functioned as a collective test to see if the balance was correct. The women were imaginary, but the vulnerability of physical weakness among civilised man was real.

One legend concerned the Sacae, an Iranian people usually classified as a subset of the Scythians who the Greeks such as Ctesisas (fifth century BCE) had always associated with warlike women. In one account of the Sacae, a young man who wished to marry had to challenge the object of his desire to a single combat. If the man won (apparently the expected and desired result), he became her husband and lord. If she defeated him, however, 'she led him off in the same manner, and made him her husband and her slave'.[46] Clearly this was a test to eliminate the weak and vulnerable from the ranks of public men. (The coexistence of matrimony and slavery is unusual though – if not distantly reflective of a lost reality it perhaps represents a sardonic Greek commentary on marriage itself.) Of course, in such stories spirited male slaves as well could challenge and examine the strength and virtue of masters as well. Sandra R. Joshel and Shelia Murnaghan write of Plautus's play *Casian* in which a male slave dresses as a female slave who his master intends to rape. At the crucial moment the man surprises his master, beating and humbling him. He has done so however on the instructions of his mistress, who has intended all along to shock and shame her husband back to a moral virtuous life. His master then has to deal with the apparent challenge to his manhood by his own male slave, but ultimately the agent for his correction has been his own wife.[47]

The challenge of women's communalism itself was another urgent problem in early Europe. It could be self-evident to men at least that young women could not order the affairs of society or state, subject as they were to the demands of their bodies. Nothing conveyed this more powerfully than the supposed difficulties of communal mother-rule. Women's intellect, barbarous or not, could not project the moral order necessary to preserve civilisation or effective governance. In alternate stories of Amazon origins, the unnatural society was created when local matrons lost their husbands in war, and governed themselves. Their unsuitability for this task was illustrated by their abandonment of their status and their turning to their own slaves for comfort and procreation. Such was the reputed case with the Scythians and a number of other ancient peoples, including those of Argos, defeated by the Spartans. As told by Herodotus, the slaves subsequently took over public affairs until the free sons of women came of age, and at this point the slaves fled the city. In the later version by Plutarch, the slaves and the women married.[48] Both in their way illustrated women's unwillingness and lack of qualification for public authority.

Plutarch also described a variation of this situation, in which the slaves of Chios, a city under siege by Philip V, are promised freedom and marriage with their mistresses if they will betray their masters. This has quite the opposite effect, however, and the insulted yet virtuous masters, mistresses and slaves unite to repel the invasion. Yet the story also indirectly demonstrates again how precarious the situation of free men could be – on the verge of changing places with their own male slaves, while their wives' mid-level status would have remained unchanged, just with different husbands.[49]

A similar set of complex political stories surrounds the aristocrats of Greek city Cumae, exiled by their own king while the aristocratic women are married off to their slaves. The aristocratic sons are shamed by being brought up socially as girls, while serving their mothers and low-born step-fathers – themselves as slaves.[50] This is closely related to the Greek convention in which the sons of Amazons were crippled in order to serve their mothers and sisters, now shifted to show the wages of mindless local tyranny.

Although the mothers themselves are blameless in this tale, similar stories could be used to discredit the legitimacy of a foreign or rival society, using the literary device of mothers acting communally. One Greek polemicist told of the origins of the Greek colony of Locris in the Italian peninsula, whose Spartan-allied men and warriors had vowed to abstain from sexual relations with their wives. In the face of this unwelcome development, the Locrian women chose to turn to their male slaves. The inevitable result was that the next generation of Locrians were defined by their mother's status. This rendered the entire society less respectable in many eyes, especially since the situation had come about not from the imposed will of a conqueror or tyrant but out of women's own choice; the women had betrayed their husbands' virtue and abandoned themselves for the sake of their lust, their sons' status politically illegitimate.[51]

In yet another kind of example, 'Amazons' of a sort could be manufactured out of sheer male laziness. The Roman historian Tacitus excoriated the men of Germania, who consumed their time in 'idleness' leaving 'the care' of house, home and fields … to the women, old men, and weaklings of the family.'[52]

This accusation could and would be ironic, as these 'weaklings' in these societies might easily be captured Romans – but that was not the point of the original story.[53]

Suspicions of communal women were later applied to ordinary assemblages: the harem (to be further discussed in Chapter 2) and the female monastery. Both these arrangements forced commentators to deal first with the complications of female authority over other women. And if the subjection of the male to female mastery had a redemptive element, the subjection of the female to another woman usually did not. Christian and Muslim male writers were even capable of regarding this relationship as specifically threatening. When represented culturally, the contact between free and enslaved women sometimes emphasised that lesbianism was not compatible with slavery. Historian Bernadette J. Brooten notes:

> A comedy of Plautus (ca. 250–184 BCE) provides the earliest extant Latin reference to female homoeroticism. In a brief comic interchange replete with puns, Plautus alludes to the possibility of sexual intercourse between an Athenian courtesan, Phronesium, and her Athenian female slave, Astaphium. Hallett notes the presence of a pun alluding to the slave's forcing sexual intercourse upon her mistress, thereby associating female homoeroticism with a known form of masculine behaviour. She does not comment upon Astaphium's slave status or upon the role reversal that a slave's forcing sex upon her mistress implies.[54]

Beyond role-reversal among women, I. Butlan in eleventh-century Cairo expressed the doubts held by men about their female slaves when he especially warned purchasers in Cairo against purchasing lesbian girls.[55] Among the inconveniences he apparently anticipated was the diminished sexual ardour the new slave might devote to her master. Equally unsettling was the strengthening of alliances among women which might be further sealed with sexual activity. Such alliances might corrupt other slaves or even their mistresses who lived in such close proximity. One reason for the presence of expensively obtained eunuchs in elite households of the Muslim world was certainly to help break up and counterbalance alliances among female household members. In Istanbul many centuries later, those who ran a sort of training academy for girls entering the imperial harem kept the lights burning throughout the night expressly to prevent lesbian activity among the girls.[56]

On the Christian side of the frontier, the communal libertinage of women might be made the subject of pointed social satire and serve as a reminder of the hazards of a non-traditional family. The eleventh-century narrative poem *Moriuht* written by Warner of Rouen attempted to expose the world's hypocrisies around him using the explosive, lurid, yet darkly comic theme of a hapless man among lascivious nuns within the real nunnery at Corbridge, Northumbria. In Warner's version, the convent walls concealed all manner of unnatural sexual practice, with no virtue anywhere in sight. The sacred mysteries of the Roman church were stripped away in the forms of the nuns' attentions to their enslaved, untalented Irish poet 'Moriuht'. The use of slavery and specifically female sexual mastery as metaphors gave the satire the power to cut into the sinew of Warner's society and religion.

In Warner's tale, upon his purchase by the nuns of Corbridge Moriuht announced that he possessed considerable abilities as a composer of epic verse. As a result the intrigued and amused women installed him as a sort of court poet. The female monastics then shamelessly abdicated the adult responsibilities of properly managing a slave, indulging instead in an immature appreciation of his limited talents as, according to Warner, 'the gaze of women love every novelty'. Quickly, though, the nuns moved from girlish distraction and turned to brute animal lust. The ersatz Homer is 'stripped of everything' and sexually exploited by the 'young heifers'. Male virtue is not impinged upon here, however, as Moriuht is every bit the willing victim – possessing an equally debauched sensibility.[57]

Imaginative satire, certainly, yet this fiction was pieced together from essential elements of the known world of the eleventh century. The slave trade internal to western Europe (in this case conveniently facilitated by the pagan Vikings) put Irishmen like this poet on the markets of northern Europe. Corbridge and Warner's own home town of Rouen were noted entrepôts of the slave trade, and monastic houses, even those run by women, could be counted on as reliable buyers and sellers of human chattel of both sexes.[58] Satire was then at least partially built on the expectation that women acting together would produce folly. Women in authority, moreover, were trapped in a perpetual mental childhood even as their bodies matured and proved capable of considerable mischief. However, this was a satire on church and state more than misogynist cultural commentary. Reminiscent of the theme of the communal Amazons, female rule was constant in character – it could not help but create situations of disgrace and disorder. The church and its secular sponsors had failed, as metaphorical fathers, in their oversight of the female. As always however, there was a human reality behind this literary construction. What of the real, slave-owning nuns of Corbridge and their male and female slaves? Their more pragmatic tales attracted no storytellers.

From deviance to paternalism

According to Cassius Dio, writing in the third century, Octavian [Augustus] Caesar excoriated the shamefulness of the Egyptians under Cleopatra for all manner of faults, the worst ones being that they were 'slaves to a woman instead of a man'. This lack of honour was apparently contagious, and would naturally be the result if Romans followed Marc Antony's descent into feminine servitude. 'Who would not be dismayed to see the Queen of the Egyptians with Roman bodyguards? Who would not lament to hear that Roman knights and Senators fawn over her like eunuchs?'[59]

European representations of slavery in writing and art frequently seized upon the juxtaposition of powerful women and powerless men, a relationship so fraught with meaning as to make up a durable cultural theme. The stock situations were simple and suited to storytelling. The principles of father-rule, understood by all, would be set against the normal day-to-day realities whereby women of the master group mixed with and sometimes managed men of the servant or enslaved group. The natural tension in the story played

out on a battleground of ambiguity, with a woman's social authority potentially endangered by a subordinated man's virtue – or alternatively physical or
sexual power. As in Warner of Rouen's epic poetry, the potential and predictable consequences served to challenge, upset, and even discredit established
family, sexual and political order.

Even by the end of the classical period, the debauched, capricious,
unsteady mistress of slaves was already a cliché in western drama and commentary. The possible purposes of this unflattering female figure were many.
The uncontrolled wives of free men cavorting with slaves either highlighted
the perceived need for more effective governance of wives and daughters – or
underlined the hopelessness of attempts to bring wives and daughters to heel.
Further, women who were shown exerting authority that exceeded their class
position could demonstrate a perceived moral or political weakness of a people collectively – a failed male government represented and embodied in the
figure of a woman out of control.

It was a small step from the story of Deborah (which as an Old Testament
account would became part of the Christian tradition as well) to discrediting political enemies by showing how they obeyed wives in exactly the same
manner as boys minded their mothers. Plutarch described the debt owed by
Cleopatra to Marc Antony's wife, Fulvia, who 'with no thought for spinning or housekeeping', had 'tamed' Antony and 'schooled him at the outset
to obey women'.[60] And it was yet another very small step from the obedient
husband and his dominant wife to the mistress and her male slaves. Diodorus
made political points by contrasting a tyrannical slaveholding female named
Megallis, lording unnaturally over her slaves, with the moral health represented
by her daughter, who was of a much more kindly, maternal disposition toward
them.[61]

Social order could be upset by excesses of masculine behaviour as well as
feminine. The western mind might prescribe corrective maternal oversight for
those men whose masculine enthusiasms had led to improper and destructive violence and mayhem. Such was the central theme in the classic story of
Heracles and Omphale, queen of Lydia. In the durable versions the hero, having lost control of himself and murdered the brother of Iole, was condemned
by the Delphic oracle to a term as a slave of the Lydian sovereign. The message of the story was remarkably consistent throughout the centuries: the
wages of undisciplined manhood would mean the loss of the prerogative to
live as a man. A startling classical Pompeiian fresco makes this clear by dis-
playing a distraught and explicitly naked Heracles being delivered over to a
delighted, smirking Omphale in the full regalia of a Roman matron. Two sets
of messages were uneasily mixed: errant 'boy' returned to his 'mother', and a
highly sexualised reversal of roles.

That lesson stayed fresh in the west during the early modern era. It was
regenerated with greater or lesser degrees of sexual frankness in the sixteenth
century by Lucas Cranach and in the seventeenth by luminaries like Rubens,
Spranger, Abraham Janssens and Giovanni Romanelli. This was followed by a
virtual craze in Omphale-related art in the early eighteenth century. Joining in
were Coypel, François Lemoyne, Tischbein and Boucher amidst many others.

A 'pre-Raphaelite' rendition in editions by H. A. Guerber Gleyre served in the Victorian age. In all these ages Heracles endured debilitating years of women's work and passive sexual servitude, all while Omphale sported his trademark lion's skin and club, appropriating the virtuous masculine activities of her captive. Yet there was also a redemptive element in how the hero's life continued after this shock. He managed, through a combination of patient endurance and gradual assumption of more traditionally masculine tasks, to be restored to the prerogatives of his sex. Omphale turned out, for all of her sexualisation, to have been maternal after all, becoming a rite of passage for Heracles. As he learned from his mistakes he increasingly took his place among mature men.

The theme of men in public sight gone badly astray and brought into line by the metaphorical mother was developed in literature contemporaneous to some of these images by such giants as Chaucer. In the *Tale of the Wife of Bath*, a 'lusty bachelor' knight forcibly rapes the maiden in the corn, and to punish this great sin King Arthur turns the knight over to the queen for punishment. The knight's new judge/jailer/mother practises a guiding form of maternal mastery by holding his life over his head, until he can answer the telling riddle about what it is that women most desire.[62]

Another mark of the early Christian faith was the redemption of those afflicted by unjust subjection to women suffered as an actual legal penalty. Here the Christian example paralleled closely the Muslim stories of transcending the feminine. Prominent Christian men, even noblemen, might be disgraced during the late Roman empire by being treated publicly as women. Emperor Constantine made a point of freeing those who had been imprisoned for 'refusal to join in idol worship', and who had been made 'by way of disgrace and insult to serve in the employments of women'. The specific conditions of the noblemen so afflicted are spelled out in considerable detail:

> if any have been wrongfully deprived of the privileges of noble lineage, and subjected to a judicial sentence which has consigned them to the women's apartments and to the linen making, there to undergo a cruel and miserable labour ... let such persons, resuming the honours they had previously enjoyed, and their proper dignities, henceforward exult in the blessings of liberty.[63]

This was just as extraordinary a forge of pious manhood as had been the tyrannical mistresses of Medina in the time of Mohammad. Here elite men of the faith underwent the trial of losing control of their property and bodies, and being trapped in cramped, stifling environments and set to work on feminine projects for which they were so ill suited that it constituted a torture working with slave girls. Men subjected to cloth-work had been a powerful metaphor when Heracles struggled with Omphale's needlework, as it would be again with Edmund Spenser's fictional male captives in *The Faerie Queene*. Yet these were not prescriptive myths but facts taken from the annals of law. With the Muslim – and to some extent the Hebrew examples – stark humiliation could be turned into triumph through the act of redemption. When Constantine freed these noblemen, their ultimate trial, working as, alongside, and under the direction of slave-girls stood as the experience that made them truly Christian men.

On a social rather than a religious level, private law could also use slavery and the maternal to provide solutions for domestic problems. In the Visigothic Code of early Christian Iberia, which continued to govern Christians even during the Muslim regime in some areas and elements of which were reconstituted during the *reconquista*, for example, women were explicitly included in the ranks of those who might personally extract private vengeance for adultery, fornication and abduction.[64] In one provision a guilty abductor (a word defined widely in this context) who consummated the act sexually was to be 'given forever to serve as a slave her who he has injured'.[65] This is a remarkable sanction in the annals of law, especially in terms of its flexibility as to social standing of both parties. There does not seem to be a way to purchase one's way out of trouble, the traditional legal escape for the wealthy elite.

We might presume that such a woman in question, likely to have been traumatised by an involuntary kidnapping or sexual assault, would be inclined to sell her accoster so as to be rid of him. But the law does take keeping him into account:

> a freeman who has been proved to be guilty of a crime of this kind, shall never be permitted to marry her whom he has violated. But if the woman herself, after she has received the man as a slave, should marry him, she shall then undergo the penalty of her base action, and shall, along with all her property, be delivered over to her own heirs, to forever serve as a slave.[66]

Nevertheless, male and female avengers as guardians of public order were not interchangeable. Under certain circumstances the malefactor could wind up preferentially in the hands of parents, relatives or a betrothed future husband rather than the woman victim herself. Brothers for example who colluded in the abduction of their sister would lose their property to her, but only their father, if living, could receive the brothers as slaves – they could not become her own property, at least until she might inherit them.

The law was restorative, directing an aggrieved woman back toward her proper role as mistress/mother, rewarding virtue, and proving especially harsh on breaches of public order violating lineages or involving excessive aggression. Yet authorities to a remarkable degree expected women to assume responsibility in the system of private justice.

It is notable that gender (and age)-blind provisions also abounded in slave ownership laws in medieval and early modern Christian world. A *Motu Proprio* (personal decree) issued by Pope Paul III in 1548 stated:

> each and every person of either sex, whether Roman or non-Roman, whether secular or clerical, and no matter what dignity, status, degree, order, or condition they may be, may freely and lawfully buy and sell publicly any slaves whatsoever of either sex, and make contracts about them as is accustomed to be done in other places, and publicly hold them as slaves and make use of their work, and compel them to do the work assigned to them.[67]

Accordingly, the Visigothic example should be seen alongside other seminal bodies of law such as the Salic Code and even the Hungarian slave law under

Coloman, providing for female participation in the course of private domestic justice. In the latter example, it was adultery that was a high-stakes affair. An accusation by the husband against the wife might, predictably enough, result in her enslavement if she was found culpable. Making the charge in the first place carried grave risk though, for if it was not substantiated the husband could be cast into slavery. Wives who accused husbands engaged in an identical, winner-take-all contest of exoneration and vengeance – though it is not clear whether the enslaved party became the property of the state or of the prevailing spouse, now free to marry again.[68]

The challenge to masculine prerogative through corrective manipulations of gender roles could even take place across hierarchies of rank and status. In one instance, a free man of some means named Juan de Molina began using one of his father's young servant women named Ana, first as an involuntary concubine and then as a hired-out prostitute to other men. She suffered beatings at his hands when she did not produce the expected amount of money. The situation was saved from being yet another anonymous tale of a woman trapped without hope when one of Ana's fellow prostitutes intervened and reported Molina to the authorities. He was, perhaps surprisingly, convicted and condemned to 'galley slavery' – to serve his ten-year sentence at hard labour. In the court records is a note Juan later sent to Ana from prison, reasserting his power over her yet also drawing an image showing the couple, with Juan having been wounded by Cupid's arrows of love. He also portrayed himself in the image as the bound prisoner he was, but with the controlling end of his chain falling into Ana's hands.[69] The irony here is actually two-fold, his reassertion of power coexisting with his apparent helplessness in the face of what he imagined to be love, and second that the free white master, who had practised rape, physical abuse and pandering with assumed impunity, was now literally in chains, facing many years of strenuous involuntary labour, while his victim would now live as a free woman in proximity to him – albeit one with a possibly compromised future. Juan seemed to recognise at some level the ageless principle that the wages of failing as a man, whether a victim of love or his own impulses, were to be at least metaphorically imprisoned by a woman.

Tension created by the coercive contact between male masters and female slaves might have been less culturally resonant than the reverse situation simply by virtue of being commonplace and unremarkable. The widely accepted encounters between free man and enslaved woman were less useful to make rhetorical points and cultural observations, because too many privileges of male mastery had to be protected and promoted – whether the relationships in question were very public or hidden away in private.

There were exceptions of course. The master–female slave relationship could be used to evaluate and classify the outside world. Descriptions of different sorts of women slaves, which on the surface might indicate the most desirable girls to buy, at a deeper level provided piquant commentary on the virtues and shortcomings of foreign societies. One notorious list was produced, again by I. Butlan. Turkish women were paid the complement of having the characteristics that would make the best female slaves – beautiful, pure and affectionate to their children. Blonde Greek slaves were especially praised for their attractiveness and good-natured temperaments – only marred by lack of generosity. Armenian females were deemed good, hard workers – but poor sexual partners. Nubians were among those Africans praised for chastity and submissiveness. Other African women, however, were criticized for possessing all sorts of vices that could lead to a woman slave becoming incorrigible.[70] An entire survey of the world was made by studying the captive young women of the city.

Lessons from the master–serving woman relationship could leave significant marks in the records if they reflected serious social concerns. Slavery and servitude had the potential to grotesquely exaggerate the degree of men's legal and customary authority over women that a society might find natural and acceptable. A slaveholding man had more opportunities to cross these lines than a man who governed only free dependants. Countless men used slavery and practices like it to indulge in violence, rape and other forms of sexual abuse deemed excessive even in societies that granted much latitude to paternal privilege. This could lead to public and official concern. Restrictions might be at least theoretically imposed if such behaviour was deemed to systematically disrupt the integrity of the free family or the larger social order.

Greek city-states set the tone for future limitations that would be set by Christian, Jewish and Muslim authorities. Investigations might follow and sanctions be imposed when social overseers found evidence of murder or gross abuses directed toward helpless women. When they occurred, these efforts countered, at least to some degree, philosophical contentions that the power of the slaveholder was absolute.[71]

Of course, sometimes the desired effect was just a matter of acceptable behaviour and self-restraint. The Roman stoic philosopher Musonius Rufus assumed women would be virtuous even when faced with the sexual temptation of slaves, and encouraged free men to 'disciplin[e] their desires' and show the same moral restraint by refusing to exploit female slaves.[72] There could of course be consequences for taking advantage of a female slave not one's own. The Burgundian Code even provided that the master of a slave girl who was taken in marriage or a sexual relationship by another free man could claim the transgressor as a slave (although a fine could be paid to the master if the assignation had been casual).[73] Other attention was devoted to master's own property. For the Hebrews of the Torah, the specification that female slaves as well as male had some prerogative to bodily integrity was contained in Exodus: '[w]hen a man strikes the eye of his slave, male or female, and destroys it, he shall let the slave go free for the eye's sake'.[74] In medieval Portugal, a man could face relatively mild sanctions even for having simple sexual relations with his own female slaves. According to historian François Soyer, in 1473 an owner named Rasto was fined for sexual relations with his married slave, on the grounds of adultery (presumably his as well as hers). Another complication was that she had originally been enslaved on the basis of having been Muslim, and though she had later converted the authorities were not pleased by either the insult to matrimony nor the crossing of religious boundaries.[75]

From failed womanhood to redeemed motherhood

Like men, sometimes women of rank could fall through no fault of their own. Just after he describes the plight of the chained Roman senators discussed above, Gibbon notes that in similar lines of captives,

> the loudest in their wailings were the nuns, who were torn from the altar with naked bosoms, outstretched hands, and dishevelled hair; and we should piously believe that few could be tempted to prefer the vigils of the harem to those of the monastery.[76]

God's people were thus reduced again to mere bodies – subject to non-believers. In addition, a virtuous mother could betray herself – and be held accountable – for actions deemed 'failures.' There was a thin line between maternal mastery and the cruel mistress who had abandoned her good office. Roman satirists, Greek dramatists and Christian observers all used the caricature of the perverse mother. She was usually described or seen in dramatic performance engaged first in flogging women and small children on capricious whims. Juvenal wrote:

> if the husband has turned his back upon his wife at night, the wool-maid is done for; the tire-women will be stripped of their tunics ... while the flogging goes on, the lady will be daubing her face or listening to her lady friends or inspecting the widths of a gold-embroidered robe.[77]

The Council of Worms (876 AD), provision 39, decreed that a Christian mistress who 'in a fit of jealousy' carried out a preconceived plan to beat a slave to death must undergo five years of penance. The mention of jealously strongly implies that the provision refers to a female slave. The reputation of women as unfit, jealous mistresses had clearly survived the demise of classical pagan civilisations, as it would carry forward into the New World. Other sorts of representations of free and enslaved females fell into familiar, established patterns of making political or religious points by describing cruelty to slaves. Seventh-century Christian tracts emphasised the trials of their slaves among Jews and Saracens – among them virtuous women fighting and resisting the perverse mastery of foreign females. One commentator, Anastasius, wrote of a young Christian 'maid' whose Muslim mistress in Damascus beat her every time she returned from receiving communion – a situation that continued until she was redeemed by a righteous Christian master.[78]

The cruel mistress – that recurring signifier of sickness within a culture – frequently found female victims on whom to vent her wrath. For two thousand years and more, afflicted female as opposed to male slaves were especially emphasised when the cause of the cruelty was a free woman's feelings of helplessness and jealously over her husband's involvement with slave concubines. Over a millennium after Anastasius and classical dramas with similar themes, scores of writers continued the theme of the double misfortune – sexual violence at the hands of the master resulting in ongoing punishment at the hands of the mistress.[79]

But as with the converse situation – the point of view of fallen men from which female mastery was apparent – views of women's tyranny had to coexist with the practical need for their management skills. Historians of early Christianity Carolyn Osiek and Margaret McDonald have observed that:

> there is no evidence that any sense of solidarity was formed between women and female slaves based on sex or the common features of their situations. In fact, the opposite seems to have been true. Women owned slaves, both female and male, and women slaveholders, as far as we can tell, were no less brutal or authoritarian than men toward their own slaves.[80]

There was virtue to be had, though. One candidate for a New Testament counterpart of Deborah the Judge was Lydia, a merchant, who when encountering Paul caused herself, and her household, to be baptised. The mastery of a mother as spiritual guardian of her ancillaries was recognised in a matter-of-fact way.[81] Although the mother is defined in the biological sense by procreation, the good mother of slaves was desexualised. Her maternal virtue transcended corruptions of the body as well as legitimised her authority, actions and prerogatives.

Yet is it possible to ascertain how the free woman/mother understood her own mastery? While textual and contextual documents make this increasingly possible to discover in the early modern Atlantic world – as we shall see – in the general absence of direct narrative testimony before about 1500 AD recovery of voices is difficult. It is nevertheless vital to balance, where possible, the weight of men's writings on the subject of female mastery against what might be learned of free women's experience.

This contrast is illuminating. As discussed above, male-created written discourse on female mastery usually began with the idea that free women and slavery made an explosive, corrosive combination that was significant and revealing in some way that transcended contacts among individuals. This made practices of female mastery anomalous even while they were ubiquitous. But numerous localised studies of slavery from antiquity right through the early modern era expose the considerable extent of women's ordinary involvement with managing slavery. While we cannot access what St Margaret felt when she ransomed English captives in Scotland, or what combination of thoughts occurred to a Visigothic woman when she received her convicted abductor as a slave, we can see that common involvements of free women with slaves made routine – even while the male writers surrounding them were making and imagining these same experiences as somehow extraordinary.

The first problem is that of social status within slavery. Women owners in writings tend to be the free women known personally to the literate male elite. Yet underneath was an entire world of free female experience with slavery that went unexamined. The master–slave relationship was not necessarily a function of the elite ruling those far below them on the social scale. Historian of Christian Byzantium Judith Evans-Grubbs draws out an ordinary scenario by which:

> [A] widow of limited means, perhaps a former slave or child of ex-slaves, who would rely on her only male slave to the point where they essentially set up house

together. She might not even see any reason to free him legally, especially since formal manumission ... could be difficult to arrange ... [and] a free woman's children by her slave would be freeborn.[82]

Although a historian's composite, here is the quintessence of pragmatic European female mastery without the political, rhetorical, legal and even scriptural hysteria surrounding it. In one sense, such a woman would have created a small topsy-turvy, female headed world such as that imagined by those who had claimed a Sacae woman would lord over her husband had she defeated him in single combat. Yet the straightforward pragmatics still bear a range of possible interpretations. Another explanation for the composite woman in question is that the female master might simply not have wished to give up control. Freeing the man would have made her former slave the master of her original property, children and body – and a slave 'husband' who later turned troublesome could always be sold. And there is the male experience to recover as well. It is possible that men slaves in such situations chafed at being denied the final and public prerogatives of father-rule by their companion-mistresses as their culture might have expected them to – but gratitude seems a more rational response, as there were far worse fates for slaves in Byzantium than being established in such an amicable domestic arrangement.

Other levels of experience included female petty traders and artisans who depended on skilled male labour for their businesses to survive and thrive. Christian Spanish women owners of artisan shops in the early modern era, for example, employed Muslim male slaves as specialised labour to make their enterprises such as textile, leather and metal work productive and profitable.[83] It is likely that many such female owners of workshops were simply widows of artisan husbands who took the enterprise over after having helped to manage it, patterns that would reproduce themselves in the New World. French nuns in southern Europe bought Muslim slaves to support their establishments and work their land.[84] 'Large numbers of women' were reportedly to be found among the vendors and purchasers of slaves in the then Italian-controlled Dalmatian coastal city of Ragusa (present day Dubrovnik).[85] Here, white Slavic slaves from the Balkans would find themselves chained together and hawked door-to-door by the Italian women merchants in a town where the original seller, trader and buyer as well might be female.[86] The practical need for modest free women to have male help was sometimes officially recognised. One local law in the time of the Spanish reconquest made it clear that an inheriting wife was eligible to retain at least one male or female Muslim slave.[87]

Muslim men in Europe involuntarily might also create a situation that was at once rhetorically fraught with sexual danger and utterly routine. In one text, Alfonso the Wise's *Cantigas de Santa Maria*, a young free Spanish woman was accused by her mother-in-law of conducting sexual relations with her male Muslim household slave. The historian who writes of this, David Nirenberg, notes that what made this case worth noting was the intercession of the Virgin Mary (and possibly as well the capital nature of the sexual crime perpetuated by the young woman). What was not sensational was in fact the most commonplace of circumstances – the presence of male Muslim slaves in Christian

Spanish households.[88] For relatives and servants to police the behaviour of young women living and working in proximity to slaves was not only a function of fear on their behalf, but a deliberate domestic structure designed to ensure that such surveillance allowed the work and ordinary functioning of the household to proceed.

Bringing us full circle is the real, not imagined, danger to Christian men in very ordinary women's slaveholding, a frontier situation that would in time echo in the New World. We know, for example, that the Christian European slaves of Bursa, in Muslim Anatolia, would be bought or sold frequently by Muslim women, typically artisans or householders, acting as their own agents in business even when they were married.[89] Then there were female slavers at the eastern and southern margins of Europe, an authentic type of gendered danger that was a far cry from imaginary Amazons. Preparing and delivering previously free western Europeans for a lifetime to be spent as a slave in the east was not a genteel profession for either a woman or a man, nor one free from violence. Yet the evidence for significant female presence in the business is overwhelming. Traders like 'Catherine of Sevestapol' dominated the fourteenth-century Crimea, processing Scandinavians and Slavs in transit from the north to the south.[90] The rise of the Ottoman Empire saw the creation of Turkish women as transport dealers as well as participants in the local markets. Most women traders dealt in slave girls, Circassian and others, catering to elite buyers, but some were concerned with European men.[91] No doubt generations of captured European soldiers and officers, such as the Austrians enslaved by the Ottoman Turks in the wake of the Battle of Lepanto in 1785, were surprised if they found women among the traders physically leading them east to their fates.

Conclusion: the emotional worlds of maternalism and paternalism

Writing of elegiac Roman poetry, scholar Maria Wyke has noted that while sexuality in ancient Rome was defined by assertions of dominance and compelled submission, the emotion of love was dangerous when expressed by men. Love made free men weak, vulnerable, like a male slave who 'must learn to endure a woman who commands':[92]

> Amorous passion, the Romans believed, was particularly to be feared because it could make a free man the slave of a woman. He would call her 'mistress' and, like a servant, hold her mirror or her parasol .... When a Roman fell madly in love, his friends and he himself believed either that he had lost his head from overindulgence in sensuality or that he had fallen into a state of moral slavery. The lover, like a good slave, docilely offered to die if his mistress wished it. Such excesses bore the dark magnificence of shame, and even erotic poets did not dare to glorify them openly.[93]

The above is reinforced by this quote from Greece: 'Or he who lets himself be led by women's shamelessness along a road which offers only coldness, while he is serving her.'[94] On the other hand, this emotion, from a wife's point of view, might prove useful: 'unite them in marriage and as spouses in love for all the time of their lives. Make him as her obedient slave, so that he will desire no other woman or maiden apart from Domitiana alone.'[95]

These examples illustrate how intimately mastery was tied to biological sex; in this schema, sexual dominance was the province of the male. It was incumbent upon this male to assume a man's gendered role, lest he lose his freedom and birthright. Biological destiny was obviously complicated greatly by the fact that both men and women could be slaves as well as be free. For women, the role of the mother continued to be the one safe ground where mastery and relative freedom were compatible with their womanhood. But in all these contests of power, authority, and mastery, gender roles were subject to a final, utterly unpredictable factor: the preferences of the individual. Even in a society such as Rome, the danger was that a person could simply choose a life that was not indicated by rule and custom. This presents one final challenge: asking about the emotional life of those who performed the roles of master, mother and slave.

Historian Jennifer Glancy has raised two important questions/examples of self-image among slaves and masters in the early Christian world, wondering 'how slaves perceived their own personhood, in particular, how they perceived themselves as women and men'. For example, she asks, did the male slaves attending women in their baths as described by Clement of Alexandria internalise the divorce from manhood that had put them in that situation?[96] With the lack of sources at that extreme distance in time, satisfactory answers are not obvious. As we have seen, there was an emphasis on stories of male redemption within these three faiths. The far more common experience of individual men lost permanently to slavery was not important enough to record.

Glancy goes on to make a useful point about the importance of the individual, that 'for every [slave] who resisted such sexual advances and perhaps even saw them as rape, there may have been another slave who accepted sexual overtures with equanimity'.[97] Masters were aware of the individual as well. According to Seneca:

> [i]f a prisoner of war suddenly thrown into slavery keeps some traces of freedom and does not jump at the idea of performing degrading and laborious tasks ... we should find out whether the slave cannot do the work or simply will not do it.[98]

Closely related to the individual is the question of how master and slaves performed their roles. Slavery raised the possibility that individuals were aware of their roles to a sufficient degree that they could consciously separate themselves from them to some extent. During the Roman celebration of Matronalia, for example, free women might serve their male slaves for the evening.[99] Although it has been stated that such ceremonial inversions simply served to reinforce established hierarchies by highlighting the ridiculousness and amusements of role playing, the specific inversion of this ceremony also restored the male–female order even as it subverted the central one of master and slave.

The effects were possibly much more complex than we can recover at this distance in time.

Gender roles within slavery were constantly available to individual caprice and the genesis of all kinds of theatrical performance. Richard Trexler, describing inter-city warfare in renaissance Italy, maintains that:

> prisoners would also be important to the triumphal degradation. One Sienese historian told how one of that city's camp followers (described as a sutler by this 'decent' source) on coming upon a group of helpless Florentines after Montaperti, tied them together with her headband and then led them back triumphantly to the Sienese camp 'like a flock of geese'; they would be used on the morrow for formal reentry.[100]

Even the personas of a harlot and her honourable soldiers were unpredictable in the presence of slavery.

Yet among these individual variations, one pattern can still be detected. Slave or free, men tended to assume the centre of the story, and take the active lead in demonstrating the lessons to be learned. Even for Clement of Alexandria, the debauchery of female mastery was described in relation to virtuous men. As Glancy states, we cannot access the thoughts of these individuals, but they were the nucleus of the meaning applied to them as those who would be redeemed by Christ. For all the attention in the annals of slavery to female mastery, a mistress was defined in relation to her slave as to her husband. Real mastery, of the utilitarian, wealth and identity-building sort, was often lost in translation. Yet as empires would emerge in the early modern era, first pitting the Christian and Muslim worlds against each other, and then serving to develop New World colonies, gendered mastery would continue to define the nature of these projects even as old suspicions and fears would remain.

2

Gender, Mastery and Frontier: Europe, North Africa and Native America

Slave frontiers: Christians, Muslims and Native Americans

Theorists, commentators, law makers and slaveholders in the Christian, Muslim and Jewish traditions developed over time the common idea that sovereignty of a female master derived from the same limited spiritual and customary taproot as a mother's authority over her children.[1] Maternal mastery, though, might remain separate from the prerogatives of father-rule – and therein lay a fundamental conflict. The maternal aspect of authority over slaves was fictional in its nature, demanding that everyone involved to some extent pretend, and play assigned roles. Therein lay the danger. Male masters were notoriously unpredictable when it came to the licence their wives, mothers, sisters and daughters should enjoy; mistresses could not necessarily be counted on to act as mothers; slaves could not be counted on to act as dutiful children. And all this fear and uncertainty rested uncomfortably on the economic reliance that husbands, male relatives and their supporters in public authority placed on the management skills of women.

As was seen in the first chapter, the complications of these ideological and practical struggles were troublesome enough for people attempting to define themselves internally. This chapter focuses on Europe's experience with gender, mastery and slavery as the continent projected itself beyond its borders in the early modern age (from 1400 to 1800). Europe at this time established two expansive and defining frontiers: one separating the (mostly) Christian continent from (mostly) Muslim territories across the Mediterranean in North Africa and to its east toward the Ottoman Empire, and one in the Americas facing the indigenous inhabitants. Slavery was such an effective and resonant symbol in defining these frontiers because it could be used to explain, rationalise and justify both conquest and defeat. Enslaved Muslims who provided some of the sinew for various projects in southern Europe (especially Italy and Spain) provided living symbols of supremacy for Europeans. And as New World colonisation advanced, the coercive treatment of various kinds inflicted of Native Americans by the English, Spanish, French and Dutch came to symbolise, sometimes ambiguously, their conquests.

However, it was arguably the enslavement of Europeans *by* Muslims and sometimes even by Native Americans that provided an even greater cultural impact. In all these processes, mastery, maternalism and paternalism gave shape to the meanings of slavery, conquest and defeat. Writings about monstrous male mastery (mostly through sodomy discourse) encapsulated the experience of subjugation, serving as a way to discredit Muslim and Native American societies while using the sexual defeat of individual European men to attempt to rally a more determined resistance. Maternal mastery held by Muslim and Native American women, who were temporarily (it was hoped) in control of Europeans, was employed to demonstrate an ancient lesson: that Christian Europeans could make themselves stronger, and masterless, by overcoming savage maternal control. Finally, the enslavement of Christian women served as a collectively experienced trauma that could be used to rally people around the abomination of abducted daughters, or to accuse inept leadership that had allowed such an insult. Captive European women who voluntarily joined Muslim or Native American society were thought to have surrendered to the savagery of their own nature. They had turned away from their natural pious submission to inflict tyranny even on their own former countrymen.

Along the first frontier to be examined, multitudes of Christian Europeans were at any given time before 1800 involuntarily entering Muslim slave markets across the Mediterranean or land frontiers to the east. The proximity of often hostile North Africans and Ottomans meant that when early modern Europeans considered the institution of slavery, their thoughts were very likely to turn to their own fears of being enslaved. This fed a still larger anxiety – the subjugation by religious and cultural enemies that would mean the loss of mastery over themselves. This metaphor of lost mastery was given its centuries-long urgency because of the genuine physical peril it represented. Monarchs, ministers, popes and bishops throughout Western Europe understood this danger – as did fisherman, farmers and villagers. The latter feared bodily for themselves and their families, who might disappear without a trace from European coasts from Sicily to Iceland, leaving families bereft of a breadwinner, wife, parent or child.

Until the European domination of North Africa commenced in the early nineteenth century, Muslims got the better by far of this expansive slave frontier. Between 1500 and 1800 North Africans, for example, made well over a million captures of Christian western Europeans in order to replenish their slave supplies destined for Algiers, Tunis and Tripoli (Libya). If we extend the census to include Morocco and the western reaches of the Sahara bordering on the Atlantic (outside and to the west of Ottoman control), the number probably exceeds that by several hundred thousand. And if we add the numerous captives taken to the Ottoman Levant, the Balkans, Anatolia, eastern Persia and the Caucasus, that original figure of one million might easily be doubled or trebled, as floods of Poles, Hungarians, Austrians, Russians, Scandinavians and others entered the East involuntarily via the Tatar or Ottoman trade. While the range of between 2 and 4 million slaves is much smaller than the 10 to 12 million Africans extracted from sub-Saharan Africa by Europeans and Euro-Americans and transported west to the Americas across the Atlantic, the number of mostly white Christian slaves was far greater than the number of Arabic or Turkish Muslim slaves taken to Europe.[2]

Nor was this perceived danger confined to the southern peripheries of Europe. Despite its location, even residents of the British Isles experienced a full-fledged crisis of public security in the early to mid-seventeenth century, because of the threat of attack by corsairs. Ordinary English and Irish men and women in coastal regions and upriver estuaries continued to be taken from their homes and cast into true slavery – a danger of sufficient magnitude to inspire political fear. In mid-June 1631, for example, amidst widespread consciousness of the danger, 'Turks' raided the Irish fishing village of Baltimore, with the result that most of its 150 residents – men, women and children alike – were taken to Algiers to begin life in Muslim bondage. Thirty more were taken from the nearby coastal village of Kinsale.[3] 'Turkish' corsairs were even spotted brazenly sailing up the Thames estuary and to the Isle of Wight, looking for and finding captives. (Although it was popularly thought the pirates around southern England were seeking beautiful young women to capture, the most valuable sort of abductee from a monetary point of view would actually have been adult men skilled in shipbuilding or making materials for the maritime trade.) Local London dramas pointedly yet indirectly mocked government impotence through stock figures of the captivity such as Carazie in the drama *The Renegado* by Thomas Massinger. Carazie was a virile Englishman made into a eunuch at Tunis and assigned as a personal servant to Paulina, an Italian woman turned Muslim, doubling the humiliation of English manhood in an atmosphere in which anti-Muslim and anti-Catholic sentiment were often conflated.[4] The sheer scale of the numbers gave such urban cultural dramas their context. At sea, no less than 160 British ships were lost to corsairs between 1677 and 1680 alone.[5] One conservative estimate of the total number of 'Britons' – those from England, Scotland, Wales and Ireland – taken captive to North Africa between the early seventeenth and mid-eighteenth century put it at 20,000 individuals.[6]

Beginning in the sixteenth century, written representations of captivity reached the Latin, Germanic and Anglo-Saxon regions of Europe. Images often accompanied these narratives to give even the non-literate access to their messages. Feeding the imaginations and the dread of ordinary people were narratives and illustrations conveying such scenes as captured men disembarking at a North African port stripped and presented *en masse* to a local ruler, who typically had the right of first refusal to them. The able-bodied might well end up rowing galleys, while young or adolescent boys might be retained for military or sexual service. Skilled slaves, especially shipbuilders, were prized and employed accordingly. Those slaves the ruler declined to purchase were then placed on the market for private buyers, where the range of typical fates was identical. Male slaves attractive by virtue of wealth, education, social status or physical beauty might be placed in the fortunate circumstance of domestic service: cleaning, carrying, gardening or attending their owner's family. Although those meeting this fate were relatively lucky, a high-born layman or cleric from status-obsessed Europe could well find that life as a household slave or personal attendant humiliated the spirit and debilitated the body. Whatever his destiny, once purchased as a public or private slave he was shorn, outfitted and affixed with a chain, and required to undergo pantomimes of submission to the new authority. Artists' renderings did not fail to capture the dramatic moment where the individual Christian was extinguished – the Muslim master might signal dominance by placing a foot on the neck of the prostrate slave and recite a few words designed to seal the new relationship.[7]

There are some similarities with the situation that European explorers and then colonisers faced regarding the native peoples of the Americas. Perceptions of Muslims and Native Americans certainly overlapped (as would have been natural – the English, French, Spanish and Dutch in the seventeenth century were establishing their American colonies in the era of ever-more damaging struggles with Muslim enemies). Certainly the physical initiations proceeded along equivalent lines, with captives prepared for a variety of fates by being divested of the clothing that had signalled their former affiliation. Unclothed or adopting the dress of their captor host, the individual was ceremonially remade. However, in many cases Europeans were incorrect (deliberately or not) about the nature of the 'slavery' or 'captivity' to which they might fall victim in the Americas.

Historically, the question pertinent to Native American 'slavery' is how wandering hunter-gatherers or quasi-settled agriculturalists, could afford to keep dependent slaves. Hungry bondsmen might simply be an expensive burden if the question of abundance or scarcity in food supply did not rely on the availability of extra labour. In bountiful areas tribal societies, generally speaking, were very well able to support themselves with astonishingly few hours of work per person per month when taken over the course of a year. Enslaved females providing reproductive services and supplementing the workforce needed for gathering and farming might have added enough value to justify the burden of feeding them in certain environments. But the technically demanding and cooperative occupations of hunting and warfare, which defined freedom for men, were not easily shared with enslaved, poorly assimilated and possibly rebellious adult males.

However, pure economic considerations were not always decisive in any tribal society's decision to keep dependants against their will. Non-essential 'luxury' slaves employed in personal service or visible domestic roles could be culturally desirable – even essential. Slaves were produced by victory in war, and the pride of keeping walking trophies enacting daily submission to the members of the triumphant people existed whether or not a given economy was convincingly complex and diverse enough to provide a surplus. Furthermore, the cultural benefits of slavery bolstered individual native tribal families who acted as guardians of spiritual practice and ritual. The word 'slave', however, poses the problem of variable meanings – including overlaps with the European definitions of 'captive', 'prisoner' and 'adoptee'. Further, the intensions of native captors were often changeable and difficult for European captives and observers to understand. In most indigenous North American societies, captives could meet a range of fates including genuine adoption, outright enslavement, fictive kinship/liminal incorporation, bondage or simple execution.[8]

'Liminal incorporation' is the most applicable of these. This anthropological term fully developed by Orlando Patterson describes a captive drawn into the family life of a captor who is nevertheless unable to enjoy full member-ship in the protecting family. Typical of this status is the obligation to serve the original family members, usually with the restriction that the captive could never marry freely into the captive or group. Patterson's second term, 'fictive kinship', illustrates the mechanism by which the outsider is assigned the formal identity of a family member – such as replacing a recently deceased aunt or brother.[9] Often Europeans who entered into Native American captivity invol-untarily reported that their 'kinship' did not accord with that of the person they supposedly replaced. These false 'relatives' might be treated with respect and honour, or as subservient and transferable beings, all according to a precise calculus which was not well understood by Europeans.

Historians and writers, then, have often been rightly cautious in ascribing the word 'slavery' to indigenous Americans. Native modes of dealing with liv-ing captives were too variable and did not fit easily into European expectations of coerced labour. However, as many Native American societies included dishonoured social subordination with forced labour among their practices (customs which were often themselves adjusted or altered due to colonial influence), slavery as broadly defined did provide some basis for a mutual lan-guage of understanding between natives and European arrivals. Yet the cul-tural distances were so great and changeable that opportunities for mutual misunderstandings and misapprehensions abounded.

Europeans among Muslims

If some have overestimated the degree to which marginal status among native Americans was true 'slavery', new scholarship has shown that western observ-ers in the past and present have tended to underestimate the degree to which European 'captives' were kept in true, permanent slavery in North Africa and the Ottoman empire. Historian Robert C. Davis has written the definitive work on Christian 'slave counting' in the early modern Muslim world. Davis has com-puted that a relatively high number of captives were necessary to replenish the number of Christian European slaves known to have been present in Algiers, Tunis and Tripoli during peak and non-peak periods. He asserts that well over a million initial captures would have been necessary to sustain the known num-bers of slaves in these cities (typically in the low tens of thousands during peak periods). This estimate takes into account the high death rate among the slaves, the generally low rate of redemption which would lead to a Christian captive's release and return home, and the fact that the enslaved population (who were overwhelmingly male) were generally forbidden to reproduce. Davis emphasises that few Christian captives, probably no more than 5 per cent per year, ever emerged from bondage. Therefore there was no doubt a significant reservoir of uncounted 'captives' who in fact were permanent slaves in North Africa, the Ottoman Levant, and even western and central Asia.[10] These findings put the fear of Europeans into proper perspective: they were justified by the irrevo-cable nature of the threat that shadowed them.

As for Muslim slaves in the various Christian lands in the early modern period, a similar comprehensive census has yet to be attempted. However,

apart from certain Spanish, Portuguese, southern French and Italian metropolitan areas and in galley service, Europe at this time generally had fewer
social systems capable of admitting or making use of large numbers of enslaved
foreigners. In contrast to the Muslim world, where Christian slaves could
meet a wide variety of fates in the hands of private and public masters, even
in southern Europe the use of Muslim slaves was focused on maritime service
(the galleys) or gang labour in cities set apart from the general population –
although domestic service could be a fate met as well, especially for captive
Muslim women. Further, Muslim naval power in the Mediterranean until the
eighteenth century ensured that more Christians involuntarily entered Muslim
lands than the reverse.

Europeans then encountered two different, overlapping forms of challenge
as their long-developed ideas about maternal and paternal mastery in slavery
reconstituted themselves in foreign, savage forms.

European slaves in the Muslim world

Sodomy and sexual danger

European imagination of the Muslim-Christian slave frontier was often preoccupied with sexuality. The image of slavery in Muslim lands that has mostly
come down to us is of the pampered but sexually exposed white European
female captive entombed in the seraglio. But these are mainly artefacts of
nineteenth-century European colonial dominance, which produced pointed,
indirect 'orientalist' critiques of Muslim men who were depicted either as distant, seldom-seen tyrant-masters of the harem, or as decadent eunuchs – an
effeminate abomination of manhood. The message to the audience of these
later works emerging from the era of high European imperialism was that the
Muslim tyrant/master needed to be conquered by civilised Christians in order
that his oriental vices might be controlled – and eliminated. Similarly, the
debased eunuch required European intervention to restore something of his
lost masculinity – never quite wholly recoverable.

Yet the central visual and literary figure of this material was the enslaved,
frequently nude Christian woman, her skin an exaggerated tone of white,
placed in the seraglio among other similarly abject yet powerfully exotic
women. The artist or writer invited the reader or viewer to sympathise with the
woman as a victim of the stark sexual peril of her new environment as well as
the religious assaults that permeated her luxurious surroundings. Yet these verbal and visual images also invited audiences to ponder to what degree the captive Christian woman might be complicit in her own plight. To what degree
would she succumb to her own sexual immorality and spiritual impurity and
betray, as a weak woman, everything she had been taught to value? Culturally, politically and morally, most other mainstream cultural art and literature
placed white women at the virtuous centre of the family during the European
nineteenth century. Fantastic, lurid visions of the seraglio were one of the few
respectable ways to present the eminently civilised middle-class western woman
as both abject and overtly sexualised. To what degree, the comfortable audience was asked, was she responsible for her own victimhood? To what extent

was she the slave of her own body – and the fate to which that body would be guided by men? Would she take the path of least resistance and become herself a willing 'savage'? And the images of course rebuked the Christian men who had failed in their duties to protect her.[11] All this, of course, reflected the culture and preoccupations of European artists and authors rather than anything significant or particularly accurate about the Muslim east, or even about white women.

Before 1800, however, when enslavement was still a tangible fear among Europeans, the sexual danger presented all these elements plus the fear that Europeans might be forced to observe these degradations involuntarily. And situations of captivity existed in a profusion of variations. Often presented was not the threat posed to Christian women by Muslim men, but rather the relationships among Islamic masters and their Christian male slaves. As the Spanish commentator Father Haedo perceived in 1612:

> The [Muslim] man who keeps more male concubines [*garzónes*] is held in greater honour, and [he] guards them more closely than his own wives and daughters ... no Turk sets out on a campaign, no corsair on a cruise, without his [Christian] *garzóne*, who cooks for him, keeps him company, and shares his bed.[12]

Popular ideas of involuntary (and voluntary) homosexuality among men of the different faiths served two basic purposes. First, they suggested the perversion and natural inferiority of an enemy. Second, stories of forced sodomy suggested the shame of Christian weakness and vulnerability. To acknowledge a European being sodomised by a Muslim master was to construct in the mind an overarching metaphor for slavery itself – an enduring disgrace marked by ongoing susceptibility to Muslim domination.

Sexual danger across the Islamic frontier also involved the unpleasant prospect that Christian Europeans would voluntarily adapt oriental, Muslim ways. Miguel de Cervantes, author of *Don Quixote* and himself a former slave in sixteenth-century Algiers, tells in his play *Los tatos de Argel* of the fate of two beautiful young Spanish boys at the hands of pleasure-seeking Moorish masters. The defilement of the young slaves also highlighted the failure of the Spanish authorities to protect their society's young. Whatever the truth of the sexual peril of attractive young Christian slaves in North Africa witnessed by Cervantes, no reader could fail to grasp the wages of Spain's own weakness and failure of collective resolve. The cultural stakes were high and the emotions involved explosive: the father of the boys in *Argel* declares he would rather see his sons dead than continue as the target of the insatiable lust of their Algerian masters.[13]

Yet the use of sodomy as a metaphor to attack enemies of Christendom could not stand up to any sort of close scrutiny by those seeking signs of hypocrisy. The well-known homosexual ghettoes in Spanish cities in the sixteenth century were not really so distinguishable from even the most lurid imaginings of the barber shops of Barbary – where young slaves were brought to service any of a wide range of needs their male customers might express.[14] On the Christian side of the frontier, homosexual lovers, including Muslim slaves, were also available in gambling houses, hospitals, inns and prisons. Cervantes, a frequenter of gambling houses, and his publisher de Robles, who operated one, would have been well aware of the associations. Second, secular and religious thinking on the theory and practice of homosexuality was not consistent across the Muslim world, and it was certainly not nearly so widely accepted there as Christian commentators invariably assumed.[15] At issue with the invocation of homosexuality was, again, simply the political and religious damage done when a non-Christian wielded a master's unlimited power.

The English, for their part, tended to publicly link sodomy to depravity, lost honour, abandoned manhood, and religious inferiority along similar lines. Complex strands of drama, prescriptive literature, scholarship, political discourse, and narratives of captivity all related sodomy to the Muslim frontier.

This served to rivet public attention on the idea of lost mastery – with the English themselves as the victims – and sexuality serving as a chief metaphor.[16] Englishman Adam Elliot, a former slave in North Africa in the late seventeenth century, directly told his audience of the sexual overtures made by his Muslim master, making it clear that his owner expected these kind of services from any Christian man he owned.[17] Joseph Pitts, an Englishman who had experienced a long period of enslavement among the Algerians in the late seventeenth century, expressed a typical view when he wrote in his account that 'this horrible sin of sodomy is so far from being punished amongst them that it is part of their ordinary discourse to boast and brag of their detestable actions of that kind'. Pitts echoed Haedo when he asserted:

> [It] is common for men to fall in love with boys as 'tis here in England to be in love in women. And I have seen many when they have been drunk that have given themselves deep gashes on their arm with a knife, saying 'tis for the love that they bear to such a boy.[18]

It was the object of Pitts and others to show steadfast loyalty to home by resisting such temptations on both religious and nationalistic grounds. The purpose of publicly presenting the sexual perils of slavery was to demonstrate what had to be overcome. At the same time, writing around the British Isles during the sixteenth and seventeenth century to a large degree avoided recording local homosexual practice at home except in court records, law, and other documents produced by official recorders. In England, as in Spain, associating the sexual and violent aspects of homosexual licence with the Islamic world was a wilful misunderstanding, or deliberate ignorance, of life across the frontier.[19]

Muslim female mastery – imagined and real

The act of enslaving a Christian European was only the beginning of an process of gendered mastery which could be extraordinarily nuanced. These nuances can be revealed through case studies of individual lives. In these cases, the struggle of 'apostasy' (from the Christian perspective) or 'conversion' (from the Muslim perspective) were presented as battles among men as well as one that pitted a Christian man against Muslim women. These females might be considered degraded slaves to their husbands, but could easily be potent female masters of Christian

Europeans. The cultural disturbance created by a Muslim woman was first that she enjoyed freedom in the sense that 'savages' were thought to be free from civilising constraints. The Muslim woman with authority, as a cultural figure in Europe, communicated something about Europeans that sodomy discourse could not. Muslim female masters served as a cautionary tale for what women could become in unsettled surroundings – oriental despots in their own right. But unlike men, Muslim women might be tamed and converted. As early as 1510, the Spanish writer Ordoñez de Montalvo imagined an isle in the American Indies called 'California', whose residents were female Amazon warriors of Moorish appearance. Their queen, Califa, led them to help relieve the Christian siege on Muslim Constantinople, but the women were captured and enslaved – made into submissive Christian wives.[20] The reality proved far more ambiguous.

Like sodomy tales, though, female mastery challenged Europeans to see that perils could be overcome. The tension was built into related narrative ethnographies, stories, plays and novels. Would the Christian man surrender to, or triumph over, his savage mistress? This test would eventually prove portable – informing how Native Americans came to be understood in the process of New World colonisation and the establishment of slavery across the Atlantic.

In 1684, an English-language edition of Dutch seafarer and traveller Jan van Struys's account of his penetration into Persia and beyond found eager readers in London.[21] Although the English had become accustomed to tales of their countrymen held in bondage in North Africa, the far eastern reaches of the Islamic world would have provided some novelty. Struys and his travelling companions managed to remain free, quite against the odds, until finally captured by bandits after reaching an ethnically complex and politically fragmented region called Dagestan. Hoping to trade, Struys instead found himself being handled as trade goods, joining the Russian and Polish human merchandise sent that way by 'Cossacks' and Crimean Tatars.

The captivity narrative by its nature, and especially that genre created by Christian men venturing beyond Europe, is one in which the natural motion of the man is temporarily stopped, allowing him to take the guise of a subservient, socially invisible observer of intimate, domestic worlds that free 'guests' could have never seen. In these circumstances, captive men began to describe their surroundings, including the lives of women they would never have encountered except for their new diminished status. Struys, trapped along the far-off margins of Persia, accordingly described varieties of Muslim women for the benefit of his readers at home.

The first distinct type of women he encountered after his enslavement were lures – sirens dispatched to entreat the industrious Dutchman to convert and serve the Muslim cause. His master twice sent 'two young Damsels' who:

> endeavoured to perswade me to turn Mahometan, neither did they desist to use all manner of Allurements they could devise, to entice me to ly with them, for so they thought that if I had done that, I must either become a Turk, or dy a miserable Death, They further did what they could to put me in mind of my present misery, and told me that I must never expect to enjoy any better than what I saw before my eyes.[22]

Stalwart resolve in the face of feminine, savage temptation was the signature stance of former captives after their return. The girls were apparently offering freedom and mastery. The Russian male slave standing by as a translator must have been a reminder to Struys, and his readers, that bondage continuing in perpetuity was a very real possibility. The consequences of failing to take the opportunity to master women would be to serve them.

The second archetype Struys presents is the female apostate. Soon after his refusal to convert and consignment to slavery, he discovers that his master's wife is a young Polish woman, brought to Dagestan through the Crimean trade. Such women converts to Islam could be described as treacherous and cruel to erstwhile countrymen, or as sympathetic saviours. Appearing the year it did, Struys's tale would have offered readers the very familiar detail of the Muslim mistress conspiring to run away with her worthy slave. In this case the Polish woman possessed a large cache of her husband's jewels, and proposed that they use the money to flee across the Caspian into Russia, and from there make their way to Amsterdam. 'If your wife be not alive,' she told him, 'we shall marry.' Struys admitted he was tempted – here was a woman offering freedom without the necessity that he betray his faith. But he knew the impracticality of such an adventure, and how it was likely to end in robbery, re-enslavement or death. He demurred – and although his duties had to that point brought him in close proximity to his Polish mistress, he was soon transferred to his master's outlying properties. Eventually the master travelled onward with Struys, leaving the mistress to compete with the two young Georgian slave girls her husband had recently brought home.[23]

The third and final archetype emerged as he travelled. Struys reflected matter-of-factly about the effect the shortage of female domestic labour could have on the character of Muslim women, and their jealous husbands:

> And by reason that Women-Slaves are somewhat rare among them, the Merchants and Citizens wives are mostly attended by men, who if they have a sprightly and airy way and Carriage, are sometimes admitted to enjoy those illicit pleasures, which in the process of time they recompense with the loss of their lives.[24]

Here is the necessary companion to the unmanned captive – the opportunistic, depraved Muslim mistress willing to engage her lusts in the undisciplined manner that a lack of Christian faith entailed. In a similar manner the 'siren' and 'apostate' female archetypes were matched with the 'renegade' and 'stalwart' male narrative figures, the women presenting the men with tests that they could pass or fail.

But what of real slavery, the actual relationships that existed quite separately from how Christian bondage was represented back home? As was suggested in the Introduction, the first task is to define mastery itself. If Patterson asserted that mastery lay in the 'lightening of the soul' of man, did owning human chattel serve as an embodiment of womanhood?[25] And if, as historian David Brion Davis has written, 'the master's identity depended on having a slave who recognized him as master', then what constituted the identity of the mistress?[26] In situations of actual mastery, how did Muslim women slaveholders' own identities reflect back upon their slaves?

First, female mastery in the Muslim world, as elsewhere, was oriented primarily around work rather than sex, and the social virility was granted by their routine management of labour. Here a wide range of Christian and Muslim commentators are in agreement. Christian luminaries from Cervantes to St Vincent de Paul, both former captive slaves in North Africa, reported on the proximity of women to working Christian slaves, unveiled to the *mahram* infidels, for the ordinary tasks of supervision. (As discussed in Chapter 1, a '*mahram*' is a category of people ineligible to marry a Muslim woman, usually relatives, servants and slaves.) For de Paul especially, the ease of such interaction between Muslim women and male Christians caused many to doubt the veracity of his accounts – his critics were clearly unaware of the deep cultural and religious roots of such contacts in the Muslim precincts of Africa.[27]

Explicit on this matter was the Christian from Dunkirk, Emanuel d'Aranda, who in the mid-seventeenth century was clear about the day-to-day mastery of Algerian women he lived among, irrespective of their marital status. He laid the groundwork by stating again the *mahram* principle.[28] One young wife of his master, for example, was described as holding control over the religious life of the household, and d'Aranda had to entreat her each time he wanted to attend mass. He also reported a matter-of-fact conversation between his own young mistress and the mistress of his friend and compatriot called Coloën, when the latter woman suspected a brewing slave rebellion:

> The next day [Coloën's mistress] came to my Patroness and said, to her, 'why do you not put your Dunkirk-Slave in irons, that he may not come to give ill advice to his companion? My patroness replied, 'Why should I do so? My Dunkirker serves me faithfully, and therefore I have no reason to put him into irons.'[29]

Coloën's mistress (likely a relative or fellow wife of d'Aranda's mistress), was not convinced of the two men's innocence and secretly arranged to have them attached together on the same chain in order that they be under her secure surveillance as they worked – the 'irons' also serving as a physical impediment to their imagined escape. D'Aranda leaves no doubt that the dispute, as a matter of course, was to be settled entirely by the two young Algerian women inhabiting their long-established roles as active overseers working in close proximity to male domestic slaves. Significantly, the two women did not sexualise their men, but throughout their conflict continued to regard them pragmatically as instruments of labour.

The unexpected proximity of Christian male slaves to Muslim women in accordance with the *mahram* principle, combined with the submergence of their romantic visions and aspirations under a sea of required work, explains the desperate attempts from those former captives lucky enough to return to embellish these relationships. The part that was difficult for their audiences (and many later historians) to believe, the proximity to the supposedly cloistered and veiled women, was in fact true. The easy part to believe, the willingness of these women to give themselves sexually and emotionally to the

Christian men, was far more difficult. These aggrieved returned captives were clearly attempting to reconstruct their own masculinity upon dubious claims of manipulating their owners. And as seen in Chapter 1, Marina Lazreg finds such claims dubious: Algerian women thought of Christian male slaves in terms of work, and surveillance by the extended family would have made sexual liaisons difficult and rare.[30] Even Christian men's work in the female baths she puts in terms of practical use rather than licentious behaviour. And on occasion the Christian slaves admitted to placid domestic labour, as when the French slave Germain Mouette describes how he became a favoured family slave when his mistress placed him in charge of her young son.[31]

Free Muslim women engaged in a wide variety of economically profitable activities relating to slaves. These included the potentially profitable business of breeding them. In one case an Arab mistress busied herself by breeding a male with a female slave when attempts to ransom them failed.[32] Such instances must have been somewhat rare because in most times and places in North Africa at least the great majority of slaves were men.[33] For this reason, there is also far less documentation on this than that relative to Muslim female economic use of Christian women. Though the Muslim mistress–Christian maidservant was a stock relationship in European drama and later novels on the hazards and lessons of this frontier, the dearth of available captured females in many areas led to the captured men being commonly employed in domestic tasks, even as galley service siphoned off most enslaved men. Struys, for example, noted that women in western Persia of whatever origin were needed as wives and daughters more than they were needed as slaves.[34] Historian Ruth Pike has speculated that among Christian owners in early modern Spain, Muslim female slaves were 'particularly close to their mistresses' – whether this might have been due to shared domestic space and agendas is not clear. This assumption of closeness is based upon the publicly performed dramas of the time, which although they are not direct sources are some of the only reflections we have on those relationships.[35]

Outside the confines of the home, women slave traders were active in Istanbul (where they may have constituted the majority by the nineteenth century). They also operated late in the Ottoman era as transport dealers, making journeys from Tripoli to the empire's capital with slaves in tow. Most such slaves would presumably be white Circassian, Anatolian or eastern European females destined for the sexual and domestic service that represented the women dealers' main trade, but even this was not an exclusively female world, since men as well appear on their slave ledgers.[36] This was also true for the black slaves of both sexes from the Red Sea and upper Nile areas.[37]

Yet in this process, the brutal business of slave trading and transportation (during which the women managers probably relied on male employees to help provide oversight), the figure begins to emerge of the female master as a cultural broker. Historian Ehud Toledano and others have shown that the slave-trading business for the women of Istanbul contained a good bit of acculturation, as new Circassian, Georgian and Albanian girls (many of them already Muslim and some of them even impoverished Turks) were prepared for lives as the wives and concubines of powerful men.[38] Such mastery exerted then by Muslim women made new worlds, for better or worse, for slaves. Such practices fed the European paranoia we shall see concerning their own women using slavery as a path of upward social mobility. As for Muslim women, male writers tended to come to a similar conclusion – that the combination of Islam, savagery and slavery created an unnaturally powerful female individual. Yet she was not unattractive, her seductions more devilish than monstrous, remembered in terms of the challenges of faith. As d'Aranda recalled on the topic of Muslim women poisoning their husbands to make way for their Christian slaves to replace them, the former captive mixes the typical ingredients of pious memoir and fantasy in which the suffering hero is at the centre, a dismissal of the virtue of Muslim men, and a roundabout admission of Muslim women's mastery of many situations:

> This slow operation of the poison causes many Spaniards and Italians to renounce the Christian faith. The reason is, that many Turks are addicted to the abominable sin, and the women are easily debauched by their slaves. Whence it comes, that having continu'd in the lewdness sometime, the women say to them 'if you will renounce your Religion, I will marry you, and, of a poor slave, make you Master of this house and all that I have.' These promises are tempting, and most of the slaves, being ordinary Sea-men, and poor in their own Country, are consequently oblig'd to get their livlihood by hard labor, they are inveigled by these taking appearances of liberty and wealth, strengthened by the sollicitations of a handsome women, and so prefer the temporal before eternal happiness. Being this agreed, the women give their husbands a slow poison, so that the husbands dying some months after, the widdow marries the Renegado slave. There is no great inquisition made into these crimes by the magistrate, insomuch as there are many who boast of their excellence in that art.[39]

Christian women and redemption

Before knowledge of the Americas was widespread in Christendom, European tradition had forged two principal roles for free women of faith facing a slave frontier. The first archetype might be called the noble, pious redeemer. Hagiographies of the eleventh-century Hungarian/English queen of Scotland, St Margaret, stand as one example. A consort might possess reflected mastery from her husband's divine right, and the particular divine inspiration of Margaret made her at once the good daughter of the heavenly father and the good mother of the afflicted. Her compassion for English slaves in Scotland at that time became one of the pillars of her reputation and sanctity. She offered general relief, including arranging for slaves to be ransomed home, for as the oft-quoted saying went, during her life no Scot was so impoverished that he did not possess an English slave.[40]

Less noble, but equally devout, was the virtuous frontier wife of men stepping off the map. The Grimm brothers' enduring folktale of 'Alexander and Florintina', which emerged from the Lorraine region of the French–German borderlands, expressed a fragment of the enduring imagination of durable Christianity. Alexander, a captured Christian knight, was held by a Turkish sultan and forced to work hitched to a plough as a draught animal. Alexander had worn a white shirt emblazoned with a red cross which had been given to him by his wife Florintina, which managed to remain immaculate and unmarked by whips, sweat and blood. The shirt attracted the attention of the sultan, who attempted to break its spell by sending an agent to Europe to seduce Alexander's wife – thus corrupting her faith and breaking the divine spell of the garment. Florintina not only refused seduction, remaining constant to her husband, but learning of his fate, disguised herself as a pilgrim and made the journey to Turkey carrying her harp. Arriving at the court of the sultan, she was offered a reward for her outstanding musical skill and voice. She chose as her gift the chance to select a one of the sultan's slaves to serve on her continuing journey. Reviewing the Christians ploughing the fields, she quickly recognised her husband, but Alexander did not recognise Florentina in her pilgrim-woman's garb. After selecting Alexander she spirited him away home, only revealing her identity when they were safely back in Europe.[41]

In this instance a strain of Christian folk tradition grants virility to female purpose above and beyond simply wifely virtue and sexual continence. While the unsullied shirt seems to reflect the faithfulness of husband and wife alike, she succeeds with the Turks where her husband has failed, emphasised by the scene of a helpless knight, hitched to a plough and denied even the dignity of ordinary movement, standing in vivid contrast to his wife, in full activity, secure in her abilities to make her way as easily in the world of powerful Muslims as she had among Christians, carrying out her plan.

The second major role assigned to women was of course that of the slave. At least in relation to Muslim North Africa, the enslavement of European females is a far more elusive subject that the enslavement of men, as women might have made up as few as one slave in 20.[42] And since far fewer women than men emerged from slavery between 1500 and 1800, the authentic voices of these women are virtually impossible to recover.

The experience of Christian female slaves and apostates however had cultural impact on both sides of the frontier, and their numbers were not absolutely insignificant. If between one and one-and-a-half million European captives were taken across the frontier to the major North African population centres (and, as previously discussed, if the Muslim world is considered in its entirety this is a conservative estimate), 5 per cent of the total leads to the recognition that at the very least 50,000 to 75,000 European women and girls were taken by force during the centuries in question – and the great majority of them would never return. A reliable overview of ransom, conversion and mortality rates between male and female Christian captives has not been attempted, and might be impossible given the lack of relevant sources.

It has been traditional to see the enslavement of European men mainly in terms of exploitation of labour, while the enslavement of white women has been defined by vulnerability to sexual violation. Upon closer examination these lines overlap and blur. As we have seen, sexual violation by masters could be a central part of slavery for many captured men. Conversely, female slaves were typically destined for a life of involuntary labour. From the hints we get from their enslaved male counterparts, it seems that Christian women were typically employed in the female North African domestic economy – as servants and attendants of wealthy Muslim women, and as needleworkers, kitchen help and similar occupations. Like male Christian slaves, a few fortunate elite women might be spared heavy or monotonous labour to preserve their value as hostages for ransom, and none seemed to have experienced life in the communal *bagno* (slave prison) for men and were dispatched instead to sequestered areas. Christian male commentators claimed that the inspections of women before sale were quite immodest and intimate in nature, and readers were directed to understand that the captives would be assessed as to their virginity.[43] It should be noted though that male captives would not ordinarily have been direct witnesses to these scenes which they wrote of with such assurance.

The imagination of the male captives often became even more loaded with innuendo when describing events that occurred after the initial inspection. 'Harems' featured prominently in the tales, with attractive young Christian women naturally falling into the hands of the local Muslim men, or rulers wealthy and powerful enough to afford multiple wives and concubines in inaccessible settings. However, stories of stalwart European women with enough mental strength and emotional courage to resist captivity were an opportunity to expand upon the too-often lurid themes of female captivity. One English slave described the fate of one of his young countrywomen sent as a concubine to the Moroccan emperor and notorious nemesis of Christendom, Muley Ismail. When the girl dared to resist the absolute monarch, he promptly turned her over to some black female slaves, who whipped and otherwise tortured her at great length until she relented.[44] (The English-born concubine later bore a few of Ismail's many children by various wives, and was popularly credited with doing what she could, like St Margaret, to bring about the redemption of Christian slaves.)

This sort of writing was a precursor to the harem fantasy characteristic of nineteenth-century orientalism. Those who portrayed women's subjugation to a Muslim conqueror sought, as would the Victorians, to illustrate Europe's own aspirations, fears, strengths and shortcomings via the highly sexualised idea of the female captive across a frontier. The earlier sixteenth, seventeenth and eighteenth-century versions, though, were more likely to deal with flesh-and-blood women as opposed to purely imaginary ones. The kind of message provided by the story of the English slave-girl and the Moroccan emperor reinforced the message conveyed by sodomy discourse. The failure of Christian Europe was represented as the failure of the girl's father, male relatives and whole society to protect her. The specific sexual nature of her victimisation was neatly designed as a companion critique highlighting the depravity of Muslim manhood and mastery. And the Englishwoman's later role in assisting slaves with their ransoms home underscored the transcendent value of feminine mercy at the heart of Protestant and Catholic ideals. The Englishwoman was able to turn her forced apostasy, her own lost hopes, into the possibility for freedom to those who might still be redeemed – a final detail that drove home the essential and defining qualities of virtue that Christians stood to lose through weakness and lack of vigilance.

In addition to sexual victims and angels of mercy, a frequently described third type of captive European woman might be called the heartless, cruel opportunist – the woman who gladly traded her faith, country and birthright in a devil's bargain for more earthly power. She was seen enacting a sort of frontier version of European belief in diabolism and witchcraft, in which the contract with the enemies of God was a route to unnatural power. Male European slaves reported encountering more than a few apostate women. Their life pathways had proceeded along the lines of the celebrated Roxelana, known in the Ottoman Empire as Khurrem – the laughing one – who rose from being a Ukrainian Christian slave girl – abject merchandise in a market – to supreme prominence and political power as the chief advisor of her husband Sultan Suleyman the Magnificent. She overcame in the process the vicious politics of the imperial harem, securing her authority, and placing one of her own sons as her husband's successor.[45]

Minor versions of women like Roxelana turned up everywhere in accounts of 'Barbary' North Africa. These were European women of typically modest birth who attached themselves to powerful Muslim men. These alliances might have been involuntary at first, but captivity quickly gave women a glimpse and then a taste for raw avarice, lust for power and wanton opportunism. Consuls recorded with surprise and dismay apostate women capable of political influence over their masters-turned-husbands, and some European male slaves recorded the authoritative presence of women converts in Muslim households. As we have seen, one of the mistresses of Dutch captive Jan Struys in the eastern reaches of Persia had been born in Poland. There was common hostility towards women who had risen through 'selling their souls for bribes'. Europeans only seemed to admire apostate women if their slavery was cast as inescapable victimisation and used to help the interests of their fellow slaves. Christian women turned Muslim who turned to petty domestic tyranny and political assertiveness were especially condemned as traitors to their faith and womanhood, as well as usurpers of legitimate social status.

For example, the Muslim world could have this transformative effect on English womanhood in reality as well as in the imagination, as the real-life consul Samuel Martin found in Algiers one day when he went to negotiate with the local caliph. He found that the ruler was to be replaced in the meeting that day by one of his wives, the de facto ruler of the city-state, an Englishwoman of a rather undistinguished social background at that, taken long ago in one of the coastal raids.[46]

Enslaved European women benefited Muslim men materially and sexually, eased the burdens of Muslim women, and provided European men with the opportunity to score ideological, political and religious points against perceived enemies at home and abroad. But these afflicted women were quite real – women who had much in common with their enslaved male counterparts, and in the end broadcast similar meanings about their lives. Were the implicit accusations that such women lived lives of relative privilege in slavery justified? European women were spared the killing labour of the galleys and the chained gangs devoted to public works, regardless of religious status. And if these women were young and fortunate enough to form attachments to free Muslim men, their lives would unfold in more or less normal, expected, and perhaps even desirable ways.

These Christian-turned-Muslim women would have opportunities for sexual expression and to bear and raise children. They would enjoy the protection and security of a new faith, a new community, and new extended and immediate families. At least anecdotally, the number of such exceptionally privileged female slaves does not seem to be proportionally different from those male apostates given the opportunity for full freedom in the Muslim world. And while the least fortunate European males suffered the most physically onerous fates, European-born females who remained enslaved and who were consigned to the most toilsome lives in household service cannot reliably be said to have borne less of a psychological burden. Nevertheless, once incorporated into a Muslim family, the opportunity to be returned home to Europe through ransom essentially vanished for women. Such mastery and privileges as the new wife possessed only existed at the pleasure of her husband. European women who achieved political power among Muslims through sheer force of personality did exist – but were hardly common. The opportunity to live a normal family life by the standards of their home societies was not in most cases a voluntary choice of the enslaved women – who entered a life that included sexual servitude to their new husbands.

There is ample evidence that many apparently privileged female captives would happily have left their circumstances if given the elusive chance. One young Irish mother brought to Algiers, learning that her about-to-commence slavery would mean permanent separation from her small children, reacted violently, holding her Algerian male captors at bay for a while, attacking them in a public square with any object that came to hand before finally being subdued.[47]

On the European side of the slave frontier, Christians were also ready to exploit some of the unexpected opportunities presented to dispose of inconvenient family problems at home. From some local laws of Spain during the earlier era of the *reconquista* we can deduce that mothers selling unwanted children into Muslim slavery produced a significant problem of civic and religious order.[48] The slave frontier, in other words, entered the European consciousness with fear of manipulated and illegitimate mastery firmly in mind.

Masterless men

Another problem posed by captive Christian men went beyond simple victimisation. Like captured women, men were made abject by Muslim slavery, but they were also potentially made more powerful. What occurred when foreign temptations, sexual and otherwise, led some European men to abandon the faith and home of their birth? The picaresque tale and legend of Dutch renegade Jan Janszoon van Haarlem is revealing in this respect.

A privateer and sea-going merchant by profession, Janszoon made his living during the first two decades of the 1600s by pirate-hunting and piracy for hire. His career accelerated after he was captured by Muslims near the Canary Islands in 1618 and taken to Algiers as a slave. Janszoon quickly converted to Islam – or was compelled to convert by those sponsors and investors who appreciated his seafaring talents. Now known as Murad Reis, the *Hollandais* captain was able to resume his privateering career, and made lucrative business of raiding European (even Dutch) ships and villages. He achieved a special brand of notoriety in the English-speaking world with his planning and execution of the Baltimore raid, which brought many Irish men, women and children to the slave markets of Algiers – an event that, as mentioned, undermined popular confidence in Charles I of England. Based at various times in Algiers and in the stubbornly independent Moroccan slaving port of Salé, his renewed plundering brought in slaves from as far as Iceland. Janszoon/Murad also apparently succeeded in moving with some assurance in the treacherous environment of Barbary politics, gaining an appointment from Morocco's emperor (no friend of the troublesome Salé) to govern the western Moroccan castle of Maladia before the trail of his life is lost in the records after 1641.

The several plausible versions of Janszoon/Murad's complex family life suggest its various cultural meanings. One tradition has the budding Christian privateer, already married to a Dutch woman, forming a liaison with a Muslim girl from an ostracised Islamic community in Cartagena in Spanish Murcia. When the Christian authorities finally expelled this isolated Muslim community about 1610, Janszoon's Muslim female concubine (possibly by then his wife), with one or two of their sons, relocated to Algiers and later to Salé, there to be reunited with Janszoon after his own capture, enslavement and conversion to Islam. In another version, there was no woman of Cartagena – but this story mentions the existence of at least one Dutch son by his original Amsterdam marriage, who was captured alongside his father in 1618. This young man grew up to help his father in privateering. Janszoon/Murad's subsequent sons were born to an unnamed woman or women in Algiers.

Whatever the actual circumstances, Janszoon/Murad's extended family may have moved with remarkable ease between the Muslim and Christian worlds – worth noting especially in consideration of the 'slave frontier' separating them. As a Muslim corsair, the captain managed a visit to his Dutch first wife in 1623 when a truce between the Netherlands and Algiers gave him the chance to stop enslaving his fellow Dutchmen and begin trading with them. Visits went the other way as well, with Janszoon/Murad's Dutch daughter from his first marriage and Christian son-in-law making the voyage to Maladia, Morocco in 1640–41 – the son-in-law's presence perhaps suggesting that this stay included trans-Mediterranean business dealings. Frontier crossings also steered the destinies of Janszoon/Murad's second, Muslim family. When political instability threatened in Moroccan Malagia, the captain sent his sons to Holland for safety – where they went by the surname of 'van Sallee' and apparently remained Muslim. The eldest son, Anthony Jansen van Sallee, who according to some assisted his father in piracy, eventually emigrated to the New Netherlands (later New York) in North America in the 1640s. There he was recorded to have carried a Koran (by some accounts the first Koran on the continent), although he later attended Christian services on Manhattan island. There is some evidence that despite his general prosperity in the New World, Anthony was marginalised as a 'mulatto' – giving support to the theory that his mother was a Cartagenan Moor rather than a Dutch woman. Certainly he was known in Manhattan, and later in Brooklyn and further east on Long Island, as the 'troublesome Turk'.[49]

The Christian–Islamic frontier could, then, create a specific kind of male slave who was endowed with anything but slavish, vulnerable qualities. This man could not only skirt around what was an unforgiving 'slave frontier' for most of his compatriots, but could actually turn the circumstances to his advantage. He did not confront his home society with tales of pious woe or pleas for redemption, but turned on them with a direct military threat one day, and offering lucrative business opportunities the next. The complexities could be hard for anyone to follow. One's Christian neighbour, 'turned Turk', could be the very man conducting one's family into slavery the very next year. Janszoon/Murad was a most dangerous type on this frontier – the masterless slave.

Janszoon van Haarlem of the Mediterranean frontier and his son Anthony Jansen van Sallee of the transatlantic frontier also show how temporary truces, shifting alliances, privateering and freebooting ensured that the contact between the two sides remained jagged and unpredictable. Technological know-how, especially relating to seafaring and warfare, ensured that some professions travelled well. For a captive with specialised knowledge in these areas, such as Janszoon/Murad, enslavement presented a mixed blessing. Their skills made it highly doubtful they would ever be permitted to be ransomed back home. Therefore we find Janszoon/Murad himself possibly claiming late in his life he still possessed the 'heart of a Christian'. We find his son Anthony embarking to a solidly Christian New World with his Koran revealing the 'heart of a Muslim'. And then there were the conflicted loyalties of the Dutch daughter who went to Morocco, and the Moroccan sons who went to Holland. We cannot be sure whether the Muslim Cartagenan paramour even existed. But it is clear what Janszoon/Murad's range of possibilities signified about the many meanings of 'slavery'.

Janszoon/Murad's slavery represents its contingency – its pattern of randomness. His entire family successfully skated on the thin ice of the slave frontier, never really falling through, but any one of these people could have just as easily ended their days in bondage on the 'other side'. The Islamic woman of Cartagena, if she existed, might well have been Janszoon's legal property when he was a Christian. Equally plausible, though, is the situation that would have arisen if she did in fact escape with her family to Algiers before 1610. Thereafter, she would not only have been in a position to witness the delivery of her former master/lover to her new city in chains eight years later, but, given the monetary resources, she could have reunited the family by legally purchasing and rescuing him. Such thoughts of sudden reversals of fortune permeated the thoughts of countless people who constituted the audiences for narratives, stories and legends about the frontier. Accounts exist describing newly captured Muslims being marched through the streets of Leghorn, searching desperately in the crowds lining their route for a face of one of their former slaves, a Christian Italian man or woman who might be in the (merciful?) state of mind to buy his or her former master. In these circumstances even a doleful familiarity could be more desirable than the panic-inducing unknown.[50]

Yet the bulk of European slaves in Muslim lands, who again were overwhelmingly male, had little of value to offer their captors beyond the capacity to perform brute labour. The experience of the majority of slaves was neither that of a sexual object nor that of a prized renegade corsair. Before techno-logical changes of the eighteenth century made oar-assisted galleys obsolete, a typical able-bodied Spaniard, Italian, Frenchman or Englishman would be assigned to a tortuous existence chained without relief to a bench in a gal-ley's stifling mid-deck, where he would work very literally under the lash. Those retained on land often laboured as public slaves at a local ruler's pleas-ure, typically in and about the port cities of Tunis, Tripoli, Algiers, Salé or smaller outposts, but separate from the local population. They worked in chain gangs on large port or building projects, kept at night in *bagnos*. The families of obscure, common slaves could rarely afford redemption, even if they were able to learn their whereabouts from afar. What pathways to freedom existed were often effected by redemptionist orders of Christian fathers, such as the Trinitarians, in place in Barbary throughout the early modern era. On occa-sion governments, local churches or regions might make a direct effort if the population of an entire European town or village had been taken and leaders felt pressure to act.

Opinions vary as to whether the heavy labour of most Barbary enslave-ments represented a new and especially unwelcome experience for ordinary Europeans. Some contend that heavy work offering little promise of reward was the lot of most men on either side of the frontier, slave or free. There is also the point that supposedly intolerable conditions were doubtless exag-gerated for effect back home. Indeed, many slaves in North Africa seem to have enjoyed some opportunity to help procure their own living. Typically this was accomplished by time being allowed for peddling water and other com-monplace necessities to passers-by in the street. For all the Christian rhetoric surrounding the 'pains' of enforced celibacy abroad, casual opportunities for homosexual and heterosexual contact were apparently not unknown to urban slaves. (Though it was illegal for male slaves to patronise, prostitution none-theless flourished in North Africa.) Even galley service could be seasonal, and any profit a slave could produce by his own efforts during the rest of the year could usually be shared. And not all slavery was outrageously burdensome – the light outdoor tasks such as gardening and general household service required of a private domestic slave for example might actually improve the hard lot of a western European peasant, although they could also be, as previously suggested, a resented indignity for elite captives.

But what constituted slavery in the mind? One English domestic slave in North Africa, who enjoyed the advantageous position of managing his master's farm in the countryside around 1640, recorded this psychological state this way:

> though i might have been there a petty lord and bashawed it over the rest of my
> fellow servants, yet slavery had in it something of i don't know what harshness that
> I could not brook. Fetters of gold do not lose their nature, they are fetters still.[51]

These slaves also carried the physical symbols of their subordination with them – compounding the alienation created by a permanent separation from home, language and native culture.

Both strains of argument have merit, but considering the meanings of male mastery grants additional insight. The most significant difference between ordinary slave life in Muslim North Africa and an ordinary free worker's life in Europe was the opportunity to live as a husband and father. Even the European peasant or soldier generally enjoyed a decent chance of heading a family; the slave in Barbary by contrast faced extremely dim prospects of the same. Even if they pursued other employments or managed occasionally to engage the services of a prostitute, *bagno* or galley-based slaves nevertheless lived in rigidly enforced single-sex environments. Christian women were scarce, and in any case were likely, if encountered, to be themselves either enslaved or turned apostate. When on occasion European-born women converts to Islam interacted with male Christians, it was generally in a supervisory rather than a sexual capacity. Such women converts theoretically at least made ideal overseers of male European domestic slaves because they could speak the language and understand the cultural behaviour of the slaves, and perhaps with some irony, teach them the womanly arts of domestic service. And in any event, the supervision of domestic workers was generally an inferior office unsuited to free Muslim men. Slavery among Muslims fundamentally reversed a Christian man's relationship to the women around him. Not only were they sexually unavailable, but they possessed in actuality the mastery that had animated so much mythological and imaginary fear among their countrymen for so many generations.

Could conversion to Islam then lead to freedom and a restoration of manhood and mastery for common European slaves? Some Muslim religious authorities and local traditions held that a convert would gain his freedom. And indeed, across the Islamic world general custom, theory and legal edicts proclaimed that no Muslim was permitted to own another Muslim. Local North African practice, however, confirmed a more complex reality. Full freedom as a reward for conversion or apostasy was most likely for prominent or useful slaves like Janszoon. The Spanish cleric Haedo reported that prominent former Christians were common in North African government administration, perhaps in some times and places more than native-born North Africans.[52] Those lucky or skilled enough, even if born into modest means, might find true freedom in apostasy and embark upon a career assisting or collaborating with their former master. Liberation might also occasionally arrive by a male slave marrying his former female owner (when widowed), but actual cases of this seem to have been very few – despite the assertions of some former captives.

Young unmarried male converts, relatively free of previous familial attachments, were most often encouraged to abjure Christianity. Their masters reasoned that they might feel less compelled to try an escape, with little left to which to return. Full transition from Christian man to Muslim man was only usually accepted when a master enjoyed a clear financial incentive to do so – as in adding a skilled employee or business partner. The trend of preventing conversion, or not recognising the freedom of a converted slave, was strengthened because of the simple fact that each slave represented a substantial financial investment. Simply awarding freedom, on the strength of a verbal profession of faith (which is all that was required), could have proved financially ruinous. The loss of public slaves could mean similar disaster for an emperor or other potentate who might employ massive numbers of captive bodies. (The value of these armies of slave workers cannot be underestimated. Moroccan emperor Muley Ismail's palace at Meknes was reportedly built by thousands of Christian slaves. Public works and harbour defences all along the North African coast were also completely dependent on bonded labour.) Religious conversion was not particularly encouraged in the *bagnos* and galleys because manumissions on that scale were not deemed practicable – slavery was too crucial a contributor to North Africa's prosperity.

Accordingly, some masters flatly refused to allow their slaves to change faiths. And even in the more common cases where conversion was accepted, many of these new Muslims were obligated to remain slaves – much to their surprise, consternation and continued misery. At most, many apostate slaves could expect to be relieved from the dirtiest and most onerous employments. The well-circulated narrative of Pitts records his own not atypical circumstances:

> And many, I know have been as little respected by their Patroons [masters] after changing their religion (or less) as before. For my part, I remained several years a slave after my defection, and suffered a great deal of cruel usage, and then was sold again.[53]

A spiritual and practical war could also be waged on the male slave's own body – one source of anxiety being circumcision. Like sodomy, circumcision became a pivotal issue, experience and metaphor for Muslim slavery precisely because European captives in Barbary were overwhelmingly male. Generally, in early modern Europe, Christian men were not circumcised, while the opposite held true for Muslim men. A successful conversion from Christianity to Islam necessarily included the ritual procedure. For the fortunate few like Janszoon, circumcision was a rite of inclusion in a new community and world – a badge of manhood and regenerated mastery.

Circumcision was obviously not reversible. Because a lack of circumcision confirmed that captives were not Muslim and thus suitable for slavery, the operation could help on the path to conversion to Islam and to hoped-for freedom. But it also might bind these former Christians permanently to the Muslim world. The removal of the foreskin held real danger for a slave's future. If an escaped male slave or renegade with a change of heart succeeded in arriving back in Europe and was found to be circumcised, he could be subject to enslavement as a 'Muslim'.

Circumcision was also *prima facie* evidence of Muslim conversion for suspected apostates. One such unfortunate was a Christian slave in Algiers who had been ordered or encouraged by his female owner to sail to his former hometown of Seville, Spain, capture his own parents, and bring them back to her as slaves. Upon discovery in Seville he was betrayed by his circumcised appearance and put to death for piracy.[54]

Although they tended to die in obscurity, we know that more than a few slaves who escaped from North Africa were re-enslaved in southern Europe on the pretext – justified or not – that the fugitive had converted while among the Muslims. Protestants regularly accused Catholics of singling out English, Dutch, Germans and Huguenots for service in Spanish, French and Italian galleys, households and monasteries. One observer spotted as many as 93 English slaves in the Christian Spanish city of Seville, their status as 'Muslims' perhaps giving the Catholics an opportunity to appropriate the labour of captive Protestants (as they would later force captured English from the Carolinas to work at the Spanish settlement of St Augustine in Florida).[55]

However, former slaves who were ransomed by their families seem to have escaped the implications of their forced, or voluntary, circumcision. That sign of apostasy could be 'erased', religiously and socially at least, by a public ritual of penance and re-acceptance. The family or public authorities seem after these ceremonials to have shown no further interest in drawing attention to what they perceived to be a mutilation.[56]

Circumcision as a popular metaphor of slavery to Europeans was illustrated in the apparently fictional Italian memoir of 'Signor Rozelli', whose Italian protagonist spends time as a slave in Algiers. Rozelli is memorably able to interrupt the surgical procedure that would force him to appear visibly Muslim, and as a result finds himself half-circumcised. In that state that he returns to Europe – a rather graphic indication of the ambiguous and contingent nature of slavery, freedom and manhood on the Mediterranean borderlands.[57] This story also accesses the bitterness Christian slaves felt when their Muslim masters, knowing that circumcision would alienate a Christian from Christendom, forced the operation somewhat cynically while continuing to hold the victims in slavery.

It was circumcision, not castration, that was the more usual visible symbol of male slavery and lost mastery. Centuries of western tradition have associated Muslim slavery with the creation of eunuchs, but that practice, known in the imperial palaces of Constantinople where black eunuchs served as harem guards and white eunuchs as palace officials, seems not to have extended much into North Africa, at least where Christian captives were concerned. The practice was probably discouraged first because officially Muslims themselves were forbidden from performing one of the various possible surgical procedures (traditionally, Christian or Jewish intermediaries in the slave trade had been charged with this task). Second, the mortality rate among the victims of surgical emasculation was high – greatly endangering the investment. Third, Muslim masters were no doubt aware that the changes effected by castration in a human male (later established to be hormonal) brought on a series of chronic medical problems (including obesity) which rendered their Christian prizes far less suitable for labour or ransom. Finally, 'harems' on large scale needing 'guards' were not common in North Africa.

Whatever the actual practices of Muslim masters, the popular image was nevertheless that captives were unmanned across the frontier, physically and otherwise. In 1773, a painting by Charles Amédée Philippe Van Loo showed a rotund, obviously castrated white European male slave in gender-ambiguous clothing holding a basket of fruit while attending his mistress, a distinctly European-appearing Turkish 'sultana'.[58]

In sum, becoming an apostate, turning away from Christianity and toward Islam, threatened male mastery in three ways and was embodied in three types of cultural figure. The first was the renegade, the masterless man, reclaiming his social virility while losing his soul under a heathen flag. He was at odds with Christian Europe not only because of his apostasy but because he was beyond the recovery of European social hierarchy – he had slipped the traces of his society. The second archetype was the brute labourer who became an object of pity, taking up his familiar lot of heavy toil on the other side of the frontier, losing his Christian prerogative of husband and father. And third was the mutilated man, the circumcised or castrated slave who bore the marks and shared the profound indignities of shameful lost manhood that slavery to Muslims represented. Such emasculation did not in the end have to be physically imposed, but could represent a mental and emotional condition of servitude.

As in all relationships of slavery, though, the individual relationships were the foundations of all possibilities and restrictions. It was a frontier in which Christians and Muslims knew one another in the collective and abstract, and the conduits of their complex relationships very much included those of gender and slavery. But for the individual, it was also a frontier of personal discovery – one that lent itself to many layers of understanding, trust, deception and testing. Emanuel d'Aranda told of this encounter with a free young Jewish woman of his acquaintance while he was still enslaved in 1666:

> [she] was about sixteen or eighteen years in age ... she [asked] me ... whether a man may have as many wives there [in Christian Dunkirk] as he pleases himself? I answr'd, No, marriage is there quite contrary to what it is here [in Algiers]; for [in Dunkirk] it is lawful for one woman to have seven husbands, and all those husbands are in subjection to the wife. She ask'd me which of the seven lay with her. I reply'd that they took their turns, but that he who gave the woman most satisfaction had her oftenest. This discourse pleased the young Jewess so well, that she took her leave with a sigh, saying, God's blessing light on such a Country.[59]

Europeans among Native Americans

The Spanish, sodomy and sexual danger revisited

Both the Spanish and English carried attitudes about fallen men and unnatural women with them to the New World. Summarising the current literature of Europeans among Native Americans, historian of the Spanish borderlands David J. Weber has illustrated the cultural importance of the many captivity narratives written by Spaniards of their time in Muslim North Africa – and the relative obscurity of the few narratives written about their captivities among Native Americans. There are several ordinary reasons for this difference. First, Native Americans presented no real danger to European Spain itself (nor a fundamental one to most Spanish American colonies once waves of disease had decimated native resistance). Second, Spanish captives taken along this far-flung and remote American frontier tended to be marginal folk whose information upon return was needed mostly by authorities to provide information and intelligence about the native tribes in question. Weber goes on to point out that in one strain of Catholic European thinking, the required main elements of the captivity tale – capture of the European, resistance (or temporary wavering), and ultimately physical and spiritual redemption – did not have nearly the cultural or religious resonance that they did in Protestant lands like England and Anglo-America. For Catholics, the meaning of captivity tended to be taken from martyrdom and death rather than a triumphal return in this life.[60]

This line of interpretation does seem to be suggested by the available record of how returned captives were variously received – but there might be more to the story. The Spanish response to the danger of subjugation at the hands of natives differed not only from their Protestant rivals, but from their own responses to the Muslim world. A captured Spaniard, like other Europeans, was statistically unlikely to ever return from North African slavery – invoking the lessons of death and martyrdom. In America however, the unremarkable returns of captives elicited no great interest. If a Spaniard remained among his or her Indian captors, it was typically interpreted by those left behind more as an individual moral failing or spiritual betrayal rather than a representative Christian falling into heathen bondage.

Sodomy discourse also reveals a link between the two frontiers. Sexual relations among men aimed at asserting mastery created a framework for how Europeans understood themselves as conquerors, rather than as slaves, once their attentions turned to the New World. Muslims of course were described as enthusiastically engaging in the active and passive sexual roles. Upon arrival in the New World, however, the assumed mantle of the *conquistador* did not mean that Spaniards assumed the role of the active sexual partner in homosexual relationships – this they left entirely to the natives. The focus now shifted from the savage as sexual aggressor to the supposed depravity of the native as the passive, 'womanly' sexual partner, so slave-like that he willingly succumbed to the carnal desires of other equally debauched native men.

One Spaniard in 1526 commented, '[t]he Indians who are lords and chieftains who sin keep young men publicly with whom they consort in this infamous sin. And once they fall into this guilt, these passive mozos then put on skirts like women.' These behaviours were described (or imagined) in order to highlight the suitability of indigenous peoples for 'natural' slavery – sodomy was above all an indication of depravity, feminisation and hypocrisy. Stories featured such details as Indian chiefs 'punishing' boys who had demonstrated homosexual tendencies by permanently dressing them as females – and then reducing them to concubinage at the service of the chiefs themselves.[61]

One Spanish writer, Gabriel Oviedo, explicitly connected the receptiveness and feminisation of native men to their suitability for being socially dominated, and any property they possessed that the Spanish might find valuable and appropriate for confiscation. Disputes over the legitimacy of enslaving Native Americans could be fought on the point of sodomy. *Conquistador*-turned-priest Bartolomé de las Casas, the prescient, gadfly defender of the humanity of Native Americans in the face of Spanish imperialism, directly disputed Oviedo's assertion that the 'Indians' of the Americas were particularly prone to homosexuality.[62] Overall, the Spanish calculus seemed to be that sodomy was the mark of deviant mastery and deviant enslavement. And while they might fall victim to the former, these Spaniards would only take advantage of the latter by material enrichment, not sexual gratification.

All this focus on perception, however, obscures possible native views of their own mastery – customs and deep traditions that the Spanish and eventually other invaders had difficulty in comprehending and explained in partial or contradictory ways, or left in total silence. These views shed light on the patterns of first contact between Spaniards and natives.

Central American Maya art forms, for example, suggest pre-conquest meanings of male-centred slavery and captivity in the regions spanning the Yucatan as well as adjacent parts of present-day Chiapas (Mexico), Tikal-Guatemala and Belize.[63] Unlike the western artistic tradition, which has traditionally displayed exposed bodies of female captives or slaves visually for a number of political and cultural purposes, the message-bearing, exposed captive body among the Maya was typically male. Most prominently featured in images of enslaved men were exaggerated outlines of male genitalia, which interpreters had traditionally thought to be a celebration of virility or male beauty. Later commentators have pointed out that this kind of bodily exposure was not associated with free men. Rather, genitals were displayed only by the defeated, and in a manner that was 'ugly', emphasising their 'imperfections', which included mutilations.[64]

Keeping slaves in a state of nudity, in life as in art, conveyed that 'captives, like animals, demonstrate a signal lack of control, an inability to cover their privates, and a wanton exposure of erections to public view'.[65] In contrast, his conqueror remaining clothed visually communicated that 'he, not the captive possesse[d] a truly disciplined body. His manliness rests on a fettered and controlled sexuality that contrasts to the less manly, undisciplined displays of war captives.'[66] Far from being a demonstration of virility, nudity in this context was unmanly. The captive was not so much 'feminised', however, as rendered a kind of animal.[67] One scholar has pointed out that the Mayan male slave is not so much a visually 'penetrated' being, but rather he is bound and nude – a presentation meant to convey his animal nature (or his abject fear) rather than his sexual power.[68]

Animality, rather than feminisation, was something obscured both to colonisers and to most historians who studied them. Nevertheless, Europeans did possibly misinterpret other signs of sexual or gender role variation not necessarily to do with slavery at all. Some colonists certainly found gender and sexual identity among natives to be as complex and ambiguous as anything in Europe. The so-called *berdache*, a catch-all term that describes a man or woman who dressed and often behaved to a greater or lesser extent as a member of the opposite sex, did not, as is sometimes thought, describe a 'feminised' male captive or a native man branded a coward. The exact circumstances varied substantially across the North American continent, but the *berdache* was generally accepted, not shamed, by male and female elements of native communities. The male *berdaches* (more commonly found than the female version) performed female labour, but were often lauded and credited for being more productive and skilled in the female arts than women themselves. They generally had a recognised place in their local warfare practices. Although widely assumed to be homosexual, some male *berdaches* had female wives.[69] However, their suitability for domestic, typically female roles was commented upon by numerous observers, including the *conquistador* Cabeza de Vaca.[70] While not directly related to the question of enslavement among Native Americans, the *berdache* phenomenon does show the exquisite complexity of gender roles among Native Americans – especially those revealing the precarious state of enslaved masculinity. 'Effeminate' men – those seen refusing to engage in warfare, for example – could be simplistically assigned the roles of women by those Europeans who did not fully comprehend what they were witnessing.

More directly to do with slavery, yet still poorly contextualised by the first European observers, was the price of social deviance among free men. Mayan men, for example, could suffer dramatic falls. At a time when European legal codes generally protected the secular and clerical male elite from outright enslavement, one Spanish Franciscan, Diego de Landa, reported that even Mayan 'lords and chieftains' could be cast into slavery for committing a crime such as theft – a particular problem in times of economic hardship. Such was the importance accorded to it that even when a high-status person was found culpable for a minor theft the guilty party would first be divested of their clothing of rank. The newly enslaved body would now be displayed before the community and further physical signs of disgrace applied in the form of painful scars over the entirety of his face 'from the beard to the forehead'.[71] Presumably, the lesson of this treatment would be reinforced in the course of a former leader of a society, body newly exposed and indelibly marked, performing menial labour among those he once influenced and commanded.

Diego de Landa's observations were put in terms of the exotic. Marvelling over the distance that a man could fall was made in (perhaps wilful) ignorance of the legal heritage of the Iberian peninsula. (As we saw in the first chapter, the Visigothic Code and its successors could bring down high-status men who violated their society's most basic rules.) Obscuring that heritage might have been necessary to convey the view of the inherent savagery of the Natives for subverting natural social hierarchy as a matter of law and custom, not just due to the fortunes of war and captivity. Of course, Spanish Europeans experienced such customs as slaves – not simply as observers. In 1511, a shipwreck off Quintana Roo, in an area of the Yucatan, delivered two Spaniards, a priest named Geronimo de Aguilar and a sailor called Gonzalo Guerrero, into the hands of the Maya. Their original captors killed some of the crew, placed the rest in cages and sold them off as slaves. Eventually Aguilar and Guerrero were the only survivors, but in very different ways. The priest had remained a slave, perhaps because of a refusal to relinquish his religious ways, while Guerrero had succeeded in marrying a Mayan noblewoman and becoming a local war-leader (his three children became iconic in Mexican history as the first known *mestizos*).

Their stories became known to the outside world when Father Aguilar managed to join the Spanish conqueror of Mexico, Cortés, after the latter's invasion in 1519. The symbolics of the captivity stories are ambiguous. The new Maya war-leader Guerrero reported that he had been tattooed, though whether this was an honorific of freedom or a permanent reminder of his former slave status is unclear, as is what he might have overcome to win his status. Guerrero for his part addressed his fellow captive, Aguilar, after the latter had escaped as 'Brother' in spite of their fates. This was in response to Father Aguilar's entreaty to the apostate to abandon his Maya sponsors and rejoin the Spanish, suggesting that their common bond of birth had survived their different statuses within the Maya community. Chroniclers maintain though that Guerrero's Maya wife, known as Zazil Ha, dismissed the message of Father Aguilar as coming from a mere 'slave' – distinguishing the two men absolutely – and demanded that the priest be removed from her sight.[72]

It is a paradox worth pursuing that for all their intense fascination with Amazonian imagery and metaphor, which Spaniards invested with such energy in the new Americas during the age of initial exploration in the sixteenth century, the Spanish seemed ambivalent about relating real elements of inverted reality where Native women were concerned. This included the details of encounters with Maya noblewomen such as Zazil Ha. This was in marked contrast to the attention paid to sodomy discourse and 'exotic' natives such as the *berdache*. Some Spanish narrators, such as the long-travelling stranded nobleman Cabeza de Vaca who wandered from Florida to Mexico as a trader, healer and sometime slave to a succession of local native bands between 1528 and 1536, recorded their impressions of women in a prosaic and detached tone. De Vaca was neither shocked nor disturbed by 'savage' female nudity, and dutifully recorded variations in dress, marital behaviour, and the fact that women often bore the brunt of physical work and sometimes were able to function as diplomats between warring parties. The only real condemnation was reserved for *berdache*-type men who dressed and carried burdens as women, and cohabited with other men, a practice the Spaniard found 'diabolical'.[73]

Nonetheless, opportunities for Spanish commentary on powerful savage women and inconvenienced Christian men, the staple of so much discussion across their Muslim frontier, were certainly present in North America if not much pursued. The Maya themselves seem to have had strong traditions on this relationship. Literary scholar Pete Sigal has interpreted one Mayan writing as expressing the potential sexual union between a Mayan noblewoman and a male slave and producing a metaphorical disease that infects the society. Sigal considers the possibility that the fear being expressed by the Mayan writer or writers, who were doubtless free as well as male, was the 'reversal of the social hierarchy, the woman was overtaken and dominated by slaves'.[74] Also plausible however was the associated fear that free women would overstep their boundaries, defying male authority by initiating relations with male slaves as an effort to assert privilege, rebellion or mastery. Accessing the Maya custom of making an enslaved man into the living symbol of an animal by exposing his body also sexualised him, making him a threat (or a temptation) to the wives and daughters of the free. This introduced a living contagion, a living infection, into the body of society.

Remarkable about the accounts of Guerrero and Aguilar is what we do not and cannot know. It is possible to presume, based on our relatively new anthropological knowledge of the treatment and position of male captives and slaves among the Maya, that they too were initially reduced to the vulnerable status of denuded animals. Not only might this treatment have had different symbolic meanings to a sailor than to a Catholic priest, but each of their stories seems to challenge and even defy what we know of the Maya. Obviously the Spanish captive slave Guerrero, discussed above, managed to defy both his animal state and the beliefs that an inferior male would pollute the entire society through a union with superior native woman (and especially with such a high status woman as Zazil Ha). Did Guerrero's foreign status make for an individual exception in his rise to freedom? Does his marriage suggest that despite all Maya prohibitions their women and slaves were nevertheless in proximity to one another? By contrast, did Father Aguilar's faith and position keep him in bondage? Certainly Zazil Ha thought of him as a despised slave long afterwards. And it might bear noting that after his experience of enslavement among the Maya, the priest joined Cortés.

To frontiersmen then, there was gendered danger associated with captivity and slavery in the New World – but comparatively little notice was taken of routine defections and humiliations along the remote Spanish frontier. Unlike urban north African centres such as Algiers, which, though certainly inhospitable to Christian slaves, had many elements of city or market town life a European would find familiar, truly foreign environments such as among the Mbaya-Guaycuru culture of the Argentine would have struck an early modern Spanish man or woman as primitive in the extreme. There, real captured male Spaniards were herded to work each day by native Guaycuruan women on horseback. The men were forced to do the women's work of farming and gathering alongside more privileged white Spanish women, who had married or would soon marry natives – a route to freedom blocked to male Spaniards.[75]

As new captives, in the course of learning womanly and wifely work the Spanish women and girls of whatever social status would have had to learn the rhythms and specific manual skills of the local planting and gathering, as well as the fine and brute labour of householding, and learned to provide the sexual service required of a slave, concubine or wife. Yet theirs was a relative freedom, for they were above and probably commanded the Spanish men who they might have known or been related to by blood or marriage. Spanish men found themselves cast from the top of a social hierarchy to the lowest rung, and were according to one historian forced for the duration of their captivity to endure 'involuntary celibacy', though their lives were defined in fundamental senses by the native and Spanish women around them. This actual reality was not apparently deemed suitable for lesson learning as were tales of wild women of the Amazon, or native or Moorish women to be met and conquered, as with de Montalvo's tale of California.

Captivity and the New World woman

Although the fallen man links the Old and New World frontiers, other aspects of gendered mastery diverged. Native American women were integrated into uniquely American versions of European experience in a way that Muslim women were not. This was wrapped in the representation and interpretation of what some have called the *criolo* effect – mixing and melding across ethnicities and social lines. Captivity and slavery were intimately involved in this through the acquisition, use, abuse and rape of captive/enslaved Indian women. The complexity of this issue is embodied in one of the foundational yet legendary female figures of the Spanish conquest, Doña Marina, more commonly known as 'La Malinche', a Native Nahua slave girl given to Cortés during his invasion of Mexico around 1519. She quickly became Cortés's essential interpreter, and later his concubine, with whom he fathered some of the first mixed-race *mestizo* children in the Americas (a rival to Zazil Ha in that respect).[76]

La Malinche's life has been interpreted in three opposed ways. Was she simply a slave and a victim of Spanish conquest? She was after all a slave-girl transferred to a powerful conqueror with no apparent ability afterwards to alter her life. Or, was she a collaborator/traitor to her indigenous peoples collectively? Her active work as a translator and interpreter in service of Cortés's goals has forever made her suspect in segments of the Latin American historical memory. Certainly her activities made her powerful relative to the Aztecs, Maya and others newly under the domination of the Spanish. But did her activities help or harm the besieged natives? And in any event, were her actions expressions of her own active will, or performed under coercion? Or finally, was she the mother of a new race, the *criolo/mestizo* people who would define that part of the Americas from then on? Could La Malinche have been the founding mother, a female version of redemption from slavery?

Versions of these overlapping but perhaps ultimately irreconcilable meanings continued to define subjugated Indian women under Spanish influence and control. The structure of this control was defined by the Spanish *encomienda* system (land grants to the private elite) and the coordinate mission system (mostly Franciscans in Spanish America). Both kinds of institutions were based on the organisation of native labour to sustain and enrich the properties, and both were at least to some minimal degree concerned with converting and 'civilising' their native inmates, who lived in a state of quasi-slavery perhaps more akin to European serfdom that any other equivalent system. This could particularly affect native women. New Spain's 'Law of Burgos' from 1512 stated:

> [a]lso, we order and command, that no pregnant woman, after the fourth month, should be sent to the mines, or made to plant hillocks, but should be kept on the estates and utilized in household tasks, such as making bread, cooking, and weeding.[77]

One of the tragic by-products of both these systems was an endemic rape culture. Native women were extremely vulnerable to sexual abuse by the free Spanish men of the *encomiendas*, and the Franciscans and their employees within the mission. And because these native societies were typically made up of artificially mixed communities already decimated and crippled by disease, natives not bound together by the usual cultural ties might prey on one another sexually as well.

Native as well as Spanish captor societies seemed to have a marked preference for female captives who could be joined with a specific male master, at least when it came to captives they desired for assimilation.[78] An adolescent girl or a woman in the early phase of her childbearing years was ideal, as bonds of companionship with a new husband, and the influence of a new culture that had engulfed the children she bore for her master/husband would be increasingly difficult to break away from as time went by. Yet the two trajectories were increasingly separate. Whereas population and sometimes assertions of societal mastery were primary goals of native captive-taking, especially as European diseases took their toll, for the Spanish such dominance over native women was a sign of increasing strength.

French Catholic versions of the *criolo* effect existed as well. When native captives and refugees began living within new, religiously mixed settlements, a female variant was personified in the famed Roman Catholic 'Mohawk saint' Kateri Tekawitha. Canonised after her death at the age of 24 from complications of self-mortification, Tekawitha arrived in the Iroquoian Mohawk Catholic mission of Caughnawaga on the St Lawrence River, Canada, in about 1677 when aged 21. Baptised a Catholic about a year before her arrival in the settlement, she was the daughter of a mixed family, her father a Mohawk and her mother an Algonquin, most probably a female captive adopted into Iroquoian society.

Kateri (a version of the name 'Catherine') inhabited a marginal place in Caughnawaga society, first apparently by virtue of her mother's status as a former captive or slave, a stigma that could be handed down to subsequent generations. She had also been disfigured and had her eyes damaged by smallpox.[79] Once among the French priests at Caughnawaga, Kateri's extreme demonstrative acts of piety assumed dramatic proportions. Interestingly, she enacted specific physical rituals of captivity and slavery in the course of her self-torture. The head of the Caughnawaga community at that time, Pierre Cholenec, noted that Kateri burned her feet 'with a hot brand, very much in the same way that the Indians mark their slaves'.[80] She also whipped her companions in devotion, and had herself whipped by them.[81] She was in essence turning the source of her marginalisation, her mother's captive legacy, into a source of power or a kind of mastery, among the Catholic fathers of the refugee village. In performing the physical rituals of her mother's debasement, the legacies of which her daughter still bore, she drew herself squarely into the centre of the Catholic community. Historian Nancy Shoemaker has noted that a Mohawk Iroquois woman along with her fellow Native Catholics may have equated Catholic baptism with the Iroquoian 're-quickening' ceremony whereby the captive assumed a new identity.[82] Using the available vehicle of female piety brought by the French incursion, she illustrated yet another complication of traditional Native American servitude by redeeming herself out of captivity.

Catholic writers constructed their hagiographies of Kateri Tekawitha to present the pious lesson that the young woman overcame her modest and 'savage' origins. While lauding the Mohawk-Algonquin girl, it is a supremely patronising perspective. Scholars have tended to adopt their own patronising images of the helpless, half-blind, frail, maimed convert and her protectors. Tekawitha's spiritual submission to the Jesuit fathers, however, must be put in the context of local memory that would have placed Jesuit priests and Iroquoian women in quite the opposite kind of relationship. Stories of capture and torture included in the meticulous *Jesuit Relations* indicate that the Catholic French were quite familiar with this sort of reversal. The Italian-born Jesuit Bressani, working in the 1640s, was 'adopted' by an 'old squaw' there

before being found an unsatisfactory son and servant by his 'mother
somed through Dutch intermediaries. Another missionary named Ponce.
a similar relationship to an Iroquois woman.[83] The clerical men's dependent
position in these communities was a direct slap at the paternal authority of
'Father' that the missionaries attempted to project. The point was that girls
like Tekawitha did not easily divorce spiritual and secular power, and would
not necessarily have recognised a hierarchy of power in which the European,
male and Catholic were always at the pinnacle. Like captives of the Iroquois,
even men, they adopted a strategy of advancement through assimilation
in exactly the same way as if they had been free, fully Iroquoian women a
generation before.

Kateri Tekawitha in fact personified a distinctly New World, female version of *self-mastery*. She emerged from societies used to mastering others and
through normal circumstances of the frontier found herself outside the structure of power. She adopted gender-specific strategies to rescue herself from the
peripheries by accessing the faith structure of the European newcomers who
were already acting as spiritual authorities in so many native places. The female
child of a captive mother did not achieve mastery by asserting it over captives,
servants and slaves (indeed, Tekawitha's abject self-humiliations as physical
signs of faith were, outwardly at least, the very opposite of exerting mastery,
even as they drew her closer to the centre of Catholic life at Caughnawaga),
but by mastery over a new sense of who she was as an individual, with the
ability to shape her own destiny. Self-mastery as an idea was common currency
along the European–native frontier.

Catholic women, both native and French, emulated the other in becoming cultural and religious proselytisers through the vehicle of fictive-kinship
slavery. Frontier women made themselves anew in processing, assimilating and
utilising border captives. So when English villagers with whom they were at
war in their colonies were plucked from their homes and fields, they entered
surroundings where authority and mastery became increasingly feminised as
they proceeded into enemy territory. The French, like their native allies, had
a varied interest in English captives mostly taken during one of the two major
periods of frontier warfare (1689–1713, and again from 1753–60). Native
societies sought to assimilate captives into their diminished numbers (as
adoptees or fictive kinship slaves), or to ransom them for sheer profit. French
Canadians also used them as labour and ransomable hostages. English female
captives then could experience remarkable continuity when transferred from
native to French control.

Setting the cultural stage for this later interaction was the iconic auto-
biographical tale of the elite Lincoln, Massachusetts minister's wife Mary
Rowlandson, who once captive found herself entreated to join in the life of her
Indian 'mistress'. One possible test for young women captives would be not
so much to overcome maternal authority as to aspire to it. Assimilation would
proceed according to the woman or girl captive's degree of amenability to the
work, language and life of the native women around her. Yet the capacity of
native and European women to retain the identity of their birth should not
be underestimated. To be torn forcibly from a home, especially in the wake of

a shameful military defeat experienced by her people, might be difficult if not impossible to overcome in a lifetime. A female captive might be involuntarily subjected to forced marriage, and even then remain subservient to other wives or new female 'relatives'. By the same token, some Euro-Americans reported generous treatment, often in circumstances of dire hardship among their hosts, in which they joined the women of their new surroundings as full sisters and daughters. In a narrative reflecting an eighteenth-century captivity, then British colonist Mary Jemison reported that:

> It was my happy lot to be accepted for adoption; and at the time of the ceremony I was received by two squaws, to supply the place of the brother in the family; and I was ever considered and treated by them as a real sister, the same as though I had been born of their mother.[84]

Yet the cost of doing so was full conversion and commitment to native life. The theme of redemption remained, though, whether for example a European female captive looked at her temporary stay among the natives and subsequent redemption as confirming her European identity and faith, or viewed redemption and acceptance as a portal into a new world. In the same vein, a network of very elite French Catholic Montreal women (and a few men) took it upon themselves to identify and redeem other English captives they felt might be suitable candidates for religious conversion and cultural assimilation in French society.

Some Protestant captive women were placed – or placed themselves – in women's religious communities. In New France at that time these were devoted to teaching, hospital nursing, missionary work and almshouse service. Three young English women placed at the Congregation Notre Dame in Montreal, a teaching and farming community of lay sisters, represent three possible fates for young women captives. One English girl from Maine, Mary Sayward, after her conversion led the community's mission to native girls at the settlement of Sault-au-Récollet. She thus became a true wilderness missionary, a profession unknown to Puritan girls. Her younger sister Esther married one of the wealthiest fur traders in the colony and became a successful businesswoman in her own right (and eventually one of the largest holders of native slaves in the French colony). The third, Lydia Longley, helped sustain the community by becoming a chief farming sister.[85]

In most representations of conquest and captivity, mastery was portrayed as simple domination of one human over another. The French and native interaction with their female captives produced a more complex, multi-dimensional interplay of mastery. The objective of subjugation was not necessarily slavery but freedom – although for the captive, 'freedom' would come at the cost of personal transformation. Mastery gained in the journey from captive to free woman was defined variously as well – it could mean mastery over the physical environment, over one's religious destiny, or the ability to control a mode of livelihood or profession. The captives also shared with their French Canadian sponsors the desire not only to redeem their captive bodies but their spirits and souls as well. Like Tekawitha, it was an exercise in self-redemption, and self-mastery.

Of course, there were complications and counter-currents to these straight-forward stories of transformation. Some English women held either by the French or by their Indian allies who managed eventually to return home during times of peace or truce in frontier warfare reported that their condition was little better than true slavery. Relations with their French and Indian 'mistresses' were especially strained. Hannah Swarton reported that pressures to convert to Catholicism was so intense that 'hard usages', probably some form of physical coercion, were for a short time applied to her to force the issue.[86]

Finally, however, these journeys of self-mastery could involve the journey from captive to the mastery of others. The New World produced a version of the older fear that Christian women turning Muslim would become unnaturally powerful. The incorporation of women by natives and their allies in the Americas realised these fears in the flesh.

The English American Exodus

English experiences as well were transferred continually to the New World. In the Anglo-American mythology of its birth, Exodus comes before Genesis. To populate this myth there were versions of Adam and Eve in North America. The first and most influential pair were the legendary native maid Pocahontas and the newcomer she saved from those of her own kind, Captain John Smith. In his original account, Smith records that during his attempts to secure the future of the early Virginia colony through diplomacy, he was captured by the local Powhatan Indians and slated to be killed:

> then as many as could layd hands on [Captain John Smith], dragged him to them, and thereon laid his head, and being ready with their clubs, to beate out his braines, Pocahontas, the Kings dearest daughter, when no intreaty could prevaile, got his head in her armes, and laid her own upon his to save him from death: whereat the Emperour [Powahatan] was contented he should live to make him hatchets, and her bells, beads, and copper.[87]

Following this unverifiable, now mythological act of mercy (although virtually all historians and mythmakers miss the unmistakeable prospect of Smith's servitude in the last sentence), the young girl (probably no older than her early teens) went on to have a factual, recorded history of her own. After being captured by the English and converted to Christianity, she chose voluntarily to marry the earnest experimenter in tobacco, John Rolfe (not Smith as often believed). If John Rolfe was in a certain economic sense the *paterfamilias* of the English project in America by virtue of pioneering the staple crop of the colony, the unlikely mother was Pocahontas. She died in England during a visit there with her husband (during which she was received at the court of King James I), and is buried in Gravesend.

This iconic and indeed quintessentially American story, of the seemingly clairvoyant New World 'savage' girl perceptively welcoming the future in the form of the Christian English, in fact has its origin in gendered patterns of traditional, Old World slavery. Smith had told a version of the Pocahontas tale before he ever arrived in Virginia or met an American Indian. Several years previously, the probably unreliable and self-aggrandising Smith claimed to have been captured in eastern Europe while fighting the Ottomans, and carried to the east as a slave. Eventually he ended up in Constantinople as a sort of trophy in the custody of his master's young bride, a Turkish woman called Charatra Tragabigza. The woman though apparently found 'little use for a slave such as he' and sent him to her brother in the countryside, from whom he was able to escape.[88]

The story casts Tragabigza as a saviour, her actions leading to Smith's redemption just as he would credit Pocahontas with the same quality. Although the Powhatan maiden was, and has been since, thought of as the indigenous half of America's unique parentage, in the first relation of her story she was not even wholly a creation of the New World. Her roots instead were in the European literary tradition of the 'gallant' in which the nature of the Christian man is sufficient to induce the Muslim woman to work against her own interests to serve his. This English New World variation on this pattern raised – briefly – the spectre of savage female power to just as quickly defuse it. Pocahontas and Charatra Tragabigza seem to have some relation to ethnographic reality, but given the demonstrated capacity for both Native American and Muslim Turkish women to organise their mastery and trade in the labour of captive foreigners, the true magnitude of their potential social power remained hidden away behind the nationalistic self-flattery of the temporary captive, transcendent gallant.

Anglo-American manhood redeemed

Smith's redemption served as an allegory of colonisation itself. Other former captives more verifiably placed within a female orbit of mastery, experienced and related a more difficult and ambiguous set of meanings. To begin, native fictive kinship practices often resembled pre-existing European fears, and we can safely assume exploited them. In Abenaki and Mohawk communities, for example, one French observer noted native 'women in charge of the slaves' at a time when most such 'slaves' were likely to be captured British soldiers from the Seven Years' War rather than native captives.[89] Earlier in the eighteenth century, English militiamen Martin Kellogg and Joseph Bartlett lived with a native woman who instead of 'adopting' them sold them on at a monetary profit. There was a perfect congruence between the work of native women, who traditionally worked in the fields, and their male captives, who were primarily responsible for farming in European cultures.[90] Economics aside, the symbolism of lost manhood was nevertheless applied and understood as such. The amputation of fingers might at first seem a counterintuitive way to achieve the purpose of making an effective labourer, yet it was necessary ritualistically – and perhaps even practically. This performance of violence, most often by women to male captives among the Iroquois, visibly and permanently separated the man from his social function, role and status by removing the fingers of the right hand which were necessary to pull a bowstring and launch an arrow. In these societies it was the warfare role of native women to enshrine these disabilities. The Jesuit Poncet lost his thumb and forefinger among the Iroquois, a symbolism which then was followed by consignment to actual female control – in this case the priest was made the domestic drudge of the females of one Iroquoian family. Similar fates could be met by English captives.[91]

Involved Englishmen then would immediately realise that Native American slavery/incorporation practices were highly gendered in nature, and they would further appreciate that they did not control these categories. Servile labour usually fell squarely in the female economic sector, with native women receiving help from captives at harvest and planting time as well as in gathering, preparing grain, setting up and maintaining structures, and even child care. Depending on specific circumstances, any incorporated family captive might be employed at virtually any necessary task. There is no way to assess accurately whether this work made the keeping of food-consuming captives cost-effective, but it is clear from accounts that tribal women appreciated being able to shift some of their burdens to others.

Native maternalism was a force driving fictive kinship slavery in all its forms. The fictive mother–son relationship was also crucial in terms of the ideal of redemption. Adult and adolescent male prisoners, for example, made to do women's tasks sometimes complained that to do so was a savagely imposed humiliation. Yet more than a few found to their surprise that resistance to the authority of women did not always bring punishment – but rather promotion to the status of 'man'. One New Hampshire captive was reported by his own family to have:

> seized a club ... and knocked down the Indians right and left, escaping himself wit barely a blow. Because of this the Indians liked him. Again, when ordered to hoe corn he, knowing they considered such work only suitable for squaws and slaves, cut up the corn, saved the weeds and finally threw his corn into the river saying: 'it is the business not of warriors but of squaws to hoe corn. Then they called him young Chief.[92]

Slavery, or in this case the fictive-kinship variety, was initially a dishonoured state, but it could again lead to redemption. The question remained, though: redemption for whose benefit? Early Muslims and Christians had used such stories to indicate how a non-believing man could be converted to pious manhood by defeating the mastery of a non-believing woman. Yet here the meaning is distinct in two ways. The natives may have intended the actual test of challenging women as providing a pathway into assimilation and manhood among the captors. In retelling the story, the Anglo-American family probably hoped to project a white man's prowess over any slightly ridiculous test the natives had in store. Naturally, they saw a white man among native men as destined to become a 'chief'.

Yet misunderstanding or misconstruing the actual American process was a real possibility. How did native captives, and their captors, understand it? One anthropologist of California natives reported that among one group, older men past fighting age might reach a point at which they once again were employed working at the behest of women in the prime of economic life – as they had been when they were young boys. This scholar assumed that the senior men (who in other native cultures might have been august and revered) experienced a 'keen humiliation' at such treatment. But whose values were being applied? Partial incorporation and the melding of gender roles might mean different things when based on age and preserving usefulness rather than on alien or captive status.[93] An elderly man might have the mastery of his youth preserved if the women he worked among recognised and honoured it, all accepting adjusted roles as right and proper for men and women of their physical ability. 'Dishonour' and 'humiliation' were highly culturally specific, changeable and vulnerable to misinterpretation. Redemption in old age was potentially no less an essential part of culture than redemption for youth in times of a testing crisis.

Finally, slave ownership, like becoming a captive slave, could be a form of adaptation and resistance for the captors themselves. Native American societies met and, successfully or not, negotiated the extreme challenges of European invasion and settlement by adapting their captive utilisation and slaveholding patterns. While ascertaining the nature and extent of indigenous American fictive kinship servitude before European contact is difficult because of the lack of written sources, after the arrival of Europeans these Native American practices of subordination, dependency, adoption and slavery underwent continual changes in response to the pressures of new types of competition.

For example, the Iroquoian people of north-eastern North America who lived in proximity to English, French and Dutch traders and settlers seemed to have altered their customs substantially as a result of the population pressures inflicted by disease and stepped-up warfare. Ritual patterns of balanced adoption, torture/execution and slavery marked an increasingly desperate effort to bolster tribal numbers through expanded adoption – and increase income by holding enemy Europeans as hostages.[94] In another prominent example, this phenomenon played out on a large scale in the early national United States with the attempts by many Cherokee in the American south-east to emulate their white neighbours by holding and using African-Americans in an embryonic plantation/agrarian economy which – or so it was hoped – would help them persist among mainstream 'white' southern American society.

The evolution, and in some cases dissolution, of complex Native American customs affected the practices of the English-speaking colonists in a slightly different way from their Spanish rivals. Redemption, as we have seen, could be made one cultural objective of captivity by natives and Europeans alike. But the captivity complex fundamentally sprang from war, not charity. Enemies within and across social groups were often as eager to exploit the unique gendered vulnerabilities of men and women as they were to test their captives for virtue and for signs of conversion. On whatever side of the frontier, the male honour of the warrior could be profoundly insulted by imposing the dependence and infantilisation of enslavement – and female virtue similarly insulted by exposure to sexual vulnerability. Both coercion and redemption coexisted uneasily in the colonial and empire-building processes.

Whereas the dominant theme among the Spanish had been to turn sharply away from the idea of the native woman as an emasculating 'savage', the English tendency to simply try to push natives out of the geographic and cultural picture in North America provided them with an unwanted and significant problem. Historian Kathleen Brown has nicely summarised the situation in her construction of the Anglo-Indian 'gender frontier' – a reality in which both sides defined what separated them by male and female difference. Along this frontier, native and English men each thought the other feminised in humiliating ways. According to the English, native men allowed women to do heavy field labour in addition to the domestic tasks of keeping a home and raising children, letting the 'warriors' lead a life of useless leisure in which they enjoyed ample time to boast of prowess in hunting and warfare while doing precious little of either. Natives for their part felt the English unmanly because they did not know their new American environment well enough to make a living off the land – and were thus unsuitable to marry or properly support a family.[95]

In Puritan New England, captivity to natives quickly became interpreted as a divine test in the wilderness. Physical and spiritual forms of resistance were expected from men and women alike. Men, especially prominent captives such as the Reverend John Williams of Deerfield, Massachusetts, had the obligation to fight back intellectually as well (which he dutifully recorded himself as having accomplished in his later narrative).[96] Conveyed through the highly edited and stylised form of the captivity narrative, these stories presented the English colonists at home with the troubling problem of what happened when the imagined threat turned real. What happened when the hazards of the foundational 'errand into the wilderness' actually did carry off one's family? More to the point given the gender divide, what occurred when a 'savage woman' in the flesh decided one's fate?

The journey into captivity for many European colonists was one during which father-rule became more remote and diffuse. One captive in the Ohio country named Jonathan Alder reported in an account published only after his death that as a 12-year-old prisoner of the Shawnees he had been assigned to his adoptive 'sister'. What quickly followed was a literal immersion in female tasks. The older 'sister', whom Alder called Sally, was a young mother of small children. Alder says that he:

> was kind of [a] nurse to take care of her children, which she seemed to produce as fast as I cared for, and a little faster than Indian women generally do. This nursing business was a new thing to me, and one that was by no means agreeable. I did not like it, for in addition to nursing I had to do all the washing of the children's clothes, which was neither a clean nor pleasant work.[97]

It might be tempting to explain away Alder's treatment simply in terms of the common native custom of not differentiating between male and female work until about the onset of puberty.[98] But according to the author, he was not treated as a typical Shawnee boy, but as a servant or slave by virtue of his race and origin. 'I received many a severe whipping from Sally', he related:

> In truth, she treated me in every respect as a servant, and when she became angry, which was very often, she would call me a 'mean, low, saucy prisoner,'

which hurt my feelings more than all the whippings, for it conveyed to my mind the idea that I was a degraded person, beneath the Indian race, and in no way the equal of my passionate sister or her children.[99]

That he was indeed right – that his treatment was not typical – was confirmed when Alder's native 'father' found out about the abuse and freed the captive from Sally's oversight, restoring him to his trajectory towards native manhood. Soon thereafter, he reported being allowed to hunt and engage generally in the life of men-to-be. Perhaps because he was young when adopted, Alder was not 'tested' in the manner of older captives. He was rescued from his feminine slavery and put back on his intended track.

Alder's fictive male relatives are praised for the fatherly, benign mastery, but how is Sally to be interpreted? How did Alder look through her eyes? Alder admits he was 'a little stubborn and contrary' when dealing with his fictive sister, which might suggest Sally was simply keeping a younger brother in line, or, if she truly thought of him as a 'servant,' disciplining him as such.[100] Sally's mastery might well have been supremely pragmatic. She was no doubt in one of the busiest and most pressured passages of her life as a young mother of multiple children bearing the full burden of communal work and cultural life. A brother-servant-prisoner might simply have been useful, and Sally acted as a rational master to make her household ran smoothly. Another possibility is more cultural than economic. Sally might have intended to provoke her brother-servant to revolt – perhaps this is what she needed to see whether her 'brother' was potentially a representative of her family in diplomacy, on the hunt and on the battlefield. It might have been the truest benevolence of a testing sister to help make a new man.

The more pragmatic explanation of her mastery seems more persuasive on balance. Sally was extremely upset at having to give up Alder and the assistance he provided. Had she been concerned about his progression to masculine adulthood, she might well have let him go to her father and brothers more willingly. Sally seems to have had absolutely no apparent intension of giving Alder up; she would have been happy to keep him as an assistant – whatever his family status.

There are other cases of arrested development for boy captives who grew to captive men without changing their demeaning occupations. Nicholas Woodbury, held by the Abenakis of the North American north-east starting in 1712, was fully adult and aged 24 when first captured. Woodbury was held and leased out to others for labour by his native mistress/fictive mother whom he described as an 'old squaw'. The woman did not agree to release her profitable slave for ransom for a full nine years, even ignoring official truces between the English and the French and her allied tribes when captives like him were supposed to be redeemed.[101]

There is finally no reason to doubt that Sally of the Shawnees was any different from the native captors of Thomas Brown during the Seven Years War who hitched the young man to a heavy pack sledge and insisted that he draw it through the snow.[102] Nor was she different from two Patawomeck women of seventeenth-century Virginia who insisted that a teenage English boy living among them, Henry Spelman, carry the young child of one of them on his back over a long journey.[103] These captors, like Sally, simply desired available male labour. But each Anglo male captive reacted to his burden in a different way. Brown tried jocularity as resistance, inviting three native women to sit on the sledge and joking about not being able to draw their weight, apparently an attempt at mirth that was much appreciated because, like the New Hampshire man who dumped his corn into the river, Brown was soon adopted. In a final twist though, Spelman's female tormentor struck him for his insolence, a physical struggle ensuing. When the husband of one of the women returned, he did not harm Spelman but beat his wife for her treatment of the captive, showing again the different and competing agendas in male and female mastery directed toward their dependants.

European adult males in Native American slavery present a vexed problem for historians. To some, taking men into slavery does not seem practicable. According to one description of tribal societies:

> prisoners could not be taken: for the only way in which they could support themselves was by hunting, and if they were given weapons to hunt with, they might use them to the total destruction of their conquerors. In ... a society like this female captives were occasionally spared; male captives almost never, unless for some very exceptional reasons the conquerors were prepared to adopt the captive as a member of their own tribe.[104]

The modern assumption here was very common, that there could have been very little or no middle ground between a dead adult male captive and one fully adopted and assimilated.

And indeed, many sources even of their time underline the prevalence of torture practices – mainly in order to pin the label of 'savages' on the Native Americans involved. Other direct observers, more sympathetic to natives, emphasised the adoptability of native male captives. William Bartram, travelling in the American south-east after the revolution, noted that among the Creeks even torture had died out, presumably, he thought, in the face of the civilizing influence of the new United States. He wrote that Creeks 'assured me they never saw an instance of either burning or tormenting their male captives, though it is said they did it formerly'. He then praised their ability, along with that of the Seminoles, to make their male captives 'as free, and in as good circumstances as their masters'. Bartram concluded with the observation that male captives were also permitted and encouraged to marry free girls of the tribes.[105]

The physical vulnerability of frontier communities could also feed public fear. On 29 February 1704, a mixed party of French and Native Americans attacked the town of Deerfield, an outpost community on the New England frontier. The psychological importance of the victory in the midst of the raging Queen Anne's war was such that the French king was soon notified of the victory. Fifty residents were killed in the attack and over 100 residents, men, women and children – as at Baltimore – were carried off into captivity. Some ended up adopted by either native or French communities to the north, temporarily enslaved by either community, or treated occasionally as guests by their captors according to individual fortunes. Most surviving captives eventually returned, although a few remained voluntarily among the natives or the French after their conversions to Catholicism.

This raid caused not only a crisis of confidence in the Massachusetts government for failing to protect the colonists (again, shades of Irish raids and the Stuart monarchy), but a questioning of the entire spiritual mission of the latter-day Puritans in light of this graphic punishment inflicted by God. Instead of ridiculing fallen masculinity through fictional characters in London dramas, the Puritans of the New World elected to try to turn actual defeat into a propagandistic victory by emphasising masculine strength in the person of Deerfield's minister, John Williams, who resisted the spiritual and temporal entreaties of his various captors and remained faithful to his home country. Again women played several roles in negotiating the fear of being conquered. Balancing the usual stories of women proving as stalwart as their minister was an actual case the Puritans could not suppress, the minister's daughter Eunice who had gone over to the enemy, voluntarily by electing to turn Catholic and remain as a white Mohawk. If men failed to protect their women, the wives and daughters could easily end up not only as slaves to other men, but ultimately slaves to the devil himself.[106]

Yet gendered mastery in frontier settings remained a situation where many could take their own meanings. No single point of view suffices. In 1709, a Frenchman transported a young Yamagoyochee woman to a Mississippi valley slave market. On that journey she murdered her French master as well as two other slaves. Recaptured by the French, she was brought to Mobile and executed there, confirming the view of many that black slaves were preferable to natives.[107] Seven years later, a young Cherokee woman named Peggy came to Charleston as an agent of her brother, leading a bound Frenchman, her prisoner. Upon arrival she sold him to the highest bidder and obtained, among other items, a 'suit of Calicoe clothes' for herself. In previous years, a family's prisoner would not have been owned by a man like her brother, but become part of the communal property presided over by a female relative 'as her Slave, if she requires it'.[108] Along any slave frontier, identities of captor or captive were never, by any measure, stable.

3

Gender, Mastery and Empire: White Servitude in New Worlds

Unfortunate noblemen and vile mistresses: legitimate mastery in Old and New Worlds

In 1743, a hefty two-volume novel appeared in London called *Memoirs of an Unfortunate Young Nobleman, Return'd from Thirteen Years Slavery in America*. It told the thrilling tale of 'Chevalier James' who had arrived from England as a 'slave' (meaning indentured servant) in Pennsylvania at age 10 after a sinister uncle had conspired to claim the boy's birthright. The story made an almost perfect allegory for Anglo-American colonists squandering their greater birthright and heritage by horribly distorting their English values and morals. The innocent, virtuous boy over time lost his 'sprightliness', the 'lustre of his eyes' and his 'fresh and rosy colour', and was reduced to a beaten-down 'paleness' and a 'dead sloth' in the New World.[1] The writer suggested that English greed was to blame for this descent into savagery – the 'wealth' produced being illusory. In America, it was suggested, the vigorous sons of Albion became defeated men – slaves to the continent itself. When these new Anglo-Americans claimed to be masters of that land, they did so at the cost of becoming monsters. Women as well could be destroyed – or elevated to a new kind of American tyrant.

The first fate of Chevalier James as the representative colonist was a life of excruciating drudgery as a field hand under the ownership of his new master, Drumon, in 'Pennsylvania' – actually Newcastle County, Delaware.[2] The reader is made to understand that this labour was spiritually as well as physically crushing for someone as naturally high-minded and aristocratic. 'His labour was toilsome and incessant,' the anonymous narrator relates, 'his fare was hard and insufficient for the calls of nature; the blows he frequently received were painful.'[3] Drumon is the quintessential New World father gone bad:

> there was not one who could do anything to please him – he seemed to take savage pleasure in adding to the misery of [the slaves'] condition by continual ill-usage, and to do everything in his power to degenerate him from the human species.[4]

Quickly, though, Chevalier James found substitute mothers to ameliorate his condition and ease his hard toils – women whose Old World maternal qualities

85

of mercy had survived in the face of all American degradation. An old woman 'slave', responsible for feeding the field slaves, was not an African but clearly white – the 'wife of a person of some consideration in England'. Her unfaithful husband had found her inconvenient and had gotten rid of her by conspiring with a sea-captain bound for the colonies. Her treatment upon arrival was as brutal as experienced by any person in slavery or servitude, the master Drumon not sparing the gentlewoman 'stripes' for perceived transgressions. The woman took James under her wing, provided him with food, and completed his interrupted education by telling him of history, poetry and philosophy. Hence the best of Europe was struggling to survive amid the brutal American environment.

Driven almost to madness by the conditions in which he lived, James, now 17, absconded from Drumon's plantation and made his way north across the border into Chester county (south-eastern Pennsylvania) and to the Susquehanna river where he fell in with the second worthy female, another victim of the continent, a young woman from a prominent family in the process of eloping with a man considerably below her in social standing. The whole party was captured, Drumon reclaimed James, and as master and slave departed the town of Chester they witnessed the public killing of the lady and her lover for their crimes. In this New World, the reader is told, the stakes of sin were raised – an adulterous woman reaching down across the social divide between master and servant meant not civilised social ostracism but a painful physical death.

Drumon then sold James to a second master, this one of base origin and of the sort that could only grow rich in topsy-turvy America, where common behaviour and brutish practices perversely produced wealth. 'Such is the temper of most, from a low fortune rise to riches and power without having been blest with an education to inspire better notions,' as 'James' put it.[5] The hero by now was in his early 20s, the point at which narrative convention might demand that he begin commanding the attention of admiring young females. James did – but the circumstances are clouded and complicated by his dual status as a nobleman in imperial theory and a 'slave' in local reality. The first free admirer James attracted introduced another necessary element to this American allegory – the 'savage' peoples of the frontier. She was a 13-year-old 'Indian maid', an Iroquois living nearby who, while pursuing a favourite pastime of watching the plantation slaves at work from a vantage point at the edge of some nearby woods, discerned that James was somehow different from the others. She began to arrange to be around him constantly while he was at work, even sharing his burdens and pledging that, once married, she would benefit him by herself being the equivalent of 'two slaves'.[6]

This admiration raised the raw jealousy of the 'fourteen or fifteen'-year-old white daughter of his master and mistress. The Anglo-American girl, Maria, confronted her native rival in a physical struggle highly flattering to the desirability of young James, who was astonished at the actions of his 'two mistresses'. The battle was inconclusive, but caused the distraught Iroquois girl to commit suicide by flinging herself in a nearby river. The guilt-ridden Maria was then delivered back home, incoherent, by James and a fellow slave. Hazarding her chamber, James virtuously, manfully and selflessly reminded the bedridden girl of the necessity to cool her ardour and for them both to remember their responsibilities.

Overhearing this discussion, James's kindly mistress pledged that he would soon be freed as a reward for his actions. Her upset husband, however, took James south to sell him to yet a third master. At this man's death, he was then sold to a fourth, this one the owner of a plantation located within a mile of site of the tragic confrontation between Maria and the Iroquois girl. Maria, he quickly learned, had continued her intense interest in her father's 'white slaves' to her ruin, and having allowed herself to be impregnated by one had been forced to marry him and move away in disgrace.

At yet his fourth plantation James happened to overhear in an outbuilding his youthful and strikingly beautiful mistress, married to the much older master, converse with a slave named Stephano about absconding together and stealing a fair bit of money to start their new life. Horrified, James decided to confront his young mistress and insist that she abandon her plans. The information had shifted the balance of power and to a degree reversed their roles, James commenting that 'chance has made me Master of your secret'.[7] Instead of standing on her legal authority as mistress, the young woman resorted to manipulation – a tactic associated with the feminine that was very familiar to readers of the Old Testament in 1734. The young mistress first claimed she was raped by Stephano, and then blackmailed James into cooperating with her plans of elopement under the threat of exposing their present encounter as infidelity, putting James himself in peril. Her second, somewhat contradictory ploy was to convince James she was now falling in love with *him*. This presented a particular hazard to James who, as we learn, when not working in the fields was frequently carrying out household tasks under the sole supervision of this young woman. Taking advantage of this hazardous isolation she continued to press her affections on the increasingly alarmed slave. Most readers could not fail to miss the Book of Genesis' allusions to Joseph and Potiphar's wife in both her tactics.

The struggle across the barrier of freedom becomes that of masculine virtue versus feminine vice – '[b]ut tho' this woman was young and extremely handsome, the vileness he discovered in her destroyed all the effects her charm might otherwise have had on him'.[8] The crisis reached a crescendo when in short order the young nobleman's fears were confirmed by a poisoned bowl of soup intended for him, and Stephano and his mistress were discovered in bed together by the unanticipated arrival of the master. James was exonerated and completed his term of service in his master's good graces, Stephano met the standard novelist's justice and died as a coward jumping out of a window. The adulterous young mistress was destined for execution herself until her wronged husband, in a weak moment of mercy, allowed her to be exiled. She was permitted to leave as a passenger on an ocean-going vessel and was never heard from again in Pennsylvania. Having overcome this final trial, Chevalier James could now embark on path of asserting his own mastery and recovering his birthright, having earned his freedom actually and metaphorically by weathering the trials of perverse feminine, and brutal masculine, American mastery.

There is some debate among historians about how much of this story might be grounded in reality, even setting aside its obvious melodramatic novelistic devices. One suggestion is that the novel was based on the actual James Annesley, whose life roughly resembled Chevalier James's. Others find the tale an unreliable example of a clumsy eighteenth-century English novel. However authentic the story of Chevalier James might be, the book nevertheless stands as a remarkably comprehensive catalogue of concerns and anxieties about the New World, often expressed in terms of gendered expectations met, exceeded and betrayed. *The Unfortunate Nobleman* also incorporates the zeitgeist of the disordered American frontier as viewed in Britain. In one respect, the story of the unfortunate nobleman is a story of masculine transcendence in the classical, Muslim, Jewish and Christian traditions – of mastery tested, regained and ultimately strengthened. However, the presence of savage new worlds *made by Europeans themselves* marks a departure in the western tradition. In the course of the triumph young James achieved over monstrous base men and tyrannical presumptuous women, the re-establishment of virtue and spiritual purity relied on overcoming the savagery that the English had imposed on themselves. James's steadfastness was an attempt to recover venerated English virtues in light of the increasing and unsettling wealth of the colonies. The idea of America remained profoundly suspect – able to turn good men and women into well-presented savages, with ease. There was even a reference to the Old World frontier, which fares comparatively well compared with the horrors of the New:

> American slavery, which is infinitely more terrible than a Turkish one, frightful as it is represented; for besides the incessant toil they undergo, the nature of the labour is such, that they are obliged to be continually exposed to the air, which is unwholesome enough, the heats and colds which the different seasons bring to these parts, being far greater than any as we know in Europe.[9]

Topsy-turvy America?

Lurking behind the story of 'the unfortunate nobleman' was the idea that America was a kind of topsy-turvy world. In the newly established colonies, would the powers of the mother and father be greatly exaggerated? Would good English men and women be made capable of inflicting gross abuses on their fellow countrymen? Would the vagaries of New World fortune-seeking and the threat of unpredictable financial disaster cause men and women to pass each other on the social ladder in both directions, with alarming results? As in European and frontier environments, a free woman, more than her husband and male relatives, invited profound suspicion and disrespect when she illegitimately superseded others amidst the natural American chaos. As the narrator writes of Chevalier James:

> He had heard that the woman who had wrong'd her husband, after having forfeited her reputation in the country where she was born, had come over there in

hope of making her fortune, and had done it effectually by marrying one of the richest planters in the whole country.[10]

Such grasping by the marginal female was problematic enough in Europe – as with the witch, the scold and the ambitious jade. But in America some assumed, or at least tried to promote, the idea that such exceptions could become a general expectation of life.

But how valid were these assumptions in reality? The picture is complex and contradictory. In one sense, the topsy-turvy thesis was manifestly false. Historian Kate Fawver has asserted that:

> Women in England were more than twice as likely to control their own households than women in late eighteenth-century America .... On average men attained the status of household head at around thirty-eight years of age, while the corresponding figure for a female heads was forty-three.[11]

Further, 'Between the ages of sixteen and forty-five, headship for women never accounted for more than fifteen percent of the entire female population.'[12]

As for women within marriage, the English common law rules of coverture existed on both sides of the Atlantic, which ensured a husband would control all the property brought into a marriage. This also gave him the authority to represent his family legally. In the legal and political senses, Carole Shammas has pointed out that the situation was probably even worse for American colonial women, as their English counterparts made more effort to undertake equity proceeding to safeguard at least part of their estate when entering into marriage.[13]

Yet the other side to American reality was that 26 per cent of the population around the middle of the eighteenth century were servants or slaves, whereas England's percentage of servants was only about 7 per cent. The question is not one of contrasting hierarchies but of judging the environments of power. Female headship of families may have been less prevalent in the colonies, but in America both the master and the mistress – married or not – possessed far more legal and customary authority over household dependants than in western Europe. This authority was backed by violence to a degree that regularly shocked European visitors. There was also the ubiquity of free women's authority. One local study of eighteenth-century Chesapeake for example found that while only 32 per cent of women heading households owned slaves, these women were more likely to own slaves than male heads of households.[14] Similarly, a slave in Bridgetown, Barbados, at about the same time was more likely to be owned by a woman than a man.[15] In both cases, women tended to own fewer slaves than men, and use them to extend a household economy or conduct petty businesses. These female owners in other words secured slaves to survive, whereas male owners in these cases at least tended to hold slaves to make profits in surplus commodities. This pattern recurred in numerous spots across the Atlantic world. Fawver argues there was a significant link in North America between slave/servant-holding and 'female autonomy'.[16]

Beyond the actualities of property management, the idea that slaveholders of both sexes held exaggerated authority helped make this idea of topsy-turvy

America. From a gendered perspective there were two elements: women rising beyond their station, and men declining. For women, historian Barbara Bush has argued that 'white women of humble origins could now aspire to the leisured, pampered position of higher-status women'. Cecily Jones adds the example of the Reverend Francis Crow, who commented of Jamaica in 1686: 'Even a cooper's wife could go forth in the best flowered silk and the richest silver and gold lace that England can afford, with a couple of negroes at her tail.' English observer Richard Ligon commented on the deplorable backgrounds of the English females eligible for such promotions, those 'lately come from Bridewell, Turnball Street, and suchlike places of education'.[17]

Male downward mobility was also a fear, but a diffuse one, with concrete examples fewer and less radical. Free man who failed financially could theoretically sell themselves into servitude, but such calamities typically befell those who had already been living on the margins of freedom. The usual examples were of recently liberated indentured servants pushed into the sketchy poor frontier lands where raids by Native Americans were more frequent and transportation of goods to market extremely difficult. Under such circumstances freedom might be short-lived, and the promise of upward mobility could turn into a closed loop, with people returning to a much-resented, absolute dependence. Among the elite, though, such a journey was very exceptional, especially in the eighteenth century as colonial hierarchies solidified.

Recent research by Eleanor Gower has shown that the American phenomenon of the 'gentleman convict', in the manner of Chevalier James, was more myth than real, at least in Pennsylvania. Those of a high status when transported from England tended to stay 'tracked' in comfortable and sometimes responsible labours which worked, intentionally or not, to minimise the humiliation of convict status and to preserve the basic privileges of high rank.[18] Nevertheless, respectable men could make such a journey, even among the English, because of misfortunes of business, war, politics or personal failings (as with the Cambridge don who ended up sold in the markets of Pennsylvania for stealing books from the Trinity College library).[19] These fallen men could be peddled door-to-door in towns or through the countryside at 'convict fairs' for the convenience of local backcountry farmers on the American mainland. In the Caribbean, they might even be bought by mixed-race shopkeepers and small business owners who tended to dominate the island marketplaces.

Even if only a relatively few white male colonisers or transported Europeans actually experienced a downward mobility that put them on par with at best self-indentured artisans, and at worst base convicts, their fate was publicly performed. So mastery also became a self-conscious attempt to insulate white men from these dangers, eventually by spinning a protective cocoon of racial superiority to replace fraying notions of religious supremacy. These protections amounted to a profoundly conservative assault on the chaos surrounding servitude and mastery in colonial life, and could, indeed, expand patriarchal privilege and power relative to the world around them.

The other essential controversy to the idea of topsy-turvy America is the aspirations of servants themselves. How were they affected by the sex of their owners? In the European colonial family, authority that was seen as legitimate by all stood the best chance of being recognised and obeyed. In the colonial arenas as elsewhere, the master–servant relationship derived from the same religious and customary sources as parent to child. Master and mistress had the rightful expectation that they should enjoy the same sort of unquestioned fealty from servants. However, they often found unsettling varieties of selective loyalty in their Old and New World servants. Servants' calculations depended not only on personal gain versus risk, but on their sense of how well each master or mistress held those offices legitimately, legally and properly. In the same way as an individual parent might succeed or fail, masters and mistresses might partially or completely lose control depending on a whole host of factors that were difficult to foresee. Most crucially, male and female masters were held to different standards by their male and female servants.

What anti-colonial propagandists such as the chronicler of Chevalier James failed to consider was that certain sources of mutual discontent between master and servant had been carried across the Atlantic. If America was topsy-turvy, so was Western Europe. In the Old World, women alone (such as widows) could be the most vulnerable to challenges of authority. In one case from eighteenth-century France, a male farm servant's expectations that he would take a place in his widow/mistress's bed showed how fundamental the misunderstanding could be. According to the sobering legal record, 'bed', as meant in this context, was the literal seat of paternal privilege (even more than being a place of mere sexual opportunity). This mistress in question refused the servant's overtures and made clear that he was to keep to his place. Eventually, the servant raped her – a case which was unfortunately not unique.[20]

The tragedy suggests more than the result of a lurid struggle for mastery. We have no idea whether the servant found his mistress charming or shrewish, attractive or repulsive. Nor do we know their respective ages, relative social backgrounds, or the nature of their relationship before the master's death. We do know that the servant sought to succeed his master through the acquiescence of his widow. So ambition played a part, the mistress standing in her servant's eyes as an instrument of social advancement while he cultivated an idea of himself as his master's second, waiting in the wings. She, however, as a widow, continued to see the servant as a fictive son, not eligible to change his status.

Other sorts of cases speak to servants using women employers as vehicles to advance themselves. Those of good education but low social status in the early modern world seem to have been especially inclined to employ such strategies. Eighteenth-century France was a particularly fraught battleground of the sexes, squaring off across the master–servant divide. Since classical antiquity, the role of children's tutor had been one laden with ambiguity, as pedagogue-slaves taught the free children of the master. In early modern Europe, it was often noted that an educated yet socially dependent tutor might be tempted to lay aside status in relationship to his relatively unlearned but socially superior young students. Viewers and readers of Shakespeare's *The Taming of the Shrew*, to cite only one possible example, would have been well familiar with this device.

In France at about the same time, it was once recorded that a tutor who aspired to social advancement via the daughter of his master was at once rebuffed and cautioned in with the cutting but justified reminder: 'I, sir, am your virgin.' With the pointed use of the word 'virgin', the student deftly combined a polite, deferential reply with the unmistakeable assertion of her own sexual integrity and her higher social authority – realities that depended upon one another. Nevertheless, the testing could be reciprocal. Elite young women would take advantage of the presence of an adult servant (perhaps the only type of non-related male in their immediate ambit) in order to hone their skills of flirtation. This situation could and did lead to considerable misunderstanding.[21] Such situations are reminders of the ambiguities produced by complex individual relationships playing out amidst the high walls separating European social orders.

More ordinary labouring servants harboured no such thoughts. Historian Sarah Maza discusses the sentimental oblivion with which wealthy French women commented on the often backbreaking agricultural work going on around them in their fields – imagining that the daily experiences of threshing, ploughing and harvesting they were witnessing must have appealed to the workers' sense of pastoral bliss and simple mirthful play. Indoors, a frankly sexual kind of oblivion was recorded in one noblewoman's diary, the writer claiming she simply could not understand the consternation and upset of the male servants she had assigned to pour water over her in the bath.[22] It is perhaps worth noting that European male writers credited Muslim women in North Africa with having the capability to cynically assess all aspects of such situations, while in Europe itself these kinds of stories suggest genuinely naïveté about the innocence of attendants. Significantly, male masters seemed more aware of what their physical gestures communicated. When a master disrobed in front of a female servant, he apparently considered it an act of connoted favour, its sexualised message clear to both parties even if not acted upon. Male mastery was self-aware. Female mastery, as portrayed, was not.

European circumstances in which a mistress was of unusually low status could also make her vulnerable, if not to violence, then at least to a distinct lack of respect. The colourful narratives that make up part of the Newgate Prison calendar reveal the 'autobiography' of James Batson, a sometime peddler and sailor from a family of performers and puppeteers who was finally put out of the misery of his life of petty crime in England by hanging in 1666. He had previously spent time scratching a marginal living out of selling counterfeit odds and ends to charming young ladies on the streets of London. One, an 18-year-old wife of an actor, was sufficiently impressed to engage the slightly older Batson as her *valet de chambre*. (The French term was probably employed as an amusing if perhaps slightly rueful swipe at the French, a play on the term *homme de chambre* – the colloquial term for a male body servant who might serve either a man or woman – which Batson seems to suggest was more a normal part of French culture than of English.[23])

Batson described his four duties as being respectively 'tiresome', 'uneasy', 'sluggish' and 'dangerous', this meaning of this last adjective being further revealed when he told of the jealousy of his mistress's actor husband, who 'supposed I was no eunuch'.[24] Yet Batson writes not in shame or anger but in the lighthearted, mocking trickster's tone worthy of a colourful gallows narrative. His actress-employer conveniently helped him stave off starvation during a desperate time in his life, but she was not taken seriously. His ability to amuse his mistress was itself a diversion for the Englishman until something else came along. Slipping away to gamble one evening he found himself in a tight spot and was reduced to slinking back home and stealing one of her petticoats to pay his debt. Unable now to return to his employment, he moved on again, almost regretfully because now he would be bereft of the actress's kindnesses and favours. Perhaps it was the demand of the picaresque narrative, perhaps the actress was a character meant to provide comic relief or serve as an object of salacious suggestion, that caused him to present her in this manner. But it bears noting that mistress and man were of practically identical social background – which is to say a desperate one – and her legitimacy as someone who might conceivably possess mastery was even further undermined by her youth and willingness to arouse the suspicion of her husband and others by being reckless with her virtue. This was a great distance from the maternal.

In these portraits from England and France, the mastery of a fictive mother provoked a life-or-death confrontation, as with the French widow, or an amusing diversion, as dictated by Batson from prison. But the colonisation of the New World raised the cultural stakes of these kinds of strategies considerably. The social contract binding master and servant was one of greater complexity for all parties. In typical western European contract labour, the social superiority of the master and mistress naturally conveyed the legitimacy of their authority, sanctioned by religion. The social class differential between masters and servants served the same function as the age difference did to awe a master's biological children. Paradoxically, though, New World indentured and convict servitude both increased, and narrowed, the social distance between master and servant. The distance increased because the master now held the body of the servant at least temporarily against his will, and traded or leased him as if he were, for a time, a slave. But at the same time, indentured servants – and even transported or local convicts – might at least aspire, however unlikely that aspiration might be, some day to be the equal or superior of the master. And it was always possible that a servant might be equal or superior to his master in terms of original status.

Seen through a new North American servant's eye, using a master or mistress as a vehicle of true upward mobility was not simply a function of desperate and unlikely opportunism, but was built into the servitude system. In exchange for giving up freedom for a number of years, the servant would receive a long-term tutorial in the very specific skills and strategies necessary to succeed in the New World environment. In one sense, servants now at least theoretically had some sort of stake in the colony's future. The promise did not always, or often, live up to the theory, especially for males. In seventeenth-century Virginia and Maryland, as well as eighteenth-century Pennsylvania, some men would die before gaining freedom, and some would face such poverty after emerging from bondage that they would forever live marginally even if they were lucky enough to avoid reindenturing themselves or turning to crime to survive. Some returned to Europe. Perceiving the American mistress as vehicle or shortcut to advancement now had special hazards, and the experiences proved dark and ominous in tone.

New World servants of English extraction could find strange juxtapositions of male and female mastery blocking the hoped-for upward mobility that colonial migration had promised. These frustrated hopes highlighted for all to see the social tensions and distortions inherent in some colonial realities. Thomas Hellier, from Whitchurch, Dorset, was not a character in a novel, nor was he a self-romanticising trickster but rather the subject of propaganda. Hellier was an ordinary indentured servant who had let restlessness uproot a fairly routine path in early life. He had been apprenticed with a barber-surgeon and eventually was able to settle, with a wife, on 50 good acres.[25] Saddled with debt, however, Hellier eventually bound himself on a ship headed for Virginia, where his contract of indenture was purchased by a plantation owner named Cutbeard Williamson. Hellier originally thought he was to be engaged as a tutor for the family's young children – but quickly found the Williamsons' 'dealings contrary to their fair promises'.[26] Assigned instead as a house and field servant, he was haunted and distressed that his life would be run, inside and in the fields, by his 'vile' mistress. Hellier blamed the physical and psychological burdens he bore on the:

> unworthy ill-usage which I received daily and hourly from my ill-tongued mistress; who would not only rail, swear, and curse at me within doors, whenever I came into the house, casting on me continually biting taunts and bitter shouts; but like a live ghost would impertinently haunt me, when I was quiet in the ground at work.[27]

His first act of resistance was to run away from the plantation, which he called 'Hard-Labour'. Recaptured, his life continued much as before, with his plight sealed and symbolised by Dame Williamson's 'odious and intemperate' taunts.[28] So acute was his torment, which seemed to be more mental than physical, that he felt himself driven to murder, and proceeded in the dead of night to violently dispatch his mistress, his master and an unlucky nearby maidservant.

The entire tale appeared in a 1680 London pamphlet. Hellier's prison confession was prefaced and concluded with a lengthy, anonymous commentary for the edification of English readers. In that year, indentured servitude ensnaring Englishmen and women had begun to wane in the tobacco-based Chesapeake colonies (Virginia and Maryland). Most now agree that one principal reason for this transition was economic, slaves of African descent becoming more readily available and living longer. Another reason was social, as in the so-called 'Bacon's Rebellion' of the mid-1670s, in which desperate groups of disgruntled ex-indentured servants temporarily overthrew the royally sanctioned colonial government. Once order was restored the chastened ruling elites eventually allowed the development of what would become a sense of racial solidarity among whites that could to some degree transcend class standing.[29] And as the Hellier pamphlet indicates, aspects of the hierarchical order in Virginia and the Chesapeake in the midst of all these developments had become discredited in English eyes. With their physical cruelty on display, Anglo-Virginian masters had, to some, ripped asunder the social compact that in England bound master and servant in voluntary, reciprocal relationships. Highlighting the juxtaposition of the virtuous English man and the monstrous American woman was an effective way for sceptics and critics of the colonies to illustrate the chaos.

Hellier, it was understood by all, had to be executed for his crime of triple murder. But the anonymously written conclusion makes it clear that Dame Williamson, the 'vile' mistress, had ultimately been to blame for the tragedy. By contrast the killer servant is pitied and even described as the passive victim: 'the poor desperate wretch ... by the overpowering violence of temptation seduced and prevailed upon to extricate himself out of this seeming Hell upon earth'.[30] Dame Williamson for her part was more than one woman with a bad, unnatural temper. She was a symbol for the depraved colony itself. 'His mistress continually bent to load him with abuses ... all ... ought to be cautious and wary, whom they trade with on this account, that they be not abused ... to their own destruction.'[31] Female mastery went hand-in-hand with extreme continental disorder.

Indeed, English culture at this time also abounded in cheap, unimaginative ways to titillate while at same time discrediting English domestic matriarchy: in other words, the unnatural 'rule' of women in the home. This metaphor was so often employed in early modern England that there are signs even London audiences were becoming weary of its constant repetition by the late seventeenth century. Edward Howard's late entry to this genre, *The Women's Conquest* (1671), lasted only six performances. Its departure was unlamented – but the playwright held out hope that its failure was mainly because of poor acting.[32]

The shrew or domestic female tyrant, an especially enduring figure, also entered the home by possessing the spirit and character of ordinary wives, sisters, mothers and daughters. Even female witches were endowed in early modern Western Europe with certain Amazonian characteristics, particularly the desire and sometimes the ability to emasculate through a devil's bargain. The ultimate controlling authority was Satan, not the witch (just like the power of the household mistress was ultimately the master's). The witch, like the mistress of servants, could be the instrument of malevolence. Some men testifying to their own experiences of bewitchment described themselves as physically subject to sexual violation, likening their experience – in graphic detail – to that expected of passive, female servants or slaves.[33]

The discourse of the shrew and the scold also often used the vocabulary and visual elements of servitude to describe these unchecked women supposedly so corrosive to domestic order. In early modern European drawings used to illustrate tracts on domestic (and sometimes political) disorder, unfortunate husbands were portrayed as receiving the same demeaning physical treatment (akin to that applied to a convicted prisoner) from their overtly masculine wives. But these put-upon husbands were hardly in exotic situations to which no man would be subjected. As contemporaneous illustrations tell us, male servants, along with their female counterparts and children, regularly experienced physical disciplining. Myth could be closely related to experience, especially when these relationships assumed new dimensions and intensified in America.

By the time race-based slavery was established in parts of North America on a foundation of white servitude after 1680, about 80 per cent of the population were already legal dependants.[34] Adding to the discourse of the European domestic Amazon was the American scarcity of white women. In early seventeenth-century Virginia and Maryland, men outnumbered women about six to one in some tidewater areas.[35] In such settings, settlers might acquire a wife and a male servant off the same boat carrying contract labourers. Thus a woman seemingly destined for servitude could quickly be promoted by marriage above her expected social station. Those who wrote of Chevalier James and Thomas Hellier faithfully recorded the inevitable results. Considerable competition of well-to-do white men for the companionship and help of a white woman meant that the terms of indenture for some might be of extremely short duration – though it is certainly doubtful whether such strong-armed marriages actually represented 'freedom' for these young women.[36]

In theory, a quick rise in status might prompt objections from socially elite neighbours and peers resisting socially marginal women in their midst, but the advantages of securing any free white women in these frontier environments seem to have muted this type of objection. However, the circumstance might have been behind planter men sometimes not accepting widows as business partners as readily as one of themselves. The male–female divide was exacerbated when the woman in question did not share the manners and heritage of elite Englishmen. It might have raised resentment among male servants who were usually denied similar opportunities for rapid upward mobility, as well as for those female servants excluded, for whatever reason, from the marriage market. Another fertile field for the female tyrant.

Accordingly, the editor and framers of Hellier's story took great pains to emphasise the protagonist's gentility, at least relative to that of the owners of his contract. The farmer-debtor-voyager in England becomes the respectable teacher in Virginia, and it is deeply lamented that such a man should be exposed to the cruel work of the tobacco fields. And as apologist for the institution of indenture, George Alsop (himself a former servant) observed in 1666:

> The Women that go over into this Province as Servants, have the best luck here as in any place of the world besides; for they are no sooner on shoar, but they are courted into a Copulative Matrimony .... Men have not altogether so good luck as Women in this kind, or natural preferment, without they be good Rhetoricians, and well vers'd in the Art of perswasion then (probably) they may ryvet themselves in the time of their Servitude into the private and reserved favour of their Mistress, if Age speak their Master deficient.[37]

A similar, if smaller-scale and muted, dynamic existed in the French colony of colonial Canada. Indentured servants who typically served three-year terms, called *engagés*, tended to be respectable artisans aged between 30 and 50. They seem unlikely to have accepted easily the rustic farm girls or recently arrived immigrants from the asylums of Paris as fictive mothers, caretakers and disciplinarians.[38] They had little choice in the matter, though, and such alienation from the colony might explain why early servants fled back to

France at an alarming rate and at the first opportunity. Of course, the disadvantageous sex ratio in New France (a ratio that did not even out until some time between 1690 and 1710, depending on the region and source) made it difficult to contemplate raising a family on the free land that was provided by the colony when an *engagé*'s term expired.

In one sense, that master and servant were further apart in America than in Europe tied in with a New World master's ability to treat a servant 'as a slave', albeit temporarily. However, the boundaries between the classes were paradoxically more fluid and permeable. Some male as well as female indentured servants eventually succeeded in marrying into their masters' families, but in doing so they crossed a wider gulf of social status than those entering into the common marriages between male apprentices and masters' daughters under the guild systems in Europe.[39] For male servants in North America such a move upward in status might be accepted, especially if master and servant shared specific ethnic and religious identifications. The German settlers of eighteenth-century Philadelphia tended to view their 'redemptioner' servants not only as former countrymen but as future neighbours and fellow community-builders. So intermarriage did not always bridge a significant cultural or social divide.

These opportunities were not always without suspicion, bad feelings and controversy, however. Sarah Osborne of Salem Village, Massachusetts, was thought badly of by her neighbours because of her quarrelsome temperament and the fact that in middle age she took her former and younger male indentured domestic as a husband. The breach might have cost her life at the hands of those who in their hysteria cast this vulnerable woman in with the others unable to save themselves from execution in the witch craze that swept the region in 1692.[40]

The suspicion and social disability could apply to the male servant who married upward as well. In 1660s Maryland, indentured servant William Price succeeded in marrying his mistress, a free woman named Hannah Lee. Because Price had a criminal reputation, court authorities essentially placed him as the spouse under coverture to his wife, the English common law provision by which the husband assumed legal responsibility for the couple. In the eyes of the court, there was little difference between his free/criminal status and his previous disability as servant.[41]

Such resistance could also be a function of 'false adoption'. Youth was not a bar to the same kind of resentment launched at an imperfect 'fictive mother'. Within the loosely defined border zone between indentured servitude and apprenticeship, rebellion could be inspired even among the young. Some time around 1730 an Irish indentured servant named William Hendron bound himself to 'the widow Howel' and in time married her daughter called Mara (or Mary). The basic story of upward mobility in Richmond county, Virginia became compromised when Hendron's namesake son and his wife died in quick succession, leaving grandson Robert Hendron to begin an apprenticeship to a local carpenter and joiner named Ezekiel Foster around 1791. Foster's wife made it clear to the 13-year-old boy that he was to be a servant in the house rather than an apprenticed child of their own. The couple barred

Robert from learning the master's useful trade and instead dispatched him 'to the corn field and such other work as best suited them'. Abuse both mental and physical originated from both Fosters, with Hendron's sarcasm evident when he described how his 'merciful' mistress always failed to take his part while his master 'wore out several switches' on the boy. With the help of his older siblings Robert eventually obtained a court order freeing him.[42] Clearly even youthful 'adoptees' could discredit fictive mothers and fathers who failed to live up to a standard of paternal or maternal authority.

Reflected maternalism

Historian Laurel Thatcher Ulrich, referring to the challenges faced by women who had to reconcile their maternal duties with the lack of privacy inherent to the early modern colonial frontier environment around Puritan New England, stated that according to the religiously influenced ethics there, a respectable woman simply would not undress before her male servants.[43] As we have seen, these kinds of physical proximities caused all manner of suspicion, accusations and cultural diatribes. Yet such decisions of self-presentation had to be made with practical management and domestic harmony in mind. Ordinary free women had the difficult task of simultaneously presenting themselves as female as well as effective organisers and directors of others in public and private. Customs and prescriptions could be observed for practical reasons just as easily as they could be dispensed with. This proved useful for women whose livelihoods demanded the effective management of servants, slaves and children.

Maternalism within servitude demanded further that an operational compact be reached between mistress and servant. The arrangements had to come from the woman herself, as they did from her husband or father. Sarah Lauderdale Graham, writing generally on the 'petty mistresses' in the active market economy of Rio de Janeiro, has commented on the subject that '[t]he goal for the *doñas de casas*, was to maintain among their servants "discipline and good order." Care traded for service, protection for obedience – those were the expectations in the exchange.'[44]

American conditions sometimes invested in unlikely maternal figures the confidence of management under demanding environmental and human conditions. Early eighteenth-century Englishwoman Eliza Lucas, who came to South Carolina via the West Indies, was about 20 when she began directing three of her father's plantations herself. This unusual circumstance came about because of her father's British military obligations in Antigua and her mother's ongoing infirmities. Sometime in the spring of 1742, the year before the sensational tale of Chevalier James appeared in London, Lucas wrote to her friend about the range of her daily activities:

> In general then I rise at 5o'clock in the morning, read till Seven, then take a walk in the garden or field, see that the Servants are at their respective business, then to breakfast. The first hour after breakfast is spent at my muisck, the next is constantly employed in recollecting something I should have learned least for want of practice it should be quite lost, such as in French and in short hand. After that

I devote the rest of the time till I dress for dinner to our little Polly and the two black girls who I teach to read.[45]

The high social status of Eliza Lucas's family would certainly have qualified her for the occupation of plantation mistress eventually. The exceptional factors were her youth, her imaginative inventiveness (her botany experiments which in concert with some other interested colonists created a commodity grade of indigo in the colony), and that she acted without direct male oversight until her marriage. Historian Rose Grey has proposed that Lucas proceeded through stages of her life: 'imperial daughterhood' and 'colonial matrimony' as precursors to her fame as an honoured 'mother of the republic', renown she gained as an elderly woman and after her death for having raised two distinguished American patriot sons.[46] At each stage, Eliza Lucas consciously and determinedly assumed the mantle of the maternal to her dependants, even while acting as a daughter to her father and then wife to her husband.

As an 'imperial daughter', Eliza supervised slaves, fired a white servant/overseer her father had hired, forged business partnerships with would-be indigo growers in the community, taught young slave girls (illicitly) to read, and generally transacted business to build an economic presence in the Atlantic world. In matrimony, this independence of action receded, as evidenced by the fact that immediately after her marriage in 1744 Eliza's father started to direct his business correspondence to her new husband, the established Charles Pinckney.[47] Upon her early widowhood though she was cast back into a familiar managerial role, often using her sons, son-in-law, daughter and overseers as intermediaries through upheavals including the American Revolution, during which time her slaves burned one of the family properties.[48] The hard-won wisdom of maternalism was apparent in a letter written to Eliza's daughter Harriott:

Be calm and Obligeing to all the servants, and when you speak doe it mildly, Even to the poorest slave; if any of the Servants commit small faults that are of no consequence, doe you hide them. If you understand of any great faults they commit, acquaint y'r mother, but do not aggravate the fault .... Be kind and good natured to all your servants. It is much better to have them love you than to fear you.[49]

Age as well as youth presented challenges of self-constructed mastery. Two-thirds of slaves held by women in Sao Paulo, Brazil between 1750 and 1850 were owned by females over 50 years of age. By contrast, less than half the slaves owned by men over the same period were owned by males over 50. This was clearly due to the demands of widowhood, which would be expected.[50] Before the advent of large-scale race-based slavery in the Americas, and in areas where it was not widespread, older women bore these burdens and opportunities even within marriage.

In colonial French Canada, elite widows no less than married women who managed joint property during the frequent or long-term absences of husbands tended to employ French indentured servants (*engagés*), convicts, free labourers and New England captives (forced to work in New France until freed by the next peace treaty), as well as occasional African or Native American slaves. These mostly young adult servants were the most versatile of help, being eligible to perform any task from heavy outdoor labour to attending members of the family within the household. The sometimes significant age differences and social gap between women of the French *noblesse* and their various servants probably introduced a significant amount of maternal mastery felt to be legitimate on all sides. These advantages, typical of mature women, would tend to offset any lack of physical confidence the advancement of age might bring.

Interestingly in this colony, however, some younger women employers acquired older, more experienced male servants. French Canadian entrepreneur Louise de Ramezay, presumably in concert with her long-time business associate Anne Hertel de Rouville, in 1755 bought the services of convict Frenchman Jacques Huet, a man in his 50s when they themselves were considerably younger.[51] Their motivation is suggested by the practices of neighbouring women's religious communities who collectively provided education and nursing care to the embryonic colony. The women monastics relied as much as possible on experienced *engagés* (serving three-year terms and enjoying favourable terms upon release) to develop the landholding that provided the sustenance and security of the communities. In the Congrégation Notre-Dame in Montreal, for example, the median age of the male indentured servants rose from the low 20s to the mid-30s, as the median age of the sisters in the community fell to about 25 over the same period. This gives a hint that younger women relied on more experience male help, while their older women, when a choice was available, might have preferred versatile labour who could occasionally even act as surrogate sons to be brought up in the faith, yet would not be invited to marry into the family.

There was always a heavy element of supportive sponsorship in Canadian mastery. Servants of the Congrégation Notre-Dame in the early days were called 'brother' and given the remarkable freedom to eat at the same table and worship alongside their women employers. Encouragement to live a godly life was a defining part of Catholic maternalism in this setting, one that was not always welcomed by the men, who seemed to regard this regime as surveillance as much as redemption.[52] Widows or wealthy wives who sponsored the purchase of a young New England servant had an additional motive for their patronage: converted young men could be freed and choose to wed (usually a modest Frenchwoman or a fellow converted captive; they did not marry into the French *noblesse*), thus winning another body for the fragile, underpopulated colony. The same dynamic worked with scarcer women servants (a minority of the New Englanders and virtually non-existent among the indentured French). Sponsorship for dependent females meant guidance towards marriage.

Of course, individual decisions confounded trends, as when the young widow Pachot secured the services of a gentleman named Sieur Lagarde, probably a convict. Pachot was only a bit older than Lagarde and both possessed social status, but the context of the acquisition made the motive clear. With ten children to educate, he was most probably employed as a tutor (an appropriate and not too unusual occupation for elite, literate prisoners or indentured servants).[53] In all these cases, the search for real skills that complemented the abilities, ages, and capacities of their masters guided servant choice. Whether or not individual souls were saved or lives were redeemed, women sponsors certainly helped in these ways to build their respective colonies and empires.

However, the first task of mastery that women made for themselves regardless of status or age was physical work – an unending task and the source of serious conflict in these settings. One of the most useful complex and relevant case studies on this has been put together by historian Terri L. Snyder concerning Anne Batten of seventeenth-century York County, Virginia. In the absence of her travelling husband, Ashaell, Anne attempted earnestly to maintain order, physically if necessary, on her property. On one occasion that we know of because it entered the court records, Mrs Batten took it upon herself to discipline her indentured servant Andrew Hill for some offence. Hill, enraged at his treatment, seized the stick and began to beat his mistress in retaliation, for which he was publicly prosecuted.[54]

The simplest lesson of the rebellion of Andrew Hill is that male and female mastery were not necessarily seen as interchangeable. While the courts upheld Anne's authority as mistress, Andrew Hill obviously had not. All other factors being equal, it might seem that to be disciplined by a woman crossed a boundary Hill was unwilling to accept. Yet is this why he attacked her? Would he have been as likely to attack a man beating him 'in correction'? The evidence trail quickly grows cold. The only further information is that Anne Batten was Ashaell Batten's fourth wife – the only one who survived him – and that the beating of Hill occurred about two years after this marriage.[55] Therefore it is possible that Anne Batten was a young woman, and as such would have had a more tenuous hold on authority than an older, more established, more maternal woman. If Anne Batten had been promoted from a status similar to or perhaps even lower than Andrew Hill's (a possible dynamic in that colony), her maternal assertiveness would have been much more subject to dispute and misunderstanding.

Violence intensified the conflict because to be 'beaten' in this time and place was not even at its core the act of applying an instrument to the body of a victim. It was a compelled performance of infantilisation, deliberately designed to return the dependent adult to his place as 'fictive child' from which he had strayed. A servant could not keep his body private from his masters any more than a young child could from its parents. The status of the child and the servant became fused. While to a master or mistress these performances might have been anything but sexual, there were unavoidable implications if the master and servant were of different sexes. Puritan theorists in England were very aware of this potential danger. The right of masters to beat female servants in this manner was affirmed, as it was for mistresses to apply this sort of correction to menservants. But these same writers discouraged these practices purely on the grounds that it was immodest and unseemly to do so, implicitly sexualising the performance.[56]

Virginia was not a Puritan colony, but the sensitivity of this issue was at least indirectly recognised 20 years after the attack of Andrew Hill on his mistress during the large-scale introduction of race-based slavery into the colony. To more closely associate servitude with race, it would become illegal in the colony to whip a white servant naked.[57] Before such legislation was in force, it is not difficult to see how an attempt by a woman such as Anne Batten to establish her maternal mastery could easily have provoked a violent backlash. Of course, differences were discerned in male and female patterns of disciplining that their critics did not always seem to appreciate. As Snyder herself has observed regarding branding: 'it was extraordinarily rare for female planters to have the bodies of their slaves branded or marked with their initials, practice commonly employed by male planters'.[58]

It bears noting that this sort of scene set the American context apart from its English antecedents in the 1670s, when the Andrew Hill episode took place. As Gwenda Morgan and Peter Rushton observe:

> Private whipping was sometimes admitted freely in the advertisements for white servants in the colonies, something that was certainly socially impossible in England by the eighteenth century (except for apprentices and very young servants, perhaps, and seafarers) .... It seems that by the eighteenth century adult servants in Britain would not be subjected to private corporal punishment, and certainly not to branding. In the colonies, it was the private character of legitimate violence that was so distinctive. In Britain, by contrast, the state – in the form of magistrates and the courts, had achieved a near monopoly on legitimate violence.[59]

Clearly, in legality and custom, the status of children and fictive children had diverged according to region as the eighteenth century advanced.

Even American patriot, founding father and source of New Word wisdom *extraordinaire* Benjamin Franklin took up the issue of the battleground over the body that had inflamed passions and fears from those involved in cases like those of Andrew Hill and Thomas Hellier. Franklin, writing in his newspaper two and a half decades before the American Revolution, warned his fellow residents of Philadelphia about a menacing 'desperate villain' missing one hand who had been seen about town. 'The publick are therefore cautioned to beware of him,' Franklin wrote, because:

> From Maryland we hear, that a Convict Servant, about three weeks since, went into his master's house, with an Ax in his Hand, determin'd to kill his Mistress; but changing his purpose on seeing, as he expressed it, *how d——d innocent she look'd,* he laid his Left-hand on a Block, cut it off, and threw it at her saying, *Now make me work, if you can.*[60]

Again, this was a very great distance indeed from any kind of sexualised situation. Resentment over the labour assigned by a fictive mother, or an unacceptably young, low status, or shrewish woman posing as one, had provoked attempted murder and extreme self-mutilation on the part of an aggrieved male servant.

Limits of behaviour were drawn around both mistress and servant, evidently for the protection of both. In the seventeenth-century Plymouth colony, '[o]ne servant was whipped for his profanity against God, while another was whipped for "Abuseing his mistress"'.[61] However, in a case from mid seventeenth-century Maryland involving a servant called Watson, who belonged to the Bradnox family, the master and mistress were held equally responsible for abuse. One witness observed that 'Watson had "very bad usage, not fit for a Christian"'. The account continues,

> Captain Bradnox had followed the youth all one morning with a stick in his hand to make him fetch wood, and had whipped him 'more like a dog than a Christian.' Both [witnesses] said that before his death Watson had complained of an abscess on his back which was due, he said, to a blow which Mrs. Bradnox had given him with 'a cowl staff.'[62]

Captain Bradnox died before a verdict was rendered. Mrs Bradnox got off apparently because of her high status, a detail revealing in itself. On the other side:

> A law of New Jersey provided that in the case 'any master or mistress be guilty of misusage, refusal of necessary provision, or clothing or cruelty ... to any apprentice or servant' the justice of the peace might set the servant at liberty.[63]

Women's own very real prerogative and agency in designing mastery, even indirectly, could also lead to criticism on an imperial scale. In the aftermath of the Monmouth rebellion five years after Hellier's story appeared in London, for example, about 1300 captured men and women who had opposed the accession of James II were tried in the 'bloody assizes' of Baron Jeffreys of Wen in September 1685. Of these, between 800 and 1000 were transported to Barbados and other isles of the West Indies, there to be 'sold as slaves' – actually more akin to convict servants – for a period of ten years. This human surplus provided an opportunity for patronage at court, with James's Catholic Italian queen, Mary of Modena, claiming a significant share of the men – and the profits gained from the sale of the white prisoners accrued to her. Not wanting to miss such a lucrative opportunity, many of Mary's ladies-in-waiting were awarded other convicted rebels as their own human property to be disposed of overseas. Much later, the historian Macaulay, among others, condemned this 'unwomanly cruelty'. Trading in 'white slaves' was an empirical reality and an example of what might be called indirect mastery.[64]

Resistance and the New World body

In 1736, North Carolinian George Cummins discovered that his white indentured servant woman, Christian Finny, has given birth to a mixed-race child. He secured a court order extending her service for one year, with the child bound to him for 31 years.[65] Indentured Scotsman John Harrower later reported from neighbouring Virginia that masters there routinely impregnated their white servant women and then procured convictions for unlawful pregnancy, thus extending their terms indefinitely.[66] This was not topsy-turvy America, but a monstrous one, made so by the increasingly unnatural men and women who populated it.

The struggle over gendered servitude was frequently fought on the battlefield of the body. Sexual aggression, violence and resistance defined mastery for many who experienced coerced labour of various kinds in North America. Pion-eering historian of the African-American experience Carter Woodson recog-nised the importance of the racialised sexual encounters by using the example of cynical owners of white female indentured servants who forced them to have children with African slaves. Voluntary liaisons would be punished, of course, as with Christian Finny. When forced by masters, though, the practice was strategic and economic – resulting as it might in valuable mixed-race slaves.

Maryland especially became notorious for this practice during the dec-ades of transition between the dominance of white indentured servitude and race-based slavery (roughly 1680 to 1720). One statute provided that white women 'forgetful of their free condition' who 'intermarry with negro slaves' should themselves be enslaved and serve the masters or mistresses of their hus-bands for as long as their spouses lived. Crucially, the law also provided that the mixed-race children of these matches be permanent slaves.[67] The tempta-tion to take advantage of these provisions proved irresistible for some. One such case involved a Maryland servant called only Irish Nell, who had formerly served the proprietor Sir Cecil Calvert, the second Lord Baltimore. Calvert sold her contract to a planter called Butler who 'married' Nell in some form to one of his slaves for the purpose of 'producing slaves'. According to Woodson:

> Upon hearing this, Baltimore used his influence to have the law repealed; but the abrogation of it was construed by the court of appeals not to have any effect on the status of her offspring almost a century later, when William and Mary Butler sued for their freedom on the ground that they descended from a white woman.[68]

The position of such white women servants was sexually perilous – their vul-nerability was imparted by the early colonial systems. In Virginia, feeble efforts to sanction masters who had made their female servants pregnant were over-whelmed by more determined actions designed to control the sexual 'danger' of these women. Blaming the victim became rampant as even those victims of rape who were removed from the custody of their master would have to serve out their terms with another master, plus two additional years for their 'role' in the illicit intercourse. Even children, very young female victims, could be held somehow responsible for provoking their much older male owners. Very little in the way of social sanction curbed such behaviour.[69]

The famous secret diary of planter William Byrd gives us some unique insight into the mind of those taking such licence, who felt mentally and emo-tionally able to indulge in violence that debilitated their victims. Sex was intim-ately tied to punishment on Byrd's properties. On 8 February 1709, Byrd wrote that 'Jenny and Eugene', two servants or slaves, (the diary does not make clear which) were whipped, after which the master noted that he 'danced his dance', apparently a euphemistic coded term for masturbation.[70] Even while his wife was living, Byrd recorded the 'woman hunts' in which he and his friends 'made sport' of native and black girls in the neighbourhood.[71]

As the eighteenth century progressed however, white masters found their sexual mastery over female indentured servants curbed, a trend that continued through the American Revolutionary era. Historian Sharon Block records the story of a Pennsylvania girl named Rachel Davis, who for some months in 1804 (when she was 14) suffered the repeated sexual attentions of her Philadelphia master, William Cress. Family and community sanctions eventually curbed this unacceptable form of mastery, but it proved a drawn-out process. First, William's wife Becky, finding the situation intolerable, succeeded in having Rachel removed from the house. However, the assaults continued even with Rachel not in residence. Eventually, in 1807 Rachel's father took action and pressed a successful rape prosecution. The family of the victim, though of lower social status, succeeded in acting in concert with authorities to enforce a public rather than a private conception of mastery. William Cress, the owner of the girl's contract, was sentenced to ten years at hard labour.[72]

The tale ends there with the sentencing, but it is worth considering the consequences of such a sentence at that moment in history. The Walnut Street Jail, the most likely place of incarceration, was in 1807 experiencing the breakdown of its hoped-for solitary confinement model, with prisoners being employed in stonework, weaving, making nails and shoes in a rigorously single-sex environment.[73] This was the prescribed corrective and like the early modern Spanish case of the servant Ana described in chapter 2, authorities had intervened to free an afflicted and relatively powerless woman in the face of a brutally exploitative mastery. As in that case, a natural sort of justice followed, the master who had illicitly used the body of a fictive family dependant found his own body appropriated and deployed against his will. Yet the time had recently passed when Rachel Davis or her family could be compensated privately through his labour, or that his work might continue to support his own wife, Becky Cress, Rachel's mistress. Unable to right the domestic problems in her house, she was deprived of the family's breadwinner by society at large acting through the courts, and afterwards very possibly faced significant hardship. In the name of reform, the victimisation of many participants had been narrowed to a simple relationship between lost mastery of a man and the new mastery of the state.

At the very edge of historical recovery is mastery among black men projected outside their immediate families and indeed out into the white community. Up to about the beginning of the eighteenth century, free black families might own white indentured servants; although this was certainly rare. Free blacks did own and trade in other blacks as long as the institution existed. In these ways, mastery exerted by free African-American families might even be manufactured, at great cost, under extremely disadvantageous circumstances.

The odds were indeed significantly above zero that black male mastery over white women actually existed. However, such fears were far larger than the reality. Anglo-Americans even took steps to end their own literal servitude, at least to those not of their own kind. Whereas free blacks in Virginia had been prevented from holding white 'servants' (usually indentured) since 1670, white women and men could 'fall' by virtue of criminality.[74] Aspects of the reversal could be graphic for free people, at least of lower social status and most frequently female. Free white women could be sentenced to five years servitude for bearing a mixed-race child as decreed by a 1705 law.[75] The option of a monetary penalty kept truly elite women from being so ensnared, but most ordinary women so convicted faced the same uncertain fate as other white women, including 'shame' or purchase by a free 'coloured' family skirting the law. In 1755, an Orange County, Virginia court ordered the release of white female servant Margaret Irwin. She had been owned for some time by William Jones, a man found by the court to be a 'mulatto' and thus ineligible to hold her further. The finding however did not negate the fact of her service.[76]

Finally, yet another potentially explosive site of bodily resistance was that involving an imperial perspective. In 1731, Ignatius Sancho was born on a British slave ship en route to the West Indies, ending up at the age of two sold to three unmarried sisters in Greenwich, London. An obviously bright boy whom the sisters dubbed Sancho after the Cervantes character, he was nevertheless denied an early education on the grounds that ignorance begets obedience. Yet obedience was not the only function for such a slave, or 'ward', as Ignatius was sometimes characterised. As Orlando Patterson notes, 'young black pageboys were the rage in the boudoirs of eighteenth-century England and France, although what they did with their leisured mistresses as they grew older is best left to the imagination'.[77]

What are better analysed than left to the imagination are the crucial signs and symbols imparted by such relationships. (Some Europeans ladies in this fashion had formal portraits painted with African boys in the manner that others used spaniels for personal adornment.) Several Old and New World themes operated at once. First, the benevolent mistress of English maternal tradition is to be found in the those cases where former pages lived out lives of greater privilege than would have been possible, or so the mistresses believed, in Africa or on an American plantation. The famous Soubise, made notorious as the lover of the Duchess of Queensbury as well as others of her cohort, was dispatched to comfortable exile in East India by the aggrieved male nobility of the country.[78] Yet race-based slavery and dependent servitude crossed the ocean in reverse, a New World export to Europe.

Young male slaves in Europe who had outlived their usefulness and favour were more commonly demoted or sold to be coerced in the American fashion into more ordinary, strenuous lives as common slaves. Records reveal such ordinary details as one young black male slave in England sentenced to a month's hard labour in the Southwark House of Correction for recalcitrance – sent there by his aggrieved mistress.[79] And there was the question of the maternal. Igantius Sancho was rescued from his life of obedient ignorance by the Duke of Montagu, who ensured the young man was properly launched into his future as a man of letters. The male then rescued the slave from the hopeless stasis of servitude to females. But as we shall see it was the opposite of the representation of many black male and female slaves in the nineteenth-century Americas, like Frederick Douglass, who would credit their kindly mistresses with secretly educating them against the wishes of their pragmatically minded husbands.[80]

Introducing race: the birth of Atlantic world communities

Ultimately, however, the experience that English-speaking colonists had accrued with white servitude turned, although unevenly in time and place, to race-based slavery. A small but usually overlooked part of this gradual transition may also be traced through gender and mastery away from the metropolitan centres and established plantations. New communities, some small, some tiny, began to incorporate mixed mastery into the gender relations of these fast-changing environments.

The life of Molly Walsh is illustrative. As a young Irish girl, she had been transported to colonial Maryland in the late seventeenth century, served about seven years as a convict, then struck out on her own to try to establish herself on the land while still in her twenties. To help her with this project she entered the Baltimore slave market and purchased two adult men just arrived from West Africa. (Other sources claim one of her purchases was a white indentured servant.) After marrying one of these African men, the three of them worked Molly's land together and made a success of it. The couple raised their children as fierce opponents of slavery. Taking the responsibility to redeem African bondsmen as a matter of faith, Molly's own mixed-race daughter bought a slave, freed him and married him. The product of that marriage, Molly's grandson, named Benjamin Banneker, achieved a measure of fame as North American's first prominent mathematician considered racially African-American – a visible positive product of this micro-community devoted to the social success of race-mixing.[81]

It is worth pausing to consider how this situation built upon and then rebuked the dominant racial and gender trajectories of the eighteenth century. In one sense, Walsh's actions were utterly conventional. She served her convict sentence, became legally a free woman, and entered the slave market to acquire the labour she thought she would need. She was legally entitled to do this even as a single, unattached woman. In that sense, she fulfilled a permitted role. As the three lives then unfolded though, it was the young white woman who directed the black men (and possibly a white man) on a daily basis, and whose choices influenced their long-term fates. (It is even possible that after Molly Walsh married her African slave, the white man served them both.) The pattern we are rightly expected to anticipate from the legal and cultural structure around them is that not only will the white man be in charge, it will be his duty to separate the woman from the threat of the black slave and divorce her from active decision making. Even in this era, the ways of micro-communities could act contrary to the dominant ones.

This unique case at least indicates that individual lives could be remade according to contrarian values. Young women could be agents. Racial boundaries could be crossed and challenged across the generations. A black man could be made master and husband of a white woman who had previously owned him. A white man could fade into obscurity without triumph. In an important respect this factual arrangement was a neat rebuke to the attitudes that had fuelled the novel of the 'unfortunate nobleman', Chevalier James. The point of America was not to provide the trial that redeemed manhood and restored Old World values, but to work within established servitude to remake reality on wholly new terms. Of course, this alternate reality could only have existed because it was marginal and beyond the oversight of mainstream colonial life. But its existence speaks to the creative dimensions of female mastery, and the communities and attitudes that could spring from it.

The second story of a community defining itself is a mix of legend of the past and the memory of a present community. The local story holds that in the early 1750s, an Atlantic storm blew a ship bearing African slaves into the safe haven of the Lewes river estuary in the British Delaware colony of North America. The slavers, forced to cool their heels in the calm of the river for a few days, saw an opportunity to offset some of the added expense of the delay when they were approached by a tall girl in her teenage years, apparently Irish. The slavers may or may not have been surprised by the girl's request – that they please turn out some of the men chained in the ship's hold for her consideration of purchase. Following an inspection, the girl selected one of the ablest-looking of the African men, escorted him away, and installed him in her farming household – where she lived alone with her other slaves. The African was to replace one of the men slaves who had 'gone' from her recently – died or run away. A few months after the new slave's arrival, the Irish girl, known only as Miss Ragua, married him – but she was careful to keep her new husband in legal bondage. Childless before, Miss Ragua would spend the next years bearing and raising numerous children by her slave husband, all of whom became well known to the surrounding communities for their unique and striking physical appearance. These children, although legally free by virtue of the status of their mother, were not accepted into the white society of Lewes, Delaware. And Miss Ragua, as family matriarch, was likewise afflicted with a measure of pride – her self-perceived racial superiority would not allow her children to consort and interact personally with the local community of free blacks. By default, excluded from white society and self-excluded from black, the family found social allies among the tiny remnant of the local Nanticoke band of Native Americans, with whom the children eventually intermarried.

Over the next several generations, Miss Ragua's reputed descendants remained a matter of interest and curiosity to nearby white residents of coastal Delaware – the combined characteristics of Europe, Africa and Native America inspiring the creation of a local mythology about this visually exotic group of 'Indians'. Somehow, white neighbours became convinced that this unusual strain of Nanticokes had resulted from a Spanish or even Arab Moorish presence in the dim swashbuckling distant past of the region. Their over-active imaginations seized upon the name 'Ragua' – which seemed to some to be more Mediterranean or Arabian than Irish. And they consulted their imaginations to answer various questions. How had the Irish Miss Ragua found her way to the Delaware shore? Had she been captured by Spanish pirates who routinely passed close by that coast to catch the Atlantic currents home? Or, better yet, was she made prisoner by Barbary corsairs and abandoned after forced marriage by a cruel Muslim buccaneer-captor? How had she become, at a very young age, established as the independent free matriarch of a bizarre 'family' consisting only of herself as head of a varied collection of enslaved

African men? And for that matter, by what path had the men come into Miss Ragua's care? In the neighbours' way of thinking, there had to have been a shadowy, secret, foreign man somewhere in the story.

The descendants of Miss Ragua created their own mythology about their origins. In nineteenth-century versions of family stories, Miss Ragua became at once ingénue and matriarch, combining with the vigour of her youth a tall and commanding stature crowned with a romantic halo of light auburn hair, piercing blue eyes, all brought to life by a preternatural, masculine managerial intelligence unusual among women (all characteristics associated with reddish hair in the literary conventions of the time). Her slave husband, as family patriarch, was similarly honoured, becoming in repeated tellings not only the tallest, most physically attractive specimen on the slave ship, but a 'king in the Congo' – the royal distinction serving as a private conceit to overcome the negative public associations of the man's African race (after the fashion of some profoundly race-conscious white Virginian slaveholding elites then claiming an incongruous pride in their descent from the Native American 'princess' Pocahontas – on the basis that her pure royalty negated, to them, her distinctly impure origins.)

From these increasingly embroidered mythologies of this slave–mistress relationship there was created the community self-described as the 'Moors of Delaware'.[82] The story does not represent a typical circumstance of slavery in the mid-eighteenth century British American colonies, or indeed anywhere else. What does this case, involving some of the most obscure individuals imaginable at the very margins of the first British Empire, tell us about the mythological uses of slavery for the sake of a community? The story itself has been too subject to legendary embellishment to judge its merits as possible facts. The significance, though, lies in the way a highly unconventional – even scandalous – situation served to build an imagined community from disparate imperial ingredients to create something uniquely American.

Surveying the ideological heritage of slavery explored so far in this book, it is difficult to imagine a more suspect arrangement in the tradition of the Christian west than one young Irish woman, holding and directing a team of enslaved African men. Further, that the female master might be seen to have surrendered to her feminine weakness, giving herself to one of her Africans, could well have confirmed the suspicion anyone might have taken from prescriptive condemnations of women in close proximity to slaves. Also, the very product of this union was an abomination to the growing racial divide in the British American colonies, a pollution of whiteness, however marginal the wild Irish-Arab Miss Ragua might have been. Yet the mixed race community developed and embellished, rather than hid away, the exoticism of their origins. Vulnerability, weakness and betrayal of womanhood became the strength of the competent mistress, racial mixing an inspired act of American creation, forged by ostracism. Slavery enabled this beginning, and the maternal was the root of all.

The third example moves back and forth across the Atlantic and considers the mixed race, mixed gender micro-communities, sometimes just extended families, that grew up around the slave trade and the women who facilitated it.

These women combined maternalism and mastery to pursue business interests, yet another way to rewrite the conventions of gender and slavery. These sprang up from the west coast of Africa to the coastal British American colonies.

Such relations were created, for example, by the *signare* – the renowned mixed-race African women (typically having local mothers and European fathers) who became the consorts of wealthy white men from Bissau to Saint-Louis (Senegal) during the seventeenth and eighteenth centuries. They were liberated in business by a law that allowed them to trade separately and in concert with their husbands, dealing in a wide variety of goods including gum arabic, gold and leather as well as the ubiquitous slaves. These partnerships with white husbands or lovers were culturally complementary alliances – with the *signare* especially facilitating the slavery end of the business with contacts in the interior. The husband's eyes would naturally be focused on the Atlantic. These couples combined indigenous and European cultural forms, providing an outlet and use for the *signare*'s potentially marginal status in both European and African societies.[83]

Signare were romanticised by witnesses who encountered them as well as in historical memory. One of the French officials of the Senegal company described them collectively as tender, charming and faithful, with a certain 'sweetness' – but also 'an insurmountable urge for love and lust'.[84] The last word hints at the separation between the image projected by *signare* and that of white French women of similar social standing. Behind the image was a complex, decidedly unromantic world of sexual calculation. George E. Brooks points out that to enter into a marriage to a company official of sufficient status for the woman to be considered a *signare*, it would have been necessary for her to first gain notice, wealth and experience through liaisons with less prominent European men. These would be soldiers and the like whose possible brutality and dissipation might diminish a woman's prospects just as easily as advance them.[85]

The African phenomenon of the *signare* and other women operating in a similar fashion elsewhere along the coast could reach America directly. Trader Fenda Lawrence (sometimes referred to in the literature as 'Venda') conducted her slave business in contact with British traders in Gambia around the 1760s. She apparently married one of them based in Kau-Ur, a slaving centre processing humans for the transatlantic and local trades. In 1772 however she alone with five of her slaves (three female and two males) emigrated to the Georgia colony which was soon to be in rebellion against the British Empire. Her status as a respectable woman was vouched for by the captain of the vessel on which she had travelled – a ship that had also carried slaves in transport to the markets at Savannah. It is unknown if Lawrence had a financial interest in this particular shipment of slaves, but the diligence of the captain in establishing her reputation on the American shore suggests a past or ongoing business relationship. Remarkably, she was issued official letters that allowed her to settle and trade by Georgia officials, and was not forced to ply her trade at the margins.

In its most obvious respect, the acceptance of the African Fenda Lawrence as a respectable free businesswoman in revolutionary, slaveholding Georgia suggests a transatlantic understanding that disabilities of race and gender could be overlooked in recognition of a higher form of citizenship – membership in a guild that supported the foundations of Atlantic world prosperity. But that such pains were taken to issue the letters, similar in some respect to the paper licences enslaved black women had to carry with them to trade in Savannah, indicates that race was not ignored in her case. The allowance made for her seems to have been exceptional. As Lilian Ashcroft Eason points out, Lawrence would have stood out more in Savannah, Georgia than along the African slave coasts where a female trading presence was far more common. Eason also raises the valid point that perhaps newly arrived black slaveholders threatened the white status quo of the colony much less than newly arrived free blacks who were not so established – to say nothing of unattached slaves. Although it is possible, given the potential hysteria regarding the potential for 'disorder' perpetuated by specifically female slaveholders, here at least the 'gentlewoman' aspect of Fenda Lawrence seems to have provoked a gentlemanly, money-oriented response among white Georgian men who had the option to accept or reject her. She certainly did not challenge them.

Although obviously highly unusual, Lawrence was apparently not unique. According to Eason, who brought that story to light, another black African woman named Elizabeth Holman, from Sierra Leone, settled to the north in South Carolina where her white slave trader husband had come across the ocean to establish a rice plantation.[86]

Along with indigenous African and Euro-African women adapting their traditional roles to the demands of the Atlantic trade, a white woman who assumed the same kind of role adds another dimension of complexity. Mary Faber, of Nova Scotian parentage, was born in Freetown, Guinea-Conakry about 1798. She married an ambitious young American ship's master/slaver named Paul Faber at some point after 1816, when their joint career in the business began in earnest. Trading activities took him far and wide while Mary built up and ran the upper Rio Pongo slaving 'factory' – a large operation eventually disguised as a coffee plantation to avoid the interference of the Royal Anti-Slave Squadron. Exports of slaves were directed at least in part to Cuba.

The significance of Mary Faber is not so much in the entanglements across oceans or with empires, but the degree to which she and her husband, also white, enmeshed themselves in the complex and often deadly tribal rivalries and power struggles among local merchants and slavers. Mary herself commanded her family's private 'slave army' against rival slaver/warlords, and proved herself adept at acquiring political allies and sponsors among the locals.[87] In partnership with her husband, she traded and slaved as a free agent, guided by canny self-interest and apparently unencumbered by her origin, appearance or biological sex. She was utterly a creature of the Rio Pongo environment, and mastered its rigours.

White women in Africa, then, might have the opportunity to transcend race given special circumstances, just as Fenda Lawrence transcended her race, at least to some extent, in American Georgia. Yet such assessments of business prowess are potentially sanitised representations of what was involved with running a slave factory. According to Sylviane A. Diouf, in slave outposts in

Upper Guinea, '[t]he objective was to kill any spirit of rebellion, to "tame" the detainees, and make them accept their fate ... shackles and guns safeguarded the body, while the spirit was broken in'.[88]

As for how these women and their forms of mastery might have been viewed, one glimpse we have – and it is only just that – of women traders from a slave's perspective concerns Olaudah Equiano, an apparently Igbo captive destined for American slavery. His 1789 narrative includes a passage on his 'wealthy widow' owner, who left two distinct impressions on the slave, then just a boy. After his initial capture, the African widow purchased him and seemed to install him almost as a guest – or an adoptee – in what was to Equiano the most impressive property he had ever seen. Physical comfort, and the dignity of being treated akin to his mistress's own son, brought the captive to the point at which he felt reconciled to his slavery. Without warning, he was spirited away, bound for the Atlantic coast, having been traded, or intended all along, for transit to a slave ship at anchor.[89] The female merchant was first a would-be mother, then very quickly the author of his doom. It was a combination likely to be felt by other merchandise of these women, who gave their confused slaves mixed signals about their complex roles and, to them, unpredictable intensions.

White men's role in these micro-worlds was often controlling, but could be marginal as well. West Africa, like Native America and North Africa, was a geographic location where the Europeans developed a fear of captivity. Although apparently rare, white captives were held and sometimes enslaved in sub-Saharan Africa. In 1785, a French nobleman named Lajaille reported seeing (but apparently not freeing) a French sailor who had been enslaved for 28 years on a West African island off Bissau.[90] Much more important however were white men as free employees of the African and Euro-African women prominent in the slave trade. These women relied on a variety of male Europeans for at least their start in the business, producing confusion in the nebulous zone where freedom, captivity, slavery, race and gender interacted uneasily.

Such an example, which closes some of the many circles of this chapter at a single nexus, is that of John Newton, an English slave trader turned clergyman whose life spanned from 1725 to 1807. Newton remains celebrated for his enduring hymn, 'Amazing grace', written at some point in the 1760s. The first line, concluding 'how sweet the sound, that saved a wretch like me' expresses the overlapping experiences of conversion and redemption. In Newton's own case both the conversion and redemption were related to African slavery. Whereas captives in Muslim North Africa could usually claim only to have been victims of a powerful Muslim scourge, and draw ironies to the European-orchestrated slave trade to the Americas indirectly, Newton was an example of direct inversion, an actual crewman on a British slave ship who by accident of fortune found himself a 'slave' in black Africa, to a black African, and specifically, to a woman.

In his writings he described this descent into hell, which began at one point in his slaving adventures when he became a land-bound servant to a British slave trader named Clow on an island trading outpost off Sierra Leone.

A severe illness there coincided with one of Clow's regular absences, providing the trader's African wife with the opportunity to step into the breach and take charge of Newton. This woman, whom Newton calls 'P. I.' (as he was apparently unable to render her entire Sherbro name accurately) took an active role in her English husband's business, assessing the human merchandise on visiting ships and running the trading house in the place of her husband when necessary. In retrospect 'P. I.' seems to have been acting in a *signare*-like manner as a cultural, linguistic and economic go-between to facilitate Clow's transactions.[91]

Newton was much less interested in her commercial role than in the woman's grasping for personal power:

> She lived in plenty herself, but hardly allowed me sufficient to sustain life, except now and then, when in the highest good humour, she would send me victuals in her own plate, after she had dined; and this, (so greatly was my pride humbled,) I received with thanks and eagerness, as the most needy beggar does an alms. Once, I well remember, I was called to receive this bounty from her own hand; but, being exceedingly weak and feeble, I dropped the plate. Those who live in plenty can hardly conceive how this touched me, but she had the cruelty to laugh at my disappointment; and though the table was covered with dishes (for she lived much in the European manner,) she refused to give me any more.[92]

This description of her manipulation of his food, only allowing him that left over from her own plate for example, might have seen as the height of depraved cruelty to Newton, but if accurate, it seems highly calculated and imbued with ritualistic meaning – a variant on the pattern seen in many traditional cultures of a woman master asserting control metaphorically and sustaining it practically with control over the preparation, distribution and style of food consumption. Through these actions, 'P.I.' might be understood as simply exercising the traditional rights of a Sherbro wife over her husband's dependants, disregarding what Newton saw as the natural prerogatives of his race and national origin, which he as a matter of course expected to be honoured regardless of his modest station in the household. And therein lay the conflict.

His complaints only became more acute after his white master returned, and to Newton's horror he was not redeemed by the fellowship of Englishmen, but resumed his slide into a sort of enslavement:

> I was busied in planting some lime or lemon trees. The plants I put into the ground were no longer than a young gooseberry bush; my master and his mistress passing by the place, stopped a while to look at me; at last, 'who knows,' says he, 'who knows but by the time these trees grow up and bear, you may go home to England, obtain the command of a ship, and return to reap the fruits of your labours; we see strange things sometimes happen.' This, as he intended it, was cutting sarcasm. I believe he thought it full as probable, that I should live to be the king of Poland.[93]

Newton's evocations of what was the unmistakable work of slaves, labour in groves while being casually overseen by his owners, conveys the belief that he had indeed reached the same degraded state of being as the Africans he had himself traded. Nevertheless, his firm view of legitimate hierarchy, gendered and racial, is on display. He referred to these owners as '[m]y master and *his* mistress' [emphasis added]. Although Clow had the authority to end Newton's humiliations he did not. But even as he chose not to override the savage authority of his black African wife, he still had not relinquished his rightful title of 'my master'. P.I. however was not 'my mistress' to Newton, but 'his', Clow's mistress, a neat word trick which also deflated the meaning of the word 'mistress' of any content of authority. Here it simply means a dependent sexual partner of a white man who has lost the ability to read his moral compass.

And there is more. In the discussion of his master, the man of cutting sarcasm, eager to cast aside the solidarity of race, the bonds of Englishmen, and above all the transforming humanitarian attitudes of eighteenth-century Christianity, Newton locates what was to him the corrosive core of slavery. He himself is the returned captive, literally and metaphorically, having been redeemed by his transformative ordeal of illness and abject helplessness in the hands of an African woman. But haunting him, mastering him, were the thoughts of the wreckage that remained of a human being when the storm of slavery had passed over. A slave was a man barred from the faith and civilization of home. As a historical figure he stood on the cusp of all the past and present worlds of gender, mastery and slavery. He was the biblical and classical slave afflicted by the natural tyranny of women; he was the redeemed captive, passing through the fire of savage bondage; he was the unfortunate Englishman, victim to countrymen who had sold their souls. And then as a free man he would come to represent an empire and nations that would enrich themselves on the slavery of Africans, a sin that had to be atoned.

The final story is that of gender in the history of American racial slavery, to which we now turn.

4

Gender, Mastery and Nation: Race and Slavery in the United States

Antebellum mastery in perspective

Students of world slavery often grasp by virtue of comparative training what is not so often clear to those who have studied exclusively American practices. Antebellum southern slavery in the United States was exceptional in a number of essential respects. It existed as a very large (4 million by many counts at the beginning of the American Civil War in 1861), enslaved population that was self-reproducing (with no significant external slave trade after 1808), and masters and slaves were separated by race. This system became especially remarkable because of its durability, lasting well into what most would define as an era that was ideologically and economically modern. Certain strains of thought after the American Revolution (1775–83) concluded that eventually the resonance of the American political enlightenment would end human slavery in North America. Indeed, most of the northern United States abolished slavery on their own shortly after the war, and similar sentiments in the British Empire would end the fading practice of slavery in Canada by 1833. However, the explosion of the south-eastern American cotton economy starting in the 1790s created the seeming anomaly of a vast slave-based economic system rising in the midst of modernity – a phenomenon that seemed distinctly backward to those standing outside of it. Whether American slavery was in fact, an economic throwback or something that was suited to supply the intensifying industrial revolution has been a matter of intense, long-standing debate among historians.

Antebellum American slavery produced gender dynamics which, while sharing some of their aspects with what the West Indies and Brazil experienced simultaneously, were unique. However, this chapter will reveal ways in which the ideologies and experiences of gender, slavery and servitude, in public and in private, resembled their antecedents in the greater and much older Atlantic world. Especially emphasised in its latter-day incarnation was sexually coercive mastery; this defined slavery to its internal and external critics as well as its practitioners and apologists. These relationships damaged humans physically and psychologically on all sides of racial, gender, age and regional divides. Rape and other sexual violence graphically demonstrated the vast social distance between master and slave.

Familiar racial and gender hierarchies still developed unexpected conflicts in this modern American environment. Social angst, moral and legal ambiguity, and mixed motivations between women and men were as private as they were troubled, and often hidden from view. However, private life left a public trail, resonated legally, and ultimately assumed political importance in America's north–south crisis. In the south, local and regional governments expressed the will of the male portion of the owner class by seeking to erase these ambiguities between black and white, as well as women and men. These legislative actions were even sometimes pursued at the expense of achieving maximum efficiency in their slave systems. First, elaborate legal and social structures were designed to protect white women from supposed sexual danger posed by enslaved men. Second, anti-miscegenation (interracial sexual relations) measures attempted to control not only the enslaved male rivals of white men but also the master's wives and daughters – making voluntary assignations subject to the full apparatus of state power. Third, the offspring of a slave mother would also be a perpetual slave – meaning widespread practices of miscegenation and rape could serve the twin purpose of adding to a master's slave stock with the taint of African blood and alienating mixed-race children from any claim to legitimacy or their father's privileges of citizenship.

But this theoretically ordered state of affairs became far more complicated in reality. Free women's own ambitions might mix in unpredictable ways when their conceptions of their family status, values and religion varied slightly or sharply from those of their male relatives. Further, what was considered a normal gender divide in roles between master and mistress differed substantially from the work roles expected of enslaved men and women. Enslaved females could be relegated to masculine roles they might resent, and men slaves similarly feminised. Masters who assigned female slaves to fieldwork did so without consideration of their norms of white regional femininity, and indeed performing men's work consciously distanced female slaves from ideas of themselves as women. Yet most west African cultures from which these women had been forcibly separated or were removed by one or more generations often had universally prized female agricultural expertise.

Perceptions of what was appropriate gender work was therefore a contested area depending on the point of view involved – but by the nineteenth century, as narratives of enslaved women themselves tell us, the virtues of female domesticity, of a similar nature to those valued by middle-class southern and northern white women, had become the badge of freedom. For black women as for white men, outdoor work bore the indelible stigma of a degraded servitude. And even when male slaves performed traditionally 'male' heavy fieldwork, they made that very work no longer virtuous for their masters. For a white man to do work with one's hands was not a betrayal of one's sex, it separated him from the aspirations of the entire white race. Role manipulations of various kinds often resulted in upsetting chain reactions.

Free women fully exploited whatever fluidity existed within locally defined gender roles, in order to define themselves and the families economically and culturally. The cultural ideas of elite plantation mistresses, rich townswomen devoted to consumer culture supported by lands elsewhere, and modest farm wives, were constantly shifting. Multiple levels of mastery enabled women to adapt to the often treacherous conditions under which making a living was imperative. For free women of all backgrounds, cultivating mastery under the rubric of maternal management could become an essential skill of womanhood.

One of the other distinguishing characteristics of latter-day American slavery was its remarkable contingency at its margins, which is to say, intriguing exceptions to the strict rule of racial and gender hierarchies. Between the American Revolution and the Civil War, African-Americans owned others of their own race, and European visitors were astonished at the ubiquitous presence of slaves of both sexes they could only conclude were 'white'. Rather than dismiss these rarities as insignificant, these gendered dynamics reveal once again how dominant attitudes toward slavery were both limited and reinforced in the context of modern America.

The cruelty of women and the abolitionist sensibility

The perpetual theme of the cruelty of women slaveholders, written about to attack and discredit a slaveholding society, intensified and reached a crescendo around the antebellum United States thanks to British and American abolitionism. Even luminary Charles Darwin weighed in on the subject after a stay in Brazil. Imbued with a strong anti-slavery sentiment, he recalled in *Voyage of the Beagle* with revulsion that he had once 'lived opposite to an old lady, who kept screws to crush the fingers of her female slaves'. He recorded his desire, God willing, that he should 'never again visit a slave-country'.[1]

The nineteenth century had not dimmed the capacity of Europeans in general, and the English in particular, to associate alien worlds other than the Americas with wanton female cruelty. It is worth pointing out that such condemnations could be universally applied if found elsewhere. On an 1817 visit to Russia, an interesting parallel to the American form of depravity was recorded by a young student of Christ Church, Oxford University, named John Thomas James. He had encountered a woman 'suffering under the most acute pain, and had, it appeared, burst a blood vessel in consequence of the violence she herself had exerted in beating one of her male slaves'. This sort of behaviour was apparently endemic. James continued, 'A second person will speak of the cruel Madame Soltigoff, who was confined at Moscow for murdering her servant'.[2]

However, it was America that was the great moral evil in British print, a spectre made more resonant by the shared heritage of the two peoples. London publications expounded upon – mixing shock and a discernible degree of outright fascination – the lurid details emerging about slaveholding women. Embodying all the necessary themes was a former slave named Lewis Clarke, who wrote this passage that appeared in London in 1846 about the people he pointedly referred to as the 'Algerines of Kentucky':

> Of all the animals on the face of the earth, I am most afraid of a real mad, passionate, raving slaveholding woman …. She is forever and ever tormenting. When the master whips, it is done with; but a mistress will blackguard, scold and tease, and whip the life out of a slave. Her instruments of torture were ordinarily the

raw hide, or a bunch of hickory-sprouts seasoned in the fire and tied together. But if these things were not at hand, nothing came amiss. She could relish a beating with a chair, the broom, tongs, shovel, shears, knife-handle, the heavy heal of her slipper, or a bunch of keys; her zeal was so active in these barbarous inflictions, that her invention was wonderfully quick, and some way of inflicting the requisite torture was soon found. One instrument of torture is worthy of particular description. This was an oak club, a foot and a half in a length, and an inch and a half square. With this delicate weapon she would beat us upon the hands and upon the feet until they were blistered. This instrument was carefully preserved for a period of four years. Every day, for that time, I was compelled to see that hated tool of cruelty lying in the chair by my side. The least degree of delinquency, either in not doing all the appointed work, or in look or behavior, was visited with a beating from this oak club. That club will always be a prominent object in the picture of horrors of my life of more than twenty years of bitter bondage.

This much might have been expected even to the point of routine far into the nineteenth century. But then came the twist:

> Mrs Banton [Clarke's owner], as is common among slave-holding women, seemed to hate and abuse me all the more, because I had some of the blood of her father in my veins. There are no slaves that are so badly abused, as those who are related to some of the women, or the children of their own husband; it seems they could never hate these quite bad enough.[3]

And so the shock was accomplished. What Clarke had been describing all along has been the vicious abuse and wanton cruelty inflicted by an aunt on her nephew. Nor was there any reason to think this was some sort of singular case. Even the inaugural First Lady of the United States, Martha Washington, had held her half-sister in bondage.[4]

American abolitionists themselves emphasised precisely the same theme from inside America. This narrative by Peter Bruner illustrated that slavery not only could obliterate feminine qualities of mercy but could twist it into an assertive tyranny, in this case a woman who wished to buy a slave quite literally to personally brutalise him into submission:

> After a week [in jail] Joe Bruner and his nephew came and told me they wanted me to go home and I told him I would not go home. He then went out and purchased a cotton rope and his intensions in buying this was to tie me behind the buggy like people do their horses. And then I came to the conclusion that I would go with him. On our way from Nickleville he took me to his sister's, Elizabeth Muer, and there I remained all night. She said she wanted to buy me for the sole purpose of whipping me; she said that if she could whip me and break me in she could stop me from running off. She went and got a lock and chain and locked me to a post on the porch. She would not let me come in the house and then she was afraid I would run off. Joe Bruner told her he did not think I would run off but she thought it the safest plan to lock me to chain so she would have me. While I remained at that house I saw a house where she whipped her slaves. She had large staples driven into the floor, then four large rings were in them and straps to strap you up.[5]

The Antislavery Examiner, also an American publication, generalised about the spells cast by slavery which ruined white women. This example was from Bridgetown, Barbados:

> White females would order their male slaves to be stripped naked in their presence and flogged, while they would look on to see that their orders were faithfully executed. Mr. Prescod mentioned an instance which he himself witnessed near Bridgetown. He had seen an aged female slave, stripped and whipped by her own son, a child of twelve, at the command of the mistress. As the boy was small, the mother was obliged to get down upon her hands and knees, so that the child could inflict the blows on her naked person with a rod. This was done on the public highway, before the mistress's door.[6]

But did this behaviour, according to those who publicised it, have an immediate cause beyond simple monstrousness? One, it was claimed, was jealousy, and those writing for the English-speaking world cast a wide net through the Americas to find suitable examples. Dutch-born Scottish soldier John Gabriel Stedman, writing of Suriname, recorded the case of a crying infant, yanked from her slave mother's arms and drowned by a household mistress. The slave was then punished for attempting to save her baby's life. The underlying cause for the murder had apparently been the white woman's jealousy.[7] This was a common theme in such writing. E. S. Abdy, a fellow of Jesus College, Cambridge University, wrote:

> Many cases of extreme cruelty were related to me. One was that of an unfortunate girl, whose mistress, from ungrounded jealousy, employed some of her slaves to hold her down, and then, with her own hands, cut off the fore part of her feet. This was done in the absence of her husband. She was then carried bleeding into an adjoining wood. And there left to perish.[8]

Brazilian women as well often proved suspect, making the United States, a bit uneasily, a companion in moral crime with its South American counterparts. This had the potential at least to be mortifying to Americans because English observers were keen to associate the savagery of white mastery with the savagery of the land as well as the savagery of the slaves themselves. It was the same story carried over from colonial times. The wildness of the American continents themselves would make civilised men savages, and ultimately 'enslave' them – whites having become prisoners of the physical and human wilderness they chose to inhabit. The famous racial blending and complex colour-based hierarchies of Brazil gave British writers licence to narrow the gap of civilization between master and slave. Both states of being were depraved – and depraved mastery was closely associated with female-perpetuated violence.

The precursor for this violence was a lack of moral, ethical and religious values on the part of Brazilian women. The Irish-born chaplain to the British embassy in Rio, Robert Walsh, offered this description to London readers in the 1830s:

> I have frequently seen ladies at these [slave] sales. They go dressed, sit down, handle and examine their purchases, and bring them away with the most perfect

indifference. I sometimes saw groups of well-dressed females here, shopping for slaves, exactly as I have seen English ladies amusing themselves at our bazaars.[9]

The contrast between the objectives – and the very nature – of the Brazilian ladies and their idealised English counterparts could not have been more pointed. Walsh used Brazilian women slave-buyers in the same narrative manner as had British commentators on North American slavery, to attempt to show that the degraded status of Euro-Americans was caused by the institution of slavery itself.

Brazilian stories might also be framed in terms of male virtue seeking to curb women's supposed natural propensity to cruelty. In a case related by historian Mary Karasch, German writer F. Friedrich von Weech told two separate stories of men acting to curb the violent tendencies of neighbour women. Both slaveholding women engaged in the typical practice of compelling their slaves to form a line each evening in order to give any money earned over to their owner and/or receive any punishments earned that day. In the first case, the mistress sat out on her veranda each evening, continually applying manual corrections to slaves in succession, which created a disturbing nuisance to the free families living around her. In response, a notice was published in a local newspaper sarcastically inviting all to assemble in front of the woman's house and witness 'a fine display of domestic disciplining'. The mistress did not interpret her new audience appearing each evening as an admiring crowd, so withdrew her 'performance' indoors. In the second case, a male neighbour turned off the offending woman's lights in the attempt to end the noisy violence. In this case though the woman prevailed when her retaliatory threats forced the man to flee Rio de Janeiro.[10] Brazilians themselves of course, also might register objections to excessive violence committed by men.[11] But the effect related back to Europe by the German writer was one of male calm fighting against female abandon in a hot, barely controlled climate.[12]

Sometimes, societies of the Americas were compared directly. In *Travels in South and North America*, Alexander Majoribanks wrote of Brazil and the United States that:

> Female owners of slaves are also proverbial in both countries for cruelty to their slaves. I observe that the same takes place in Cuba, as Walton in his work on the Spanish colonies says, 'the females are often found more inexorable and severe to the slaves than the men.'

In the immediately preceding passage, Majoribanks points out his belief that in both countries as well, 'negroes who had been slaves, when they come to be slave-owners themselves, almost invariably treat their slaves worse than the whites'.[13]

This not only puts the United States in the context of its non-Anglo neighbours, but puts female mastery in the context of linked disorders. Blacks are more fearsome slaveholders than whites. Women slaveholders are more depraved than men. This would be the result any time white males lost control of their surroundings. That very old idea was still alive and thriving in the Christian west. And for the unfortunate white women, their debasement by slavery was the perfect symbol of the evils of human bondage itself. Scotsman Zachary Macaulay, seeking to indict the 'excessive rigour of the slave code' in the French and Dutch colonies he had visited in the Caribbean, personified their depredations in the forms of free European females. Slavery, he offered, 'serves to divest the female character of its most amiable attributes, rendering not the masters only, but the mistresses of slaves, dead alike to the feelings of tenderness and delicacy'.[14]

On the general topic of womanhood, critics of slavery observed several ancillary but crucial aspects of monstrousness. First was the shocking phenomenon of how quickly young girls could be socialised, contrary to all good forms of feminine compassionate breeding, into growing supporters of this system. The very same characteristics however could be lauded in the south. A letter from one plantation owner noted in amusement that when his young daughter, Anna, became frustrated with her black nursemaid she requested that her father 'cut Fanny's ears off and get her a new maid from Clarksville'.[15]

Next, critics of slavery writing, editing or publishing material about American slavery by extension critiqued the unseemly physicality of white southern women, certainly undercutting any claim to gentility. Interestingly enough, even southern newspaper writers could share these accusatory writers' opinion of assertive physical presence, even when applied to white men. Wartime stresses brought these kinds of tales to notice. In 1864, with Confederates hard pressed on all fronts, the Augusta, Georgia *Daily Constitutionalist* reprinted this item from the *Macon Telegraph* under the headline: 'Escaped Federal Prisoner Arrested by Woman'. The story told the thrilling tale:

> Mrs Patterson, of Sumpter County, a few days ago, arrested and returned a federal prisoner who had escaped from Camp Sumpter. Prisoner came to her house, she being alone, asked for breakfast. Under pretence of preparing it, she procured a double barrel gun from another part of the house, and presenting it to Mr Prisoner, told him to march before her or she would kill him. In that position she had turned him over to the guard at Camp Sumpter.[16]

The connection of physicality to slavery is important when considering a phenomenon rarely discussed by historians of gender and slavery, that of the female overseer. British observer George Pinckard, whose tour of Dutch settlement areas of Demerara-Guyana in South America (some of which at that time were coming under *de facto* British control) included a sight that seems to have genuinely startled him:

> In one of the fields we passed a gang of negroes employed at their labour, with a female driver carrying the whip at their backs. On my remarking that it was not a becoming duty for the beau sexe – that the nature of the lady might be too tender to admit of her correcting the strong – and her arm too feeble to enable her to chastise the idle, my companion replied that I was much mistaken, for that to the contrary the women drivers, 'were sometimes peculiarly severe, and often corrected the stoutest slaves with no feeble arm.'[17]

The references to the 'strong' and the 'stoutest' slaves leaves no doubt that the workers are men. Who is the woman? That she is described as a member of the 'beaus sexe', of 'tender' nature, of 'feeble' arm, and above all a lady makes it highly unlikely the woman in question was a black or mixed-race female overseer. Such terms would be used only for a white woman, leading to the first conclusion that Pinckard is describing the function of some of the Dutch plantation mistresses themselves. This is probable – especially given the use of the word 'lady'. Yet elsewhere in his lengthy account he specifies the identity of the 'lady of the house' when he encounters one. The references in the passage to 'women drivers', as if it were a specified occupation, also raise the possibility that Pinckard is describing, whether or not he was aware of it, socially marginal but able-bodied white female servants who had been given the task of overseeing black men in the fields. The crucial bit of missing information here is whether the plantation in question was a sugar concern, with its large-scale, highly differentiated tasks. An industrious propertied mistress might have been more likely in this case to manage overall production rather than to concern herself with the work of a single gang, leaving this to free white servants. If it were a smaller outfit, engaged in growing something other than sugar, experience elsewhere shows the mistress herself might have been more likely to supervise fieldworkers.

Pinckard also stressed that what he saw was not just the activity of a single, eccentric woman. Rather, female supervision of field slaves was an ingrained part of the social system. This is distinct from Pinckard's standard treatment elsewhere in his *Notes* of the individual moral failings of elite Dutch women 'accustomed to scenes of slavery'. At one earlier point in the journey Pickard and his company hear the 'bleeding clang of the whip, and the painful cries of a poor, unfortunate black'. Decrying the 'insensibility, and want of feeling' slavery engenders in the white female, Pickard notes the excited glee in the lady of the house when she asks the visitors if they saw the tormentors 'flogging the negre'.[18]

It is interesting that this English observer uses the term 'white' rather than 'Dutch' to describe the women in question, perhaps intending a general indictment of womanhood, including his own countrywomen, in that category rather than making this a nationalistic attack on the Dutch. But the woman overseer account goes well beyond the typical story of the depraved individual mistress, with the contention of his Dutch hosts that female drivers were 'by no means uncommon' – it became part of the established practice of an entire sex gone wrong. The physical weakness of women had become capable of correcting the 'stoutest slaves with no feeble arm'.

What Pinckard chose to highlight can be seen as just another portrait of free women corrupted, unusual only in that driving field slaves was not usually represented as a common occupation for white European women elsewhere. The description raises the question of actual practice. If Dutch free women, whether mistresses or servant overseers, routinely entered the fields to directly manage outdoor slaves, it would represent an exception to usual practice in the Americas. If Pinckard's 'drivers' were also the ladies of the house, were their practices related to something specific about Dutch colonial culture, especially the culture of elite free women, that was not present among the British, French, Portuguese or Spanish? Or might it have been because of the unique environmental conditions of the area that would later become Guyana-Suriname? Was planter society arranged in such a way that the normal management structure of plantations, such as male overseers, was missing?

If the female drivers were instead skilled white women servants, what were the physical or human factors, routinely missing in other colonies, that encouraged women to undertake that kind of employment? Much earlier in colonial history in places like the North American Chesapeake, white female indentured servants were known to be sent out to work the tobacco fields. While there they might have picked up the knowledge and skills to direct a gang. But if such experienced women ever were put in charge of groups of white indentured or enslaved black men or mixed-sex groups, we are not so informed. And finally, what of the boundaries of sex and supervision so often mentioned by cultural commentators on the ills of slavery? What would have been the response of the black slaves to their Dutch female supervisors, if any? Pinckard's free Dutch male host seems to have accepted this phenomenon as being part of the scenery, part of the established order. Did other free men share this view, or were they troubled by their wives, daughters or female servants in such positions of direct, physical mastery?

The relationship between what was written of the supposedly depraved free women of the Americas and their experiences, as mysterious as they were to observers on the north-east coast of South America, would continue to be worked out and contested in all slaveholding areas into the nineteenth century. There were transformative effects of living at the ends of the world.

Another avenue of attack against free women was modesty of the body:

> In all the states where slavery is permitted, the women tolerate nakedness which would disconcert the least modest of European women. They declare that in the southern part of Virginia, in the two Carolinas, in Georgia and even in Charlestown, young Negroes, 'absolutely naked,' appear before their mistresses, serve them at their table, without their suspecting that that is indecent. I have seen young girls, standing behind a paling fence, staring at the naked form of a Negro man who was being whipped.[19]

The historian who unearthed this quote, Catherine Clinton, goes on to state:

> White women trained themselves to respond to blacks, not as humans, but as animate property of favored status, like pets. Naked slaves, whether children or adults, were no more indelicate than livestock in the barnyard. Despite white women's exaggerated modesty, the body of an unclothed black gave the plantation mistress little offense. The relationship between plantation mistress and slave was never personal; this dehumanized naked object could present no threat to a woman's propriety. Although adolescent belles might make mention of the indelicacy of 'naked Negroes,' they soon outgrew this notion. If the issue ever arose, it was instantly repressed. White women had to render themselves immune – or, failing that, to present themselves as immune – to the black sexuality perceived by any outside observer. In doing so, they made themselves into stereotypes of sexlessness, and naked blacks to nonhumans.[20]

This self-training was doubtless part of a free woman's armoury in dealing with her environment. Yet there is no reason to suppose that white southern antebellum American women were any less sophisticated than free Muslim North African or Ottoman women on the complexities of 'gaze'. Both the demands of negotiating sexual relations and the worlds of work made this issue one of great individual nuance. It was the centuries old problem of the rituals of infantilisation – especially involving rituals of nakedness and dress – also were ones of indelible sexual significance. What, after all, was the interior world of this relationship:

> A mile further up, on the same bank of the Cape Fear River, is the home and estate of the American General Howe. While he amuses himself in dissipation elsewhere, his unfortunate family lives here; the wife has the manner of a divor-cee, and one lovely daughter, eighteen years old, has just had two sons by one of the Negro slaves.[21]

Had the 'lovely daughter' trained herself to 'see' differently?

Of course, there were local, virtually unknown occasions on which slavery could corrupt women, some of them not even southern. In one notorious local case from Putnam County, New York (a free state), a white wife con-vinced her free black husband to go south with her, and there disposed of him by selling him into slavery.[23] Sometimes, though, stories of the unusual might relate something not altogether horrible about the women in question, as in the next case, in which the free mistress in question was herself black. When some anti-slavery activists visited a court house in Barbados immediately after abolition there, when the island was experimenting with an 'apprentice' system:

> a complaint [was made] by a coloured lady, apparently not more than twenty, against a coloured girl – her domestic apprentice. The charge was insolence, and disobedience of orders … [complaints included] the same morning she delayed coming into her chamber as usual to dress her, and when she did come, she sung, and on being told to shut her mouth, she replied that her mouth was her own, and that she would sing when she pleased, and fourth, That she had said in her mistress's hearing that she would be glad when she was freed. These several charges being sworn to, the girl was sentenced to solitary confinement, but at the request of her mistress, she was discharged on promise of amendment.[24]

In stark contrast, episodes of female cruelty that provoked a violent response from their slaves could be savagely punished in the south – giving us the sense that the worries of their critics did not necessarily affect slaveholders for whom security was the primary issue:

> Dr. Parsons gives another instance which occurred not long before his visit to Georgia, the particulars he received from eye-witnesses. A slave had received from his mistress some punishment of great severity, when he seized a hatchet, and, as he supposed, killed her, though she afterwards recovered. On commit-ting the deed, he ran at once to the court-house and surrendered himself to justice. Justice in civilized countries would have been hanging. In Georgia, it was this: The slave was given to the mob, who first gave him fifty lashes a day for five days to prepare him for what was to follow. On the following Sunday,

he was taken from the jail, and suspended, naked, from his two hands, from the limb of a large oak tree near the court-house. A fire made of hard-pine shavings was kindled beneath him, and 'then the clear bright flames quickly ascended, curling about the limbs, encircling the body, scorching the nerves, crushing the fibers, charring the flesh – and, in mortal anguish, he was (in the words of an eye-witness) "sweating it as it were, great drops of blood." But before life was entirely extinguished, the lungs, the heart, the liver, were cut and torn from the body, with knives fastened upon poles, and with these quivering organs elevated above the crowd, the executioners shouted, 'so it shall be done to the slave that murders his mistress.'[25]

Similarly, incidents of violence with the mistress as the perpetrator or victim did occur even when there was no critical commentator in sight, leaving the locals, sympathetic to slavery, to interpret the event according to their expectations. One such incident involved Caroline Turner, the wife of a retired judge in Lexington, Kentucky. She was renowned – or notorious – for her brutality to slaves, and was reputed to have killed several with her own hands. Her behaviour was not deemed criminal so much as evidence of insanity, and Turner was institutionalised for a short time in an asylum. After gaining her freedom in 1844 she resumed her old ways, and in the act of beating a male slave upon her return he lashed out in violence, killing his mistress.[26] Like the earlier case of Thomas Hellier seen in the preceding chapter, in which a male subordinate had dispatched his mistress for (apparent) cause, Turner's slave nevertheless had to be executed to preserve social order. Also like the Hellier episode, the mistress was highly suspect.

The southern Kentuckians must have wondered about the connection between Turner's behaviour and the fact that she was not local but instead from a wealthy Boston family. This northern woman was not interfering from the usual stance of a pious, meddling abolitionist, but as one who had joined their system but had failed to understand it. The customs and manners by which southern women supported slavery quietly without provoking violence was the ideal. This sort of ostentatious brutality could potentially be seized upon by northerners to further discredit the south. In this case the irony of a northern woman perpetuating the excess is clear. Without a white male's humanity to consider, as with the case of Hellier, writers dealing with racial slavery could focus on the white woman herself more exclusively, another in a veritable parade of female depravity brought about by the curse of slavery.

Maternalism claimed and resisted

The common view that slaves remembered their mistresses more as benevolent mothers than the kind of vicious monster described above also needs to be subjected to scrutiny. Other factors might have produced these recorded memories. Whether or not the slave in question had been born within the woman's household and thus identified her in a maternal light, accounts were generally mixed. The question was not always whether the slave recalled a mistress as good or cruel, because many experienced both types.

Cuban slave Juan Francisco Manzano was looked after as a boy by his female owner. He lavishly praised her later for always keeping the best interests of her young slave at heart. But his next mistress tormented Manzano with harsh, painful punishments for minor transgressions.[27] A crucial difference existed between true autobiography and those testimonies presented and edited for other purposes by non-slaves. To those who had actually experienced slavery, the goodness or evil of their owners was a function of their individuality. They were not always typecast by age, appearance or even sex.

In contrast to the constant stream of vilification, some slaves recounted that the sanctions against them had been routine and mild, more the product of a mother than a monster. In response to her male gardener's 'insolence', for example, plantation mistress Rosalie Stier Calvert simply changed the man's employment, sending him out to the fields, and ignoring his repeated begging to be restored to his former post.[28]

Outright maternal benevolence accompanied with paternal benevolence also served as a tactic and strategy of control. This found particular resonance in the collective memories of white families that had previously held slaves. In the case of the author's family's oral history, Rebecca Jane Foster, before her death in 1907, reminisced that her grandfather had been 'a very kind man to his family and to his slaves, never known to whip a slave which was uncommon at that time. The slaves worked much as they pleased, most generally pleased to work.' This method also had a female analogue:

> Grandmother, too, was very kind to slaves. Many a jar of sugar at sugar-making and a jar of lard at hog-killing were sent to the negro quarters for their extra use ... [s]he also looked after them in sickness and made them as comfortable as possible.[29]

These passages are good examples of the foundations of family slaveholding memoirs. First, they cast the family as exceptions to the prevailing opinions of the time to the effect that slaves could only be controlled through violence. Somehow, the family in question found a way to rule successfully through kindness and generosity. Second, the *paterfamilias* and his mate are shown in complementary roles, helping and guiding their slaves as if they were separate sorts of children. Even women on their own could be credited with this attribute. One enduring story centred around mixed-race Louisiana free slaveholder Marie-Thereze Coin-Coin. Essential to the memory and family mythology was that her experience as a non-white woman made her a more benevolent mistress. She apparently never ordered beatings or whippings but rather in a judge-like way ordered definite periods of incarceration in a special slave-prison built for the purpose.[30]

Of course, the maternal position of women, especially vulnerable widows, might inspire acts of filial loyalty from their slaves acting, in a sense, as 'sons'. The future hero of the Haitian revolution (the only large-scale slave revolt that resulted in the overthrow of a European government and the establishment of an Afro-Caribbean republic), Touissant L'Ouverture, had a somewhat unlikely beginning as an enslaved apprentice hairdresser in New York, working to benefit his French owner then living in the city, Marie Elisabeth Bérard. By all accounts his fealty went beyond the common obligations of a slave. As the only male living amidst a group of free French and enslaved black women, he assumed the protector's mantle at the age of 20 – his extra industry relieving for instance some of his retiring mistress's threatening debt.[31]

Another purpose for the highlighting of maternal benevolence concerned lessons of private redemption and public welfare. In one unusual Kentucky tale from the 1830s, a black woman pie-maker known locally in Lexington, Kentucky as 'Aunt Charlotte' apparently took pity on a down-and-out white vagrant convict named William Soloman and bought him at a jail auction. According to the town lore, Aunt Charlotte's motivations were purely benevolent, as she felt a 'white man would have worked him to death'. Her faith was well placed when Solomon, who went by the ironic sobriquet of King, heroically kept up with the gravedigging necessary to accommodate the many victims of a cholera epidemic that had struck the city the day after he was purchased. Aunt Charlotte's motherly authority, expressed by her rescue of the luckless man, was a private act of virtue of a black woman publicly rewarded.[32]

The case of Aunt Charlotte and King Soloman also indicates the degree to which whiteness could be compromised by those who did not both fulfil the role and act the part. During the 1840 presidential election campaign, Democratic campaign rhetoric warned voters not to support Whig candidate William Henry Harrison because he had once supported a law that would have allowed the hiring of convicts to private individuals. Such arrangements, those Democrats claimed, would lead to respectable white 'neighbor men sold at auction ... to some free negro'. Worse peril would be to 'your poor but respectable and good neighbor-women' under the orders of a black master, 'compelled to obey them, whatever they might be'.[33] That 'some free' black women might buy 'respectable and good' white men at auction was apparently beyond the possibility of mention – although more likely under such a law as free black women outnumbered free black men in many places, and the overwhelming majority of convicts were men. Yet in at least one actual circumstance, the maternal power of a respectable black woman, and the temporary loss of manhood of a white vagrant, had inverted, and in a benevolent way transcended, the hard divisions of race.

Wills and testaments can give a more direct view of maternal benevolence at least attempted. The 1778 will of Ann Philips of Barbados concerned a slave named Kate, bequeathed presumably for the benefit of Ann's daughter Eleanor:

> Kate shall not be put to any labour or slavery for or by any person but is to be allowed free liberty the same as if she had been freed, and I also order that Judy, Kate's sister be and remain with Kate in the capacity of a slave to Kate during her life, and be in no way ordered and controlled by any person except Kate.[34]

Under this form of maternalism, the words 'a slave to' are synonymous with 'under the protection of'. What we might call 'freedom' would likely have been thought of as a dangerous cutting-off of supporting family. Judy was to remain dependent on Kate, Kate on the white daughter Eleanor. What the black women thought about this is unknown and open to question, but the white female notions of slavery as maternal protection are revealing.

Free men might place or attempt to place limits on female mastery. Male observers of the same social class who were not related to woman slaveholders sometimes expressed doubts that free females could or should exert their legal authority. One mill owner seeking to lease slaves expressed his doubts to one Virginia mistress who wished to send 'her boys' to him that female-owned slaves could or would do well back in a male-regulated regime. The man wrote to her:

> I think it my duty to add that I would not advise you to send your servants if they have been accustomed to an idle life. For whilst they are abundantly fed and clothed with us, they are required to do their duty.[35]

The underlying assumption seems to be that a mistress, as a sort of mother, would naturally coddle her 'children'. Echoing this sentiment, a South Carolina man named Robert Raper observed that the slaves of his female neighbour 'have been very troublesome lately having had too much of their way for a long time'.[36] This comment reveals the belief that female ownership of slaves might erode everyone's security by producing unruly, undisciplined slaves. Maternalism might also be distorted into infantilisation, with female slaves serving to watch over young free women. Nancy Naro has observed that 'Women of the household were subject to surveillance by trusted household slaves, widowed or maiden aunts and siblings, who aimed to safeguard the family from the deception and disgrace of a dishonourable match.'[37] Mistresses could be prisoners of maternalism as well.

Paternalism tested

On occasion, male masters received the same treatment from critical observers about lost manhood as did women owners and overseers who had supposedly lost their womanhood in the process of sustaining mastery. George Pinckard, touring Barbados in the last years of the eighteenth century, expressed shock at seeing four 'almost naked' female slaves working in a line, driven by a white overseer who held a 'whip at their backs'. This was no business, Pinckard implied, for a 'stout robust looking white man'. Pinckard and his companion approached the overseer and needled him by asking why such a healthy male did not 'partake of [the women's] tasks'. The overseer of course claimed race privilege, using oblique terms. The story was presented as an example of how slavery had made vigorous white English manhood soft and lazy, reduced to the pitiful state whereby the able-bodied 'had only to keep the women at work, and to make them feel the weight of the whip if they grew idle'.[38]

On the other hand, many efforts to limit abuses of male mastery amounted to empty, unenforced laws. Curbs on masters might be imposed in order to project the image of more humane societies than actually existed. This would especially be desirable in new European colonies in the Americas sensitive to criticism that they had become hives of savagery and barbarism. One attorney in Dutch Guiana expressed amusement when presented with the idea that a white master might be punished for disciplining a black slave. Though there existed a law on the books that such masters were restricted to the application of 39 lashes, the penalty was a tiny fine, which was rarely, if ever, levied.[39]

The same author also took New World masters to task for sexual irregularities with their slaves. He found to his particular interest the unusual design of a bed that masters shared with their slaves, allowing sexual access and at the same time asserting the hierarchy of the household. What he called 'West Indian luxury' featured 'a bedstead [in] two stages, the one about eight inches higher than the other, so as, while lying under the same covering, completely to separate the mulatto nymph from her lord'. He then addresses his complaint to his audience back home: '[w]hat would the fairer dames of Europe say to such a contrivance, calculated to drive them away, at pleasure, to the lower stage of a husband's bed?'[40] Of course, European American women of the Indies were being driven away entirely from their beds in such circumstances. But the symbolics were crucial. As Winthrop Jordan has written, '[w]hite men extended their dominion over their Negroes to the bed, where the sex act itself served as a ritualistic reenactment of the daily pattern of sexual dominance'.[41]

The mastery of men was supposed to be systematic and controlled, an expression of the masculine ideal in antebellum America. Historian Stephanie Camp has expertly contrasted this ideal with the manifest behaviour of slaveholding women during the Civil War years. Perhaps unaccustomed to management of the entire property while their husbands were away, white women practised what Camp calls 'moody violence' – essentially lashing out in anger at a slave's transgression. This sort of badly attempted mastery by means of pulling a slave's hair, or burning or stabbing them with random implements immediately to hand, was deemed by one publication to be specifically 'unmanly'. The ideal at least was to maintain an air of detached, unassailable 'cool' while supervising, for example, an overseer administering an orderly whipping to a slave.[42] As witnessed by many slaves including Frederick Douglass, however, the master losing his cool in fits of violence cannot have been uncommon.

Sexuality remained the core of antebellum mastery on other stages. Edward E. Baptist discusses in his examination of one slave trading firm a 'relentlessly sexualized vision of this trade' pursued by men 'devoted to their picture of the slave trade as a fetishized commodification of human beings'.[43]

> Traders catered to the desires of planters when they selected and marketed 'fancy maids.' Women like the fair maid Martha … and our white Caroline – both for sale by Isaac Franklin at Natchez [Mississippi] in May 1832 – were so light-skinned that they were called 'white' by the traders, although their legal blackness was clearly understood by all.[44]

Baptist usefully concludes:

> The only distinction between commodity and sexual fetishization in this history of the slave trade comes from our own habit of intellectually separating economic

om those of sexuality … [t]he two sets of desires were remarkably com-
d, indeed, the commodity and the sexual fetish were ultimately the
such men.[45]

Non-elite, even enslaved men often attempted in some fashion to replicate
the patterns of masters asserted by their propertied brethren. Stephanie Camp
reports that one escaped slave named Anna Baker explained one of the reasons
for her flight had been to escape the sexual advances of her male overseer, a
fellow black slave who supervised lines of women at work in the fields.[46] It is
clear that at least to some extent enslaved male overseers felt entitled to a limited version of the sexual mastery enjoyed by their own white employers. But
even among non-elite men there could be a sense that slavery was not adding
to the master's virility and mastery but rather taking away from it. It has to be
stressed that while masters looked upon their sexual dominance over female
slaves as realising and extending their manhood and mastery over the humans
and lands surrounding them as colonisers and later as nation-builders, there
were those, more sceptical about the benefits of slavery, who felt mastery over
slaves led directly to male weakness. English soldier John Gabriel Stedman
observed in the last decade of the eighteenth century that 'too frequent intercourse with the negro and mulatto fair sex' had produced, instead of men,
'poor wither'd mortals – as dry and sapless as a squeezed lemon'.[47] The words
'wither'd' and 'sapless' were especially unflattering in reference to male sexual
prowess, an insult doubtless intended.

Sodomy even played a role in defining nineteenth-century mastery – used
to describe the corrosive effects of contact with subordinated Africans. Historian of Jamaican slavery Trevor Burnard has found that plantation owner
and overseer Thomas Thistlewood twice recorded in his journals cases of masters sexually abusing their male slaves. These entries though, seem to discredit
individuals rather than to criticise the entire master class of the island – of
which Thistlewood himself was a part – for their behaviour.[48]

From other sources, it was the presence of strong American women that
might contribute to man's weakness in America. Still another line of thought,
however, maintained that female strength added to and confirmed that of
American men. The incomparable Alexis de Tocqueville, a French commentator
on the American character during the early republic, felt that:

> In Europe one has often noted that a certain contempt lurks in the flattery men
> lavish on women; although a European may often make himself a woman's slave,
> one feels that he never sincerely thinks her his equal …. Americans constantly
> display complete confidence in their spouses' judgment and deep respect for
> their freedom.[49]

Strong or weak, some forms of vulnerability especially haunted white masters
when they contemplated or imagined threats posed by black men. According
to one Alabama Law, 'It shall not be lawful for more than five male slaves,
either with or without passes, to assemble together at any place off the proper
plantation to which they belong.'[50] Even this kind of danger could have

gendered implications and elicit gendered fear. That female slaves tended to interpret the mastery of their male owners in sexual terms is clear when the tables turned. During the Haitian revolution of 1804, one of the rare instances where female slaves had the opportunity to take physical revenge on white men, some newly liberated women castrated and dismembered their still-living former masters and forced their victims to choke on their own genitalia, the symbol of their manhood, as they bled to death from their wounds.[51]

Finally, one of the severely underdeveloped themes in the history of antebellum paternalism was the presence of men throughout the south who appeared white, and free, but were in fact enslaved. According to a typical observer:

> While at a public-house, in Fredericktown, there came to the bar-room (on Sunday), a decently dressed white man, of quite a white complexion, in company with one who was totally black. After they went away, the landlord observed that the white man was a slave. I asked him, with some surprise, how could that be possible? To which he replied, that he was the descendant, by female ancestry, of an African slave. He also stated, that not far from Fredericktown, there was a slave estate, on which there were several white females of as fair and elegant appearance as white ladies in general, held in legal bondage as slaves … and when stimulated by avarice [these masters] hesitat[e] not to bind and sell his wife, his children, or his brother! I have received direct information from a gentleman who witnessed the fact, that in one of the slave states, a white man, having married one of his female slaves, after she had borne him several children, sold the whole of them together like he would a drove of cattle.[52]

In the 1930s historian Sterling Jordan wrote that it was 'a curious piece of inconsistency on their part, an indirect admission that a white man in chains was more pitiful to behold than the African similarly placed.[53] Whereas white-appearing women might be particularly vulnerable to the 'fancy maid' trade or other forms of sexual abuse, a 'white' man in slavery might be an embarrassment to southern society and a living affront to his owners. So it was for the London promoters of the brutal tale of the white-appearing slave Lewis Clarke, who at one point growing up was subject to a punishment inflicted by his aunt/mistress, enraged at one point by her 'white' male and female slaves, related to her by blood:

> she would fix me, so that no one should ever know I was white. Accordingly, on a burning hot day, she made me take off every rag of clothes, go out into the garden, and pick herbs for hours, in order to burn me black. When I went out, she threw water on me, so that the sun might take effect on me; when I came in, she gave me a severe beating on my blistered back.[54]

Pragmatic maternalism revisited

Yet after being the subject of so many vicious accusations, how did free women themselves understand and act to enforce the slave regime? They met attacks, as their foremothers had done for centuries, simply by living their lives pragmatically and attempting to access maternal authority – defined on whatever terms seemed the most useful for the tasks to hand. In relation to the former slave Lewis Clarke, quoted above, the mastery practised by his aunt/owner was anything but fictive. It had defined both of them. The cruelty of aunt to nephew had objectified him as the equivalent of an owned animal. And as he could not physically return the treatment he received, he instead captured her in words, using his aunt to cast all female slaveholders as something less than human – as 'animals'. This kind of retribution did not remain a private affair. Abolitionists seized upon such stories to discredit the kind of backward society that would produce such a woman. And what of the lost story, that of the aunt/mistress? How did she use and understand her apparent mastery? What pressures and opportunities ruled her perceptions and actions? What was her consciousness of authority – of mastery? Did she act out of confidence, desperation, or something else entirely? She could not defend herself in the wider court of public opinion, especially when that court was dominated by those like her nephew and like his eager publishers who sought to abolish the means with which she earned her living.

Beyond all this, in the realm of the practical, like the Muslim female slave managers of north Africa and the Ottoman empire, American women drew their identity from the many tasks demanded of them.

Often these tasks were not of the variety so often described – that of a static mistress planted in the home around whom all others revolved. Women might also busy themselves moving slaves from one place to another. In one account from the rural, inland south, a runaway man named Ben Brown persisted in absconding despite continual recapture because he was determined to continue visiting the various parts of his separated family scattered around the region. When recaptured, he was forced to run home while attached to the horse of his mistress.[55] If this unpleasant punishment was regarded as such, though, it apparently did not serve as much of a deterrent.

Other women owners, like Ben Brown's mistress and like the female advertisers in the *South Carolina Gazette*, actively engaged in reclaiming slaves. One bondsman named Bob Sterling fled to free Pennsylvania in 1851 – but under the provisions of the new fugitive slave law he was subject to recapture there and return to his original owner. Sterling's female master caught up with him in Harrisburg, the free state's capital city. There she encountered resentment to the law and to her efforts to enforce what she saw as her property rights. The local jail refused to house Sterling overnight, so his mistress secured him a room in a local hotel. A suspicious fire broke out there during the night, presumably the work of free blacks who had been demonstrating locally against the hated law. None of this though prevented the woman from returning south with her runaway slave in tow. Aside from demonstrating that women could be personally vigilant in recapture efforts, it is also an illustration of the way these incidents were not necessarily shaped by considerations of gender. The same type of resistance was routinely offered to male slave owners who came north in search of their slaves.[56]

Preference for which kind of slaves women chose for themselves is sometimes surprising as well, and challenges the idea that women would universally select other women because the latter would be easier to manage.[57]

Mrs A. C. Carmichael wrote from St Vincent in the Caribbean, claiming that for white women like herself, male slaves were far more manageable than black women, who were particularly despised by their mistresses. She advised unattached women, especially the unusually young or old, or others unsure of their authority, to buy men.[58] Free women did tend to acquire enslaved females when there was a clear economic rationale to do so – but not necessarily under other conditions.

Within the sexes, patterns of age reveal surprising preferences as well. Rosalie Stier Calvert expressed in her diary a preference for younger men as opposed to older, because the young, she found, were more docile. She had experienced particular problems with the male slaves older than she – 'insolent' gardeners and stubborn cooks – perhaps defying her expectation as well as ours that older enslaved men, grown accustomed to secure, relatively desired positions and without the rebellious energy of younger men, would not give their owners trouble.[59] Calvert found the precise opposite and adjusted her priorities accordingly. The contrast to the discussion of the American colonial era is striking, though, during which we saw that at least some relatively inexperienced young female managers and owners of servants and slaves who appreciated the help of older, more experienced male subordinates. Yet a plantation mistress did not depend on her gardener or her cook for survival, and she might be more insulated from the activities of younger male help than her foremothers. Real necessity might well have provided a way for women and ancillaries of different ages to find a way to work together in common purpose.

Rationality stood as the goal for managers. Historian of the Caribbean Hilary McD. Beckles asks his readers to think about the mastery of white women in terms of complementing the mastery of men:

> The sight of creole white women examining the genitals of male slaves in the market before making purchases, which offended the sensibilities of some European travellers, should not be considered necessarily as evidence of social degeneration, but rather as a feature of the dialectical relations between social and economic forces within the slave mode of production. Neither should such an action be considered contrary to their roles as good mothers and wives within the plantation household. Rather, it suggests that white women were acting fully within the epistemological framework of slavery by ensuring that rational market choices were made.[60]

In addition to purchase, manumission stood as another test of the rational. Beckles also claims that the type of owner least likely to manumit a slave was a white woman.[61] T. Stephen Whitman's work on manumission patterns among urban male and female slaveholders in Baltimore, Maryland, found that though women comprised 10 per cent of Baltimore owners, they accounted for 25 per cent of the city's manumissions. This seems to be strange in light of the fact that the relatively impoverished women owners depended much more on their slaves for the essentials of survival. Yet Whitman concludes that women rationally adopted practices of gradual manumission, which would cut down incentives to run away and inspire loyalty while in service. Rebellious or runaway slaves were true threats that outweighed the loss from carefully planned manumission.[62]

Non-elite, or even truly marginal, women might assume varied relationships to slavery, not always direct, straightforward mastery – actions that promised security as well as some danger. Writing of eighteenth-century British American economies, historian Serena Zabin observes:

> The market dangers faced by middling and elite female traders had their parallels in the local informal economies in which most women traded .... These women's transactions were frequently concluded with enslaved men and involved second-hand or even stolen goods .... An exchange in second-hand goods was automatically considered illegal if items were offered by a slave. As early as 1702 it was illegal to trade with slaves at all.[63]

In South America and the West Indies, as well as the US south, many such town slave owners were economically marginal working women, some of them mixed-race, who depended on their few slaves or indentured servants.[64] Even relatively impoverished free women could under some limited circumstances comprise part of the legitimate or underground economies. Of course, that might have meant slave ownership, which frequently involved owning non-white women. In the Penha district of San Paulo, Brazil, for example, one widowed white woman spinner depended upon nine black female slaves for her livelihood.[65] In Rio de Janeiro, groups of Minas African women slaveholders collected female slaves, called *mulattas claras* for their white appearance, to advertise and advance their businesses.[66] In Barbados, mixed-race female slaves desperately tried to earn enough excess money in prostitution to buy their freedom from their white and mixed-race mistresses. Slaveholding could mean survival for women of all races living at the margins of their new societies.[67]

Indeed, in the early French Antilles, one widow, Madame Jeanne Herault, owned 26 adult males, 25 females and 20 children. According to Bernard Moitt, by 1671 '15.5 percent of the estates in Guadeloupe were still female-only estates'. The popular speculation was these were 'stud farms' (perhaps also serving as brothels for this purpose). This would have been a practical choice, and in any event these women owned a diverse mix of help that could be deployed in a variety of profitable employments. Léonore Ramírez from La Montaigne Saint Louis held '3 white servants and six black slaves, 3 male and 3 female'. Another prominent woman, Françoise Benoist of la Montaigne Saint-Robert, the leader of a religious community, oversaw 'an artisan, 5 white servants, and 25 slaves – 6 adult males, 7 adult females, 8 boys, and 4 mixed-race children of both sexes'.[68] This speaks to pragmatism in action and helps us move away from a blanket assumption that women owners tended to obtain female bonded labour for a limited range of enterprises.

However, identifying the participants in these small economic worlds of purpose does not reveal problems in how they operated and their ultimate effect on how free women understood themselves. Indeed, the pragmatics of mastery seemed to overwhelm some women. Texan Lizzie Neblett during the

American Civil War found her efforts at maternal control of slaves in her husband's absence to be more than she could handle. Unable to even exert power by means of a male overseer, she found herself in despondency, interceding on the slaves' behalf to protect them from the overseer's violent attempt to keep the family's restless slaves at work. She begged her husband to sell all but 'one good Negro to wait upon me'.[69] One historian of the Neblett family concluded, with good justification, that to exert mastery over slaves was fundamentally incompatible with being a woman, with her sense of being female.[70]

Race and family

Harriet Jacobs, a former North Carolina slave and renowned memoirist, neatly summarised what she had experienced in slavery when she wrote: 'slavery is a curse to the whites as well as to the blacks. It makes the white fathers cruel and sensual; the sons violent and licentious; it contaminates the daughters, and makes the wives wretched.'[71] Slaves and ex-slaves joined white observers in feeling that slavery acted as social contagion. Jacobs further told her audience immediately before the Civil War that:

> the young wife soon learns that the husband in whose hands she placed her happiness pays no regard to his marriage vows. Children of every shade of complexion play with her own fair babies, and too well she knows that they are born unto him of his own household. Jealousy and hatred enter the flowery home, and it is ravaged of its loveliness.[72]

It is important to stress the counterpoint that Jacobs provides on the issue of female jealousy. Similarly, voluntary miscegenation was not simply a matter of moral depravity as outraged observers would have it, but also existed within the context of family-building as well as family stress and dissolution. Which principle applied was sometimes a function of social background. Post-revolutionary Southern white girls in North Carolina were sometimes regarded as being too fun-loving and undisciplined for their own good. It was noted in court records as well as in visitors' memoirs when such young women bore visibly mixed-race children. There could be a fine line to the authorities between voluntary relationships and sexual violence. In antebellum Virginia:

> [Slave] Carter was found guilty of the rape of [Catherine] Brinal and sentenced to death. Yet the judge determined that Carter was the 'proper object of mercy' because community members testified that Brinal: 'was a woman of the worst fame, that her character was that of the most abandoned insomuch as she (being a white woman) has three mulatto children, which by her own confession were begotten by different Negro men; that from report she had permitted the said Carter to have peaceable sexual intercourse with her, before the time of his forcing her.'[73]

This could affect even elite girls – as previously mentioned it was recorded that the daughter of Revolutionary War general Robert Howe had given birth to two sons by a slave before her eighteenth birthday.[74]

The family also provided an informal network that could abet the temporary, or permanent, flight of slaves from the property to which they belonged. The network of enslaved and free black relatives worked as an analogue to the white social and economic networks of mutual support that united neighbours as well as friends on distant towns and farms. This network also provided for autonomous physical space for enslaved people, frequently used illicitly.[75] These connections of family resistance have been described frequently, yet often overlooked are black families which were also connected – or not – by their own mastery and slaveholding. It was sometimes surprising even for white northerners in American free states to discover how many free blacks lived and worked in the slave states of the south – a number current scholars now put at about 250,000 by the eve of the Civil War in the areas that eventually seceded from the Union. Considered locally, free black ownership of slaves operated along recognisable gendered patterns.

In Charleston, South Carolina, more free black heads of households owned slaves than did not. As almost seven out of ten heads of free black households in that city were women, naturally they comprised the majority of black slaveholders as well, outnumbering men in one city census by the count of 123 to 68.[76] These women slaveholders tended to inherit slaves from a husband or other family member, although gifts or legacies from a former master or simple purchase for business investment were other routes of acquisition. Black women typically integrated their slaves into the urban economy of Charleston – hiring out female slaves as household domestics or male slaves as skilled artisans. Slavery was vital to these Charleston women's business interests and financial survival, and the preference of urban black women for female slaves reflected the nature of their concerns, which might include seamstressing, laundry and food preparation. In rural areas of lowland South Carolina among black slaveholders the converse gender arrangements prevailed. Black male property owners tended to own slaves who were also male and adept at plantation work. Black female plantation owners were a minority but not an insignificant one – comprising by one count 27 per cent of rural masters in South Carolina by 1860. Men and women shared the same preferences for type of slaves because of the nature of plantation work. Male slaves made up about 52 per cent of the rural bondsmen owned by black masters, male and female.[77]

Very similar patterns occurred elsewhere. Kimberly Hanger reports an almost identical phenomenon from late eighteenth-century Spanish Louisiana. While acknowledging the phenomenon of kin-purchase in US states with manumission laws requiring resettlement of freed slaves, she finds that free persons of colour purchased slaves who were not related to themselves more often than they purchased kin. In Spanish Louisiana, as elsewhere, non-white free women predominated over non-white male purchasers, but interestingly this was not simply a function of there being more women than men in this category. Hanger's research reveals that non-white women called *pardas* (light-skinned or mixed race blacks) and *morenas* (dark-skinned blacks) actually bought slaves at a greater rate than would be expected from their numbers alone – in other words women proportionally expressed in the marketplace a greater need for slaves than did non-white men. This gap however closed over time during the Spanish regime in Louisiana.[78]

Overall, this pattern accords with what seems to have occurred elsewhere along the western edge of the Atlantic world – *pardas* and *morenas* preferred to buy women slaves for their specific work and businesses, while non-white men tended to buy male slaves for the same reasons. However, it should be noted again that in New Orleans, like other areas, women certainly did not hesitate to buy male slaves when it suited their needs, nor did men shy away from purchasing women. Though Hanger draws no firm conclusion to why women owners seemed to need more slaves per buyer, the comparative perspective from elsewhere at least suggests that these marginal women lived closer to the edge of survival than did men. This compounded the ever-present social disability of doing business as a free woman of colour. Slaves might well have insulated these women from economic ruin.

However, connections of black families were also of course subject to destruction in slavery. The integrity of the family was always hostage to the efforts of masters to destroy the bonds of family and community in the name of control. Narratives featuring the voices of slaves were sometimes capable of expressing clear-eyed views of family distortion. Among the most evocative account, published well after the end of the Civil War, was that of Louis Hughes, who published his memoir *Thirty Years a Slave* while working from Wisconsin in the late 1890s. The tone of the text recalls the abolitionist slave narratives from before the war, but conveys a clinical view of the depredations of slavery in which the cruelties are allowed to speak for themselves without a heavy gloss of politics or sentimentality. It is a human document rather than a polemic, and as such in a roundabout way became one of those most powerful rebukes to slavery ever written by an American who had actually experienced bondage. As with the abolitionist-influenced accounts, punishment is central to the narrative in communicating the fundamental relationship between master and slave. Hughes describes the 'bull ring' in which a slave, male or female, would be stripped naked and placed in the centre of a circle formed by the overseer as well as his or her fellow slaves and family members – men, women and children. The overseer would then instruct the slaves making up the ring to beat the slave in the middle with the switches or makeshift whips with which they had been issued.[79] Hughes does not meditate on the deep symbolics of this particular form of punishment relating to the abuse of and based on family attachment, but they were not difficult for his reading audience to perceive. Lewis Clarke told of a husband forced by his owners to whip his own wife to death.[80]

All slavery and servitude systems to some extent were wrapped up in performances of the gendered individual. For free men, honour was universally intertwined with mastery. Whereas women masters walked a narrow and hazardous path in matters of honour, risking its loss when they overstepped perceived boundaries, men generally had much more latitude to build honour on the foundations of mastery. Conversely, cultural shame was the usual reality for subjugated peoples of both sexes. 'Shame' in this context usually means the alienation from one's social identity, membership in a family, culture or society which conveys or promises an honourable existence. But gendered resistance, as in matters of honour and shame, reflects immediately back upon the nature of mastery as well. Patterns of resistance undertaken separately by men and women indicate what, precisely, was being resisted. From a master's perspective, the ability to separate a servant or slave's biological sex from his or her gender (gender defined here as the cultural perception and meaning of one's sex) was a fundamental tactic to tighten control. So it was with the epic physical battle between slave and master described by Frederick Douglass. Douglass later wrote that when he got the better of his master, Covey, he became a true man. Attaining manhood and liberty occurred simultaneously.[81] Over the course of her own memoir of American slavery, Harriet Jacobs makes clear that her journey to freedom was, to her, a journey to recover lost motherhood, and by extension, lost womanhood. Emerging in the accounts of these and other former slaves is the implicit message that mastery was built by denying manhood and womanhood to others.

Even if the work required matched the gender of the servant or slave performing it, gender identities were also upset if the supervisor or overseer was of the opposite sex. These gendered patterns of resistance also reveal the utilitarian objectives of masters and mastery. From the perspective of a slave or servant, the denial of his or her gender identity would naturally seem to have been directed at them personally. There was often, though, ordinary pragmatism lurking behind the upsetting of gender roles for servants and slaves. Slave work was in many places dictated by the seasons, and female field workers harvesting in the autumn or males working as household domestics in winter were simply deployed where there was available work to be done.

At the heart of resistance, then, we often find profound misunderstandings between practical owners and managers who thought themselves eminently reasonable, and slaves and servants who felt they were being violently torn from the ideas of who they were as men and women and what constituted their honour. This difference in understanding also sheds light on the question of why free men, despite their cultural fears, so frequently put their wives, mothers, and daughters in charge of servants and slaves, male and female, creating that all-important 'mid-level' of authority which was so often the defining fulcrum of coerced labour. In instance after instance we see pragmatic masters genuinely surprised at the rebellious – and potentially lethal – behaviour of those working for them whose gender identities had been compromised. The array of resistance does remind us in the final instance that as much as a slave or servant might claim identity or agency, it was ultimately the gendered values and strategies of the masters that determined the realities of life in bondage.

Legacies for the nation

In the mid and late 1840s English-speaking audiences in America and Britain were artistically mesmerised by an intoxicating mix of the political and the prurient from which they simply could not look away. The object was the chained nude body of a young woman rendered in marble. *The Greek Slave* – whose wrists were enclosed by manacles attached by a double chain and ostensibly exposed for sale in a Muslim Turkish slave market – was the product of the mind of sculptor Hiram Powers. The evident compulsion to view the work sprang from the very oppositions and paradoxes it evoked – piety transposed with the abject. American and British audiences were forced, not involuntarily, to share in the gaze of the imagined Turkish buyers ready to feast on the nubile product of Greece, western civilization's and Christendom's still flowering cradle. But to many viewers, there seemed to be modesty and virtue created out of her very nudity. The stoic, obviously faithful, and arrestingly beautiful face, the way the head is turned away from potential purchasers in a way both shy and stalwart, even the manner in which the left hand partially covers her nether regions, were suggested by the artist itself as the true purpose of the work. This vision of slavery indicated the complicity of the fascinated audience itself.

As for words, we can draw on a Works Projects Administration narrative taken in the 1930s from ageing ex-slaves. Sarah Carpenter Colbert had been a slave in Kentucky, and told of her father Isaac's experiences with three white women who had defined his bondage.[82] Isaac had been owned by his own grandfather Leige Carpenter, and treated well. Upon his master's death he was sold to a Jim Carpenter, whose wife was 'very mean to the slaves', Isaac's daughter remembered, and 'whipped them regularly every morning to start the day right'. Taking advice from a fellow slave, Isaac deliberately fell to the floor one day while receiving his morning beating from his mistress, and bit her foot. Apparently now fearful of her slave, the beating stopped, but in a week he was sold. He was purchased by Leige Carpenter Jr, the son of his original master and probably Isaac's own uncle. His problems with white women continued as his 'young mistress was very mean to him'. He then tried a similar act of resistance, spreading 'yellow dust' (perhaps pollen or some other form of irritant) around his mistress's room and into her shoes. This produced a similar result as Isaac was sold yet again, to yet a third abusive household. Finally in desperation, Isaac appealed to his 'old mistress', presumably the widow of his grandfather. The woman benevolently purchased him, where he lived in relative contentment until slavery was abolished.

In this single story are all the complications of gender, mastery and slavery, acting upon a single life. The focus of the male former slave was not on the man who officially owned him, but rather the women representing those mid-levels of mastery who actually determined the conditions and limits of his life. Women were the source of tyranny and the source of maternal salvation. Also typically conflicted and subtle are the sources and manner of telling. Here the tyrannical mistress is not portrayed by an abolitionist with a political agenda but the apparently honest memory of an aged daughter with nothing material or ideological to gain in a particular telling. But the ultimate source is the man himself, the male slave, who seems to instinctively put himself as the active party, as the agent, as the origin of all action. The mistresses he manipulates react to his plans. He is the centre. Lost, as always are the agendas of the mid-levels, what the women intended, their agendas, their difficulties, in forging maternalism from a system defined by brutality and involuntary service. Their masters, for their part, tended to only wish to see white women in marble.

Conclusion

In a sensitive and astute essay called 'Marriage à la russe,' scholar of Russian culture Judith Vowles analyses the popular memoirs of a Frenchman named Charles-François-Phibert Masson, a former royal tutor in the Russian court. After his 1796 deportation by Paul I, Masson wrote a devastating critique of the society that had hosted him for so many years. Among his themes was how Russia, unlike the 'civilised' nations of western Europe, promoted the savagery of women. He called into question the entire social order based on what he had seen of women's role in Russian slavery.

Russian women, he wrote:

> engaged in business by no means suitable to their sex. To buy, sell, and exchange slaves, assign them their tasks, and order them to be stripped and flogged in their presence, would be as repugnant to the feelings as to the modesty of a woman in a country where men are not degraded to the level of domestic animals, and treated with the same indifference ... [the women] live from their childhood in the greatest familiarity with a herd of their slaves; a thousand private and even secret services are performed for them by male slaves, whom they scarcely consider as men.

Pursuing the point, Masson directly quotes a Russian girl herself: 'these are my slaves, they were brought up with me. I'd like to know if they have the audacity to think I have anything but a petticoat under my skirts, or think that I am a woman to them, or that they are men to me.'[1]

Masson captures all the elements of the durable pattern that has emerged throughout these chapters. Women, hostages to his words, are sexualised in the process of claiming that they are desexualised before their slaves. The legitimacy of their mastery is ridiculed by portraying them as masters. Women were everywhere present in the management of slaves, but their contribution was obscured by those who observed or served them. Society, in other words, depended on what it despised. And Orlando Patterson was correct when he stated that manhood and slavery were intimately connected. Yet slavery could defeat manhood as easily as it could establish it.

As the preceding chapters show, the conflicts of gendered mastery did emerge in great variation and had many cultural and practical uses from the classical period on through the mid-nineteenth century. Yet the basic outline endured. Perhaps the lesson, though, is not that gendered mastery and maternalism were a human universal, a category of which historians are rightly suspicious. They might speak more to the deep transmission of a cultural narrative that was of regular use and eligible for reinvention. I have identified here several conduits by which the narrative travelled. The story of Joseph and

Potiphar's wife from the Old Testament's book of Genesis was as recognisable to Americans in 1865 as it had been to Hebrew readers and hearers of the Torah. And the mythological allegory of Heracles and Omphale served a similar purpose. More often the lines of transmission were much subtler and more difficult to track. Yet by whatever means the expectations, performances, legal structures and narratives travelled from place to place and time to time, nowhere was slavery simply invented as something entirely new.

Mastery was at the heart of the gendered aspects of slavery, and maternalism at the heart of that mastery. Sometimes, the direction of power was expected. In Christian Spain during the *reconquista*, for example, a free Muslim servant woman in a male monastic community might be raped by the brothers. The monks would then bring the violated woman in front of a judge for the crime of having engaged in sex with free Christian men. As her punishment she would be made a slave of the community. In this way, the monasteries were able cynically to build an impressive stock of female slaves.[2]

However, another account from immediately across the land border in Islamic Spain told of a different sort of story. Brought to light by Olivia Remie Constable, the lesson was set in early thirteenth-century Cordoba, where a young woman was exposed for sale in the local slave market. A Muslim man from out of town purchased her, covering her in expensive clothes. She then revealed her true identity by speaking good Arabic. To the purchaser's horror she was actually a free Muslim woman, a turn of events that placed him in real peril. Reducing such a woman to slavery was a grave criminal offence, and the 'slave girl' threatened to bring her 'master' before a judge. Trapped, he agreed to her plan to take her to a nearby city where he could get an even better price for her, which was done. The woman's blackmail succeeded if one presumes she shared in the money paid to her victim as well as kept the expensive clothes.[3]

This as well was the nexus of gender, mastery and slavery. Two individuals, shaped by the hierarchies, societies, religions and expectations around them, together in conversation, their relative masteries uncertain, face-to-face in competitive intimacy, negotiating something new. These kinds of negotiations, with the added factor of race, would of course in time reach American shores, fuelling cultural wars over slavery.

In 1894, almost 30 years after final abolition, a book appeared by a Chicago publisher purporting to be the authentic memoirs of an aged former American slave. Called *The Story of a Slave: A Realistic Revelation of a Social Relation of Slave Times*, the effort is a mix of literary forms. It is first a straight narrative in which a man apparently recounts his life in the manner of Louis Hughes and countless others. Like the abolitionist commentary that had often introduced slave accounts before the Civil War, a publisher's preface argued that the 'Negro question' was of the same essential nature in the 1890s as it had been in the 1850s. The narrative would provide its reader with 'ample food for the serious reflection of Sociology and open up an avenue of discussion … through which alone can come a pacific settlement of the social problems of the south.'[4] Yet the memoir's focus on only one aspect of the traditional slave narrative – a male slave's 'mutual love' with his master's daughter – gave the

American audience of the 1890s something more like a novel of sensation and scandal.[5] If considered as a novel, though, *The Story of a Slave* treads a thin line between a *roman à clef* (a fictional work featuring thinly veiled social truths the author seeks to reveal), and a prurient pot-boiler of forbidden, interracial passion.

Whatever its author's intentions, the characters do faithfully reflect pre-Civil War accounts by bondsmen endorsed by abolitionists. The hero, who calls himself 'Paul', is remarkably like the mixed-race Lewis Clarke, the very real white-appearing slave who had been owned and terrorised by his own aunt Mrs Banton. And like Clarke, Louis Hughes and others, Paul was owned when growing up by a close white relative – in this case the uncle who inherited him from his father. Not only is Paul's humanity established with the blood of the white race (again like the old abolitionist-edited narratives), but like the descendants of the 'Moors of Delaware' or the family of Molly Walsh, the slave's African ancestors are royal. His mother, readers are told, came from a princely Senegambian family.[6]

Though presented to refer to specific American racial problems, the story also exists in a much broader, older context. In the narrative, 22-year-old field slave Paul is assigned to serve and protect his aunt/mistress in the women's wing of the house. There he discovers the ethics of his owners. 'The slave-holders, masters and mistresses,' Paul observed, 'had been educated to regard their negroes as they regarded the furniture, or their cats and dogs, a species of domestic fixture, having eyes to see not, and ears to hear not, senses to feel and yet to feel not.' This directly echoes laterally our observer of Russia, but also the genealogy of the older Muslim frontier – the Arab mistresses who thought their Christian slaves 'blind with the eyes of the body, as well as the soul.'[7] Conscious or not of this heritage, the author of the American narrative declares: '[t]he eunuchs in the eastern harem had no more liberty of association with the inmates of the seraglio than the southern negro slave had with the ladies of his master's house'.[8]

However, Paul considers himself anything but a eunuch. Being cast into the service of women causes him to fully realise his degraded state. When his mistress's daughter Virginia (who is also his half-cousin) returns from her women's college, he is also obligated to attend her. This, on top of his strong attraction, creates a crisis of manhood, and in turn a crisis of freedom:

> I went out from her presence that morning humbled and degraded, feeling the despised reality of my position as I had never felt it before. I was not only a negro slave, but ... less than a man, and hardly a beast. I knew very well in my secret conscience, that it was not for lack of maidenly modesty she so unblushingly exposed her person to my unforbidden sight ... but for want of decent respect for me. Had she regarded me as anything better than a soulless brute, had she esteemed me as a man, endowed with the sense and feelings of a man, she would have screamed with affright and driven me with furious wrath from the room. But I was not a man, only an animated machine, a bloodless, soulless automaton to fetch and carry, with eyes to see not and nerves to feel not. This was my despised status – despicable, degraded, emasculated – and wretchedly did I realise it.[9]

But this very recognition blazes for Paul a path to redemption, the same one trod centuries before by Heracles in the hands of Omphale, Joseph in the hands of Potiphar's wife, Salman the Persian in the hands of the Jewess of Medina. Assigned to accompany his young mistress on a horseback ride, he refuses to allow her to make a dangerous jump, raising her fury. When Virginia regains her senses and realises Paul has saved her life, her gratitude eventually blossoms into love.[10] This turn of romantic novelisation nevertheless has the same transformative effect as Frederick Douglass striking Covey. More than restoration, it creates Paul's honour and manhood. It redeems him from a slavery more fundamental than any prescribed legal status.

Yet one fundamental barrier remains. Race continued to be a divide between Virginia and Paul. By contrast, in overcoming maternal mastery Heracles, Joseph and Salman became eligible for full cultural and religious redemption. Further, they were able to advance beyond simply being free men. They could proceed onward to be leaders of peoples and faiths. But racial difference was an American barrier that could not be overcome completely, even when, like the story of the Arab girl in the Cordoba marketplace, mistress and slave negotiated new realities. Eventually Virginia had to marry her own kind, and her slave faced the obligation of stepping aside. And yet – in a final twist – history itself catches them up. Virginia dies in the maelstrom of the Civil War, while the liberated slave, the supposed author of the narrative-novel, rises to a social 'eminence' – though his identity, again because of race, cannot be revealed.[11] Even earned wealth could not fully redeem the race that had defined his slavery – the state of American reality in 1894 and far beyond.

The nuances of gender and mastery to which the writer of this novel had been so sensitive were not often recognised in twentieth-century approaches to slavery. Yet the maternal, and the redemptive, had mattered fundamentally to slaveholding peoples, as it had to those who endured slavery through the centuries. There had always been a conflict among social hierarchies and the individuals who chose their own ways to negotiate them. The telling epigraph to *The Story of a Slave* was this verse by Paul Hamilton Hayne:

> Love scorns degrees; the low he lifteth high,
> The high he draweth down to that fair plane
> Whereon, in his divine equality,
> Two loving hearts may meet, nor meet in vain.[12]

Whether this idea would be met with sympathy, or with fear and rage, was a question that defined a battleground both ancient and modern.

Notes

Introduction

1. Ella Thomas, *The Secret Eye* (Chapel Hill: University of North Carolina Press, 1990), 45, 168.
2. 'Recollections of slavery by a runaway slave,' *The Emancipator*, 23 August 1838. ser 1-1308 Davis Library, University of North Carolina, Chapel Hill.
3. Joseph Holmes as interviewed by Ila B Prine, 11 June 1937, *The American Slave* supp. Ser 2, vol. 1: 5–11, 6.
4. 'Recollections of slavery by a runaway slave,' *The Emancipator*, 20 September 1838. ser 1-1308 Davis Library, University of North Carolina, Chapel Hill.
5. Master of Equities Bills of Complaint, 1839:28, Charleston County, South Carolina. Case discussed in Larry Koger, *Black Slaveowners: Free Black Slave Masters in South Carolina, 1790–1860* (Jefferson, N.C.: McFarland, 1985), 86.
6. Orlando Patterson, *Slavery and Social Death: A Comparative Study* (Cambridge, Mass.: Harvard University Press, 1981), 78, 386n7.
7. Mary Boykin Chesnut, *A Diary from Dixie*, ed. Ben Ames Williams (Cambridge Mass.: Harvard University Press, 2002), entry 9 May 1861, 49. I first discussed the concept of maternalism within slavery in W. H. Foster, 'Women slave owners face their historians: versions of maternalism in Atlantic World slavery', *Patterns of Prejudice*, vol. 41, nos. 3–4, 2007), esp. 309–10. For Chesnut's perspective in particular see also p. 306.
8. See Gerda Lerner, *The Creation of Patriarchy* (New York: Oxford University Press, 1986), especially 76–122.
9. L. Thorsten Sellin, *Slavery and the Penal System* (New York: Elsevier, 1976), 32.
10. For discussions of female authority and the principle of exceptionalism see, for example, Margaret R. Sommerville, *Sex and Subjection: Attitudes to Women in Early-Modern Society* (London: Arnold, 1995) esp. 40–69. Sommerville skillfully qualifies the term and provides thought-provoking exceptions to the very idea of 'exceptionalism'. For a more conventional view consult Laurel Thatcher Ulrich's formulation of the 'deputy husband' social role in *Good Wives: Image and Reality in the Lives of Women in Northern New England, 1650–1750* (1980) (New York: Vintage, 1991), 35–50.
11. See especially Susan Treggiari, 'Jobs in the household of Livia', *Papers of the British School at Rome*, 43: 48–77.
12. Ruth Mazzo Karras, 'Servitude and Sexuality in Medieval Iceland', in *From Sagas to Society: Comparative Approaches to Early Iceland*, ed. Gísli Pálsson (Enfield Lock: Hisarlik Press, 1992), 289–304.
13. See Richard C. Trexler, *Sex and Conquest: Gendered Violence, Political Order, and the European Conquest of the Americas* (Ithaca, N.Y.: Cornell University Press, 1995), 14–37, esp. 23–25.
14. Trexler, *Sex and Conquest*, 23.
15. See especially Kathleen M. Brown, *Good Wives, Nasty Wenches and Anxious Patriarchs: Gender, Race and Power in Colonial Virginia* (Chapel Hill: University of North Carolina Press, 1996). To her credit, Brown's thesis of male mastery does not seek to extend beyond colonial Virginia. Others however have extrapolated

her ideas and applied them to areas beyond those in which they are valid. See also my discussion of this issue in Foster, 'Women slave owners', 306n 2, 313.

16. Drew Gilpin Faust, *Mothers of Invention: Women of the Slaveholding South in the American Civil War* (New York: Vintage, 1996), esp. 53–79.

17. Kirsten E. Wood, *Masterful Women: Slaveholding Widows from the American Revolution through the Civil War* (Chapel Hill: University of North Carolina Press, 2004), esp. 1–14. 35–60. I also discuss the Faust to Wood progression in Foster, 'Women slave owners', 313–14.

18. Terri L. Snyder, '"As if there was not master or woman in the land"', in *Over the Threshold: Intimate Violence in Early America*, ed. Christine Daniels and Michael V. Kennedy (New York: Routledge, 1999), 219–36. See also Foster, 'women slave owners', 314–15.

19. Susan Mosher Stuard, 'Ancillary evidence for the decline of medieval slavery', *Past and Present*, 149 (November 1995), 19.

20. Margaret Sommerville, *Sex and Subjection: Attitudes to Women in Early-Modern Society* (London: Arnold, 1995), 60–73.

21. This idea was pioneered especially in the field of Native American history. For the seminal works see especially Richard White, *The Middle Ground: Indians, Empires, and Republics in the Great Lakes Region, 1650–1815* (New York: Cambridge University Press, 1991); Neal Salisbury, *Manitou and Providence: Indians, Europeans, and the Making of New England, 1500–1643* (New York: Oxford University Press, 1982), and Daniel H. Usner, Jr, *Indians, Settlers, and Slaves in a Frontier Exchange Economy: The Lower Mississippi Valley Before 1783* (Chapel Hill: University of North Carolina Press, 1992).

22. K. Brown, *Good Wives*, part 1, *passim*.

Chapter 1 Gender, Mastery, and Maternalism: Christian, Muslim and Hebrew Traditions

1. Genesis 39: 7.
2. Genesis 39:12.
3. Judges 4: 1–5 (text from the King James version).
4. Judges 4: 1–5 (text from the King James version).
5. See, for example, the discussion in Michael Walzer et al. (eds), *The Jewish Political Tradition*, vol. 2 (New Haven, Conn.: Yale University Press, 2006), 205.
6. Leviticus 25: 39.
7. Exodus 23: 9; Leviticus 24: 22; Numbers 15: 15–16.
8. Exodus 21:20, 26–7; Deuteronomy 22: 25–7, 23: 15–16; Leviticus 19: 20–2.
9. Deuteronomy 21: 13.
10. Deuteronomy 22: 25–7; Leviticus 19: 20–2.
11. For Rabbi Akiba see Babylonian Talmud, Gittin 38b. For the original prohibition on manumission of foreign-born slaves see Leviticus 25. This ruling is discussed in greater context in David M. Cobin, 'A brief look at Jewish law of manumission', *Chicago-Kent Law Review*, 70 (1995), 1343.
12. Moses Maimonides, *The Book of Acquisitions* (Code of Maimonides, Book XII), (c. 12th century AD), trans. Isaac Klein (New Haven: Yale University Press, 1951), 246, 280.
13. *Schulchan Aruch*, part II Yoreh De'ah, chapter 21, 'Slaves and proselytes', 267:19 (sixteenth century). May be viewed at www.torah.org/advanced/sculchan-aruch/classes/chapter21.html.
14. MT Avadim 1:2; www.shamash.or/listarchives/top/top.mishpatim-fullstudy.2002.

15. Babylonian Talmud, Baba Mezi'a 71, notes 22–3.

16. Midrash for the Torah Portion Naso, www.jewishgates.com/file.asp, p. 2.

17. Tosefta Qid 5:9 as quoted by Catherine Henzer, *Jewish Slavery in Antiquity* (Oxford: Oxford University Press, 2005), 171–2.

18. Tosefta, Sot. 5:9, as quoted by Catherine Henzer, *Jewish Slavery in Antiquity*, 171.

19. Babylonian Talmud, Tractate Gittin 70a. Soncino 1961 edition, p. 334.

20. Yaron Ben-Naeh, 'Blond, tall, with honey colored eyes': Jewish ownership of slaves in the Ottoman Empire,' *Jewish History (Netherlands)* 20 (2006), 317–18.

21. Ben-Naeh, 'Jewish ownership of slaves', esp. 322–3.

22. Ben-Naeh, 'Jewish ownership of slaves', 325, 325n51.

23. For 'Sara' see Ben-Naeh, 320.

24. For women in Cairo see Ben-Naeh, 'Jewish ownership of slaves', 328.

25. See the hadith tradition of Sahih Bukhari, vol 3, book 46, nos 713, 719, 735, 736; also see Abdul Wasay Bhat's commentary on the hadith of Muwatta of Imam Malik on male slaves being led in *tarawih* prayer by their mistress Aisha (Bhat, 'Imamah of Salah,' University of Kashmir, India, n.d.).

26. See Taqiuddin an-Nabhani, *The Social System in Islam* (New Delhi: Milli Publications, 2001), ch. 7.

27. For Salman see Sayyid Sa'eed Akhtar Rizvi, *Slavery from Islamic and Christian Perspectives*, 2nd edn (Vancouver, BC, Canada: Islamic Educational Foundation, 1987), ch. 4, sect. 1. Rizvi cites as the primary source the ninth-century Baghdad biographer Ibn Sa'd, al-Tabaquatul Kabir (Leiden, E. J. Brill, 1912), IV:1, p. 58. For Khabbab ibn Arratt (sometimes transcribed 'Arat') see Sa'd, III: 1, 116–17.

28. Ayatullah Murtaza Mutahhari, *The Islamic Modest Dress* (Qum, Iran: Dar us Sequafe), reproduced and translated by the Ahlul Bayt Digital Library Project, ch. 6, para. 30.

29. Stephen Clissold, *The Barbary Slaves* (Totowa, N.J.: Rowman & Littlefield, 1977), 46.

30. Marnia Lazreg, *The Eloquence of Silence: Algerian Women in Question* (New York: Routledge, 1994), 22.

31. Emanuel d'Aranda, *The History of Algiers and its Slavery*, English trans. John Davies of Kidwelly (London: John Starkey, 1666), 151.

32. Lazreg, *The Eloquence of Silence*, 23.

33. Clissold, *The Barbary Slaves*, 45.

34. Anon, 'The Shepherd of Hermas,' c. 3rd century AD. The text is reproduced from its various incomplete early versions (probably involving multiple authors) by Carolyn Osiek. See 1 [1], 'Vision of Rhoda,' in Osiek, *Shepherd of Hermas: A Commentary* (Minneapolis: Augsberg Fortress, 1999), 41, 46.

35. See Osiek, *Shepherd of Hermas*, 42, 42n3.

36. Osiek, *Shepherd of Hermas*, 43n8.

37. 'First vision of the Woman Church' 2 [2], in Osiek, *Shepherd of Hermas*, 46.

38. Clement of Alexandria (Titus Flavuis Clemens), *Christ the Educator* (c. 3rd century), trans. Simon P. Wood (New York: Fathers of the Church, Inc, 1954), 226. See also my discussion in Foster, 'Women slave owners', 311.

39. Anon, 'Life of St Mary the Younger' [tenth century AD], trans. Angeliki E. Laiou, in *Holy Women of Byzantium: Ten Saints' Lives in English Translation*, ed. Alice-Mary Talbot (Washington, D.C.: Dumbarton Oaks Research Library and Collection, 1996), 260.

40. R. St. J. Tyrwhitt, 'Aetius', in *A Dictionary of Early Christian Biography*, ed. Henry Wace and William C. Piercy (London: John Murray, 1911).

41. Simeon of Durham as quoted in David Pelteret, *Slave Raiding and Slave Trading in Early England*, Anglo-Saxon England 9, ed. Peter Clemoes (Cambridge: Cambridge University Press, 1981), 106, 107n65.

42. Discourse 30, 'The Venerable Moisej the Hungarian' [c. 1015 AD] in *The Paterik of the Kievan Caves Monastery*, trans. Muriel Heppel (Cambridge, Mass.: Harvard University Press on behalf of the Ukrainian Research Institute of Harvard University, 1989), 162–7. For further commentary on the case see David K. Prestel, 'The Tale of Moses the Hungarian: from Egypt to the Land of Promise', *Slavic and East European Journal*, 42.2 (1998), esp. 203, 205, 209.

43. For a literary view, see, for example, Batya Weinbaum, *Islands of Women and Amazons: Representations and Realities* (Austin: University of Texas Press, 2000), 71.

44. Orientius, *Commonitorium*, II, 167–8.

45. Edward Gibbon, *The History of the Decline and Fall of the Roman Empire*, vol. 7 (London: Bell and Daldy, 1866), ch. 68, part 4.

46. Anon, *Sketches of the Fair Sex in all Parts of the World* (Boston, Mass.: Theodore Abbot, 1841), 177.

47. Sandra R. Joshel and Sheila Murnaghan (eds), *Women and Slaves in Greco-Roman Culture* (New York: Routledge, 1998), 10.

48. Pierre Vidal-Naquet, *The Black Hunter: Forms of Thought and Forms of Society in the Greek World* (Baltimore, Md.: Johns Hopkins University Press, nd), 209.

49. Plutarch, 'Bravery of women,' in *Moralia* (vol. III) (Loeb Classical Library, 1931) 488–9. (cf).

50. Vidal-Naquet, 210–11.

51. Vidal-Naquet, 211–12.

52. Tacitus, *The Agricola and The Germania*, trans. H. Mattingly (London: Penguin Books, 1970), 114. See also Gibbon, *Decline and Fall*, vol. I, ch. 9.

53. The representations of enemy women taking vengeance of captured Roman soldiers made this threat clear at home. For examples in the context of Dacia see the list of visual sources in Sheila Dillon and Katherine E. Welch (eds), *Representations of War in Ancient Rome* (Cambridge: Cambridge University Press, 2006), 270n67.

54. Bernadette J. Brooten, *Love Between Women: Early Christian Responses to Female Homoeroticism* (Chicago: University of Chicago Press, 1996), 43. (Refers to Judith P. Hallett, 'Female homoeroticism and the denial of Roman reality in Latin literature', *Yale Journal of Criticism* 3 (1989), 209–27, 211; as well as Saara Lilja, *Homosexuality in Republican and Augustan Rome* (Commentationes Humanarum Litterarum 74, Helsinki: Societas Scientiarum Fennica, 1983), 28, 32.)

55. Goodwin, *Ottoman Women*, 110.

56. G. Necipoglu, *Architecture, Ceremonial, and Power* (Cambridge, Mass.: Harvard University Press, 1991), 78.

57. Warner of Rouen, *Moriuht* (c.1010), trans. and comm. Christopher J. McDonough (Toronto: Pontifical Institute of Mediaeval Studies, 1995), 79, 81, 83.

58. McDonough, commentary on *Moriuht*, p. 139 n94.

59. Cassius Dio, *Rome*, Book 50 (Cambridge Mass, Loeb Classical Library, 1917), 489.

60. Plutarch, *Parallel Lives* (Loeb Classic Edition, 1920), 161–2.

61. See Brent D. Shaw, *Spartacus and the Slave Wars* (Boston, Mass.: Bedford/ St Martin's, 2001), 27.

62. Geoffrey Chaucer, Preamble and tale of the Wife of Bath, in *The Canterbury Tales*, ed. Richard J. Beck (14th century) (Edinburgh: Oliver and Boyd, 1964), 85–6.

63. Eusebius Pamphilus, *Church History, Life of Constantine, Oration in Praise of Constantine*, excerpted from *Christian Classics Etherial Library* (Calvin College), 2005. NPNF V2 01, ch. XX (first quotation), ch. XXXIV (second quotation).

64. For the persistence of the Visigothic Code in reconquest Spain see Heath Dillard, *Daughters of the Reconquest: Women in Castilian Town Society 1100–1300* (Cambridge: Cambridge University Press, 1984), ch. 5, esp. 135.

65. Visigothic Code (hereafter VC), III.4, another earlier passage III.3.

66. VC, Book III, Title IV Section XIV, edition ed., trans. and annot. S. P. Scott. See S. P. Scott, *The Visigothic Code (forum judicum)* (Boston, Mass.: Boston Book Company, 1910), repr. Fred B. Rothman & Co, 1982.

67. See the *Motu Proprio*, 9 November 1548, in 'Confirmato Statutorum populi Romani super restitutione servorum in Urbe,' in *Statutorum Almae Urbis Romae* (Rome, 1567), repub. in John Francis Maxwell, *Slavery and the Catholic Church* (Chichester: Barry Rose, 1975), 75.

68. See James Theron Wilson, 'Sinespe libertatis: slavery in Hungary under the House of Arpad,' MA thesis, Indiana University, 1998. HTML formatting by Patrick Feaster, Institute of Hungarian Studies at Indiana University: see http://www.indiana.edu/~iuihsl/wilson.htm.

69. This evocative case was uncovered by Mary Elizabeth Perry. See *Crime and Society in Early Modern Seville* (Hanover, N.H.: University Press of New England, 1980), 217. Perry notes the irony of the Molina image as a 'reversal of their roles'.

70. This taxonomy of Butlan is summarised by Godfrey Goodwin in *The Private World of Ottoman Women* (1997) (London: Saqi Books, 2006), 110.

71. William L. Westermann, *Slave Systems of Greek and Roman Antiquity* (Philadelphia: American Philosophical Society, 1955), 17.

72. Musonius Rufus, Discourse XII: 'On sexual indulgence', in Cora Lutz, *The Roman Socrates* (New Haven, Conn.: Yale University Press, 1942), 88–9.

73. Suszanne Fonay Wemple, *Women in Frankish Society* (Philadelphia: University of Pennsylvania Press, 1981), 36.

74. Exodus 21: 26.

75. For this and similarly complex cases see François Soyer, 'Muslim slaves and freedmen in medieval Portugal,' *Al-Qantara*, 28.2 (2007), 508.

76. Gibbon, *Decline and Fall of the Roman Empire*, vol. 7, ch. 68, 325.

77. Juvenal, *Satire* 6. Quoted in G. G. Ramsey, ed. and trans. *Juvenal and Persius* (London: Heinemann, 1918), 123.

78. See Robert G. Hoyland, *Seeing Islam as Others Saw It: A Survey and Evaluation of Christian, Jewish, and Zoroastrian Writings on Early Islam* (Princeton, N.J.: Darwin Press, 1997), 99.

79. Jacobs, *Incidents in the Life of a Slave Girl*, 33.

80. Carolyn Osiek and Margaret Y. McDonald, *A Woman's Place: House Churches in Early Christianity* (Minneapolis, Minn.: Fortress Press, 2006), 96.

81. Acts of the Apostles 16: 14–15.

82. Judith Evans-Grubbs, '"Marriage more shameful than adultery": slave–mistress relationships, "mixed marriages", and late Roman law', *Phoenix* 47 (1993) 139.

83. Jacques Heers, *Esclaves et Domestiques au Moyen Age dans la Monde Mediter-ranéen* (Paris: Fayard, 1981), 126, 144.

84. Marthe Moreau, *L'Age d'Or des Religieuses: Monastères féminins de Languedoc méditerranéen au Moyen Age* (Presses de Languedoc, 1988), 122–3.

85. Susan Mosher Stuard, 'Urban domestic slavery in medieval Ragusa,' *Journal of Medieval History*, 9 (1983), 161.

86. Stuard, 'Urban domestic slavery in medieval Ragusa', 161.

87. Dillard, *Daughters of the Reconquest*, 105.
88. David Nirenberg, 'Conversion, sex, and segregation: Jews and Christians in Medieval Spain,' *American Historical Review*, 107.4 (October 2002), 20. The original document in question is to be found in the *Cantigas de Santa Maria de Don Alfonso el Sabio*, Real Academia Espanola, 2 vols (Madrid, 1889), 262–4.
89. Gerber, 'Social and economic position of women,' 234.
90. See, for example, Sylvia L. Collicott, *Connections: Haringey Local–National World Links* (Haringey: Haringey Community Information Service, 1986), 15.
91. Ehud R. Toledano, *The Ottoman Slave Trade and its Suppression: 1840–1890* (Princeton, N.J.: Princeton University Press, 1982), 59. See also Toledano, *Slavery and Abolition in the Ottoman Middle East* (Seattle: University of Washington Press, 1998), 68.
92. Maria Wyke, *The Roman Mistress: Ancient and Modern Representations* (Oxford: Oxford University Press, 2002), 168.
93. Paul Veyne, Philippe Ariès, Georges Duby and Arthur Goldhammer, *A History of Private Life, Volume I: From Pagan Rome to Byzantium*, trans. Arthur Goldhammer (Cambridge, Mass.: Harvard University Press, 1987), 205.
94. Pindar as quoted in Beerte C. Verstraete and Vernon Provencal, *Same-Sex Desire and Love in Greco-Roman Antiquity and in the Classical Tradition of the West* (New York: Haworth Press, 2006), 182.
95. Brooten, 106. Since this is from a woman's 'erotic binding spell' from North Africa, it strongly suggests that men were not the only ones to cast dutiful husbands in the bound, enslaved role.
96. Jennifer A. Glancy, *Slavery in Early Christianity* (New York: Oxford University Press, 2002), 28.
97. Glancy, *Slavery*, 53.
98. Seneca, *On Anger* III, 29, in *Seneca: Moral and Political Essays*, ed. John M. Cooper and J. F. Procopé (Cambridge: Cambridge University Press, 1995), 1–117.
90. Vidal-Naquet, 214.
100. Richard C. Trexler, *Dependence in Context in Renaissance Florence* (Binghamton, N.Y.: Medieval and Renaissance Texts and Studies, vol. 111, 1994), 161. Original reference is F. Schevelli, *Siena: The History of a Medieval Commune* (New York, 1964), 182.

Chapter 2   Gender, Mastery and Frontier: Europe, North Africa and Native America

1. See especially Margaret Sommerville, *Sex and Subjection: Attitudes to Women in Early-Modern Society* (London: Arnold, 1995), 66–70.
2. See Robert C. Davis, *Christian Slaves, Muslim Masters: White Slavery in the Mediterranean, the Barbary Coast, and Italy, 1500–1800* (Basingstoke: Palgrave Macmillan, 2003), 3–26.
3. There are a number of useful sources on the Baltimore raid. For primary sources on the raid see the *Calendar of State Papers*, Ireland Series, vol. 252: 1969, 1990, 1971, and vol. 253: 2077; among the latest interpretations is Mark Netzloff, *England's Internal Colonies: Class, Capital, and the Literature of Early Modern English Colonialism* (Basingstoke: Palgrave Macmillan, 2003), 87–90. A book-length popular treatment now exists in Des Ekin, *The Stolen Village: Baltimore and the Barbary Pirates* (Dublin: O'Brien Press, 2008).

4. See William Henry Foster, 'Perceptions and realities of the Muslim threat to early Stuart England: sources of discontent and disorder,' unpublished paper, 1995, esp. 5–9, 32.

5. Robert C. Davis, *Christian Slaves, Muslim Masters*, 6. Estimate is based on the account of John Morgan's assessment of a list he had seen in London dated 1682.

6. Linda Colley, *Captives: Britain, Empire, and the World, 1600–1850* (London: Jonathan Cape, 2002), 56. This estimate is conservative because by Colley's own acknowledgement the number of captives privately ransomed by, for instance, the Scottish Kirk is often excluded from individual counts. Robert C. Davis emphasises that few Christian captives, probably no more than 5 per cent per year, ever emerged from bondage. Therefore in the English/British case there was no doubt a significant reservoir of uncounted 'captives' who in fact were permanent slaves in North Africa, the Ottoman Levant, and even western and central Asia. See Davis, *Christian Slaves, Muslim Masters*, 22, for the figure of 4 per cent annual abjuration rate.

7. See, for example, Archibald Robbins, *A Journal Comprising an Account of the Loss of the Brig Commerce* (Hartford: Andrus & Judd, 1833), 68.

8. See the discussion in William Henry Foster, *The Captors' Narrative: Catholic Women and their Puritan Men on the Early American Frontier* (Ithaca, N.Y.: Cornell University Press, 2003), 14–17.

9. Orlando Patterson, *Slavery and Social Death: A Comparative Study* (Cambridge, Mass.: Harvard University Press, 1982), 45–51, 62–5.

10. Davis, *Christian Slaves, Muslim Masters*, 3–26. As mentioned in note 6, see p. 22 for information on the rate of conversion and return.

11. See, for example, Lynne Thorton, *Women as Portrayed in Orientalist Painting* (Paris: ACR, 1994), 162–73.

12. D. de Haedo, *Topografía e Historia de Argel* (1612), 38, reprinted in Stephen Clissold, *The Barbary Slaves* (Totowa, N.J.: Rowman & Littlefield, 1977), 43.

13. See Adrienne L. Martín, 'Images of deviance in Cervantes's Algiers,' in *Cervantes: Bulletin of the Cervantes Society of America*, 15.2 (1995), 8, 10.

14. For the homosexual 'ghetto' of Valencia, for example, see Martín, 6n2 (Carrasco).

15. David William Foster (ed.), *Spanish Writers on Gay and Lesbian Themes: A Bio-Cultural Sourcebook* (Greenwood Press, 1999), 11.

16. Here I generally agree with Linda Colley's assertion that the uses of sodomy in English discourse were not so much about 'othering' Muslims, or of discomfort about certain sexual practices, but rather expressed fear over a general threat of the enemy. However, I believe that the specific dangers that prompted this fear were those related to slavery. See Colley, *Captives*, 129–30.

17. Nabil Matar, *Turks, Moors, and Englishmen in the Age of Discovery* (New York: Columbia University Press, 1999), 119.

18. Joseph Pitts, 'A true and faithful account of the religion and manner of the Mohammetans, with an account of the author's being taken captive' (1704), in *Piracy, Slavery, and Redemption: Barbary Captivity Narratives from Early Modern England*, ed. Daniel J. Vitkus and Nabil Matar (New York: Columbia University Press, 2001), 236.

19. This analysis of the English sodomy discourse is based on Nabil Matar's discussion in the path-breaking chapter 'Sodomy and conquest' in Nabil Matar, *Turks, Moors, and Englishmen in the Age of Discovery* (New York: Columbia University Press, 1999), 109–27.

20. Garci Ordoñez de Montalvo, *Las Sergas de Esplandian* (1510).

21. Jan Janzoon van Struys, *The Voiages and Travels* ... (London: for Abel Swalle and Sam Crowch, 1684).

22. Struys, *Voiages and Travels*, 219.

23. Struys, *Voiages and Travels*, 231–4.

24. Struys, *Voiages and Travels*, 271.

25. Patterson, *Slavery and Social Death*, 78.

26. David Brion Davis, Introduction to *A Historical Guide to World Slavery*, ed. Drescher and Engerman (New York, Oxford University Press, 1998), 5.

27. For commentary along these lines relative to St Vincent de Paul see especially Bernard Koch, 'Vincent de Paul (Saint)' in *Catholicisme*, 15, 1158. Representations according to Cervantes are best seen through his fiction based on his Algerian captivity. See for example the iconic description of Zorayda in vol. I, book IV of *Don Quixote* (pp. 428–42 in the Modern Library Classics edition, trans. Tobias Smollett). Ellen M Anderson has astutely noted though that much on the agency of Muslim women from Cervantes appears in his other work more closely based on his own captivity, including the plays *Los tratos de Argel* and *Los baños de Argel*. Anderson notes that in each of these plays, male Christian slaves are put in the feminine position of having to curry favour with their female owners (due to their extant mastery) in exactly the same manner as female captives must do with their male owners. See Anderson, 'Playing at Muslim and Christian: the construction of gender and the representation of faith in Cervantes' captivity plays,' in *Cervantes: Bulletin of the Cervantes Society of America*, 13.2 (1993), 42–3.

28. Emanuel d'Aranda, *The History of Algiers and its Slavery* (1641), English edn by John Davies of Kidwelly (London: John Starkey, 1666), 151.

29. D'Aranda, *The History of Algiers*, 41–2.

30. Marnia Lazreg, *The Eloquence of Silence: Algerian Women in Question* (New York: Routledge, 1994), 22–3.

31. See Ellen Friedman, *Spanish Captives in North Africa in the Early Modern Age* (Madison: University of Wisconsin Press, 1983), 68–9.

32. Clissold, *The Barbary Slaves*, 46.

33. D'Aranda, *The History of Algiers*, 171–5.

34. Struys, *Voiages and Travels*, 271.

35. Ruth Pike, *Aristocrats and Traders: Sevillian Society in the Sixteenth Century* (Ithaca, N.Y.: Cornell University Press, 1972), 180.

36. Ehud R. Toledano, *Slavery and Abolition in the Ottoman Middle East* (Seattle: University of Washington Press, 68.

37. For Klausenberg, see M. L. Bush, *Servitude in Modern Times* (Cambridge: Polity, 2000), 173.

38. Ehud R. Toledano, *Slavery and Abolition*, 68–71.

39. D'Aranda, *The History of Algiers*, 163–4.

40. Thomas Roscoe, *Lives of the Kings of England from the Norman Conquest*, (Philadelphia, Penn.: Lea and Blanchard, 1846,) 215.

41. Jacob and Wilhelm Grimm, 'Der Mann im Pflug', *Deutsche Sagen*, v. 2 (1818), no. 357. According to D. L. Ashliman, the Grimms' original source was the Flemish story 'Florentina de getrouwe'. See D. L. Ashliman, 'The faithful wife who rescued her husband from slavery,' folktales of Aarne-Thompson, type 888, 2000.

42. Davis, *Christian Slaves, Muslim Masters*, 36.

43. One of the most useful of the many general descriptions available is to be found in Ellen G. Friedman, *Spanish Captives in North Africa in the Early Modern Age* (Madison: University of Wisconsin Press, 1983), 57; see also Clissold, *The Barbary Slaves*, 39–41.

44. Francis Brooks, *Barbarian Cruelty* (London: I. Saulsbury, 1693), 35 (also reprinted in Clissold, *The Barbary Slaves*, 90).

45. See Galina Yermolenko, 'Roxolana: The Greatest Empress of the East', *The Muslim World*, 9.2 (2005), 231–48.

46. There are two competing versions of this story in the literature. This version is in agreement with Robert Lambert Playfair, *The Scourge of Christendom* (London: Smith, Elder & Co. 1884), 121. Godfrey Fisher however later claimed that the real ruler was neither the Dey nor his English wife but rather the Dey's son-in-law. Regardless, Playfair's attitude seems congruent with Martin's. See Fisher, *Barbary Legend: War, Trade, and Piracy in North Africa* (1957) (Westport, Conn.: Greenwood Press, 1974), 257. I discuss this in 'Perceptions and Realities of the Muslim Threat to Early Modern England', 32–3.

47. Clissold, *The Barbary Slaves*, 50.

48. Heath Dillard, *Daughters of the Reconquest: Women in Castilian Town Society, 1100–1300* (Cambridge: Cambridge University Press, 1984), 154, 207–8. A woman apprehended trying to sell an unwanted child into slavery could be executed.

49. There has yet to be an adequate, complete scholarly account and analysis of the career of Jan Janszoon van Haarlem in English – a worthwhile project for a future historian. The mix of perspectives here is derived from two seminal early twentieth-century secondary sources. L. C. Vriman, *Kaapvaart en Zeroverij* (Amsterdam, 1938) is a privately published account that has been usefully summarised by Mark Bruyneel of the Vrije Universiteit Amsterdam and made accessible in English at http://zeerovery.nl/history/janszoon.htm. In English the standard secondary work informing modern historians is the work of Philip Gosse, who compiled the extant information in Philip Gosse, *The History of Piracy* (New York: Tudor, 1934), esp. 55–57. For the best account of Anthony Van Sallee and his life in New York see Hazel Van Dyke Roberts, 'Anthony Jansen Van Sallee', *New York Genealogical and Biographical Society Record* 103.1 (1972): 16–28. Van Dyke Roberts usefully points out that this Van Sallee cannot definitively be proven to be the son of Janszoon, however likely. However, her contention that he was of exclusively Dutch parentage because his birth predated the father's capture by North Africans can be explained if there indeed existed a Moorish concubine of Cartagena, Spain, as other sources maintain. Colonial New Yorkers certainly referred to Anthony (and his brother) as 'mulattos'.

50. For the Muslim arrivals in Italy see Clissold, *The Barbary Slaves*, 52.

51. William Okeley, 'Ebenezer; or, a small monument of great mercy, appearing in the miraculous delivery of William Okeley,' (1675) in *Piracy, Slavery, and Redemption: Barbary Captivity Narratives from Early Modern England*, ed. Daniel J. Vitkus (New York: Columbia University Press, 2001), 168.

52. Haedo, *Topographia*, 9. As discussed in Clissold, 87.

53. Pitts, 'A true and faithful account', 307.

54. Clissold, *The Barbary Slaves*, 89.

55. For Seville see John Klause, 'The two occasions of Donne's *Lamentations of Jeremy*,' *Modern Philology*, 90.3 (1993), 347n34.

56. For a complete discussion of the reincorporation process for returned captives see Robert C. Davis's concluding chapter 'Celebrating slavery', in *Christian Slaves, Muslim Masters*, 175–93.

57. Abbe L'Olivier, *Memoirs of the Life and Adventures of Signor Rozelli, at the Hague* (London: printed for J. Morphew, 1709), 70–123, esp. 88–9.

58. See Gérard-Georges Lemaire, *The Orient in Western Art* (Cologne: Könemann, 2001), 58.

59. D'Aranda, *History of Algiers*, 175.

60. David J. Weber, *Bárbaros* (New Haven: Yale University Press, 2005), 226.

61. Quote and details from Richard C. Trexler, *Sex and Conquest: Gendered Violence, Political Order, and the European Conquest of the Americas* (Ithaca, N.Y.: Cornell University Press, 1995), 90–1.

62. Matar, *Turks, Moors, and Englishmen*, 110.

63. This review of Mayan signs of conquest is based on the thoughtful of analysis of Mayan captivity in Stephen Houston, David Stuart and Karl Taube, *The Memory of Bones: Body, Being, and Experience among the Classic Maya* (Austin: University of Texas Press, 2006), ch. 6, 'Dishonor', 202–26.

64. Houston, Stuart and Taube, *The Memory of Bones*, 213.

65. Houston, Stuart and Taube, *The Memory of Bones*, 213.

66. Houston, Stuart and Taube, *The Memory of Bones*, 223.

67. Houston, Stuart and Taube, *The Memory of Bones*, 208, 215–216.

68. Pete Sigal, *From Moon Goddesses to Virgins: The Colonization of Yucatan Maya Sexual Desire* (Austin: University of Texas Press, 2000), 194.

69. See the superb anthropological overview of the *berdache* phenomenon across early North America in Charles Callender and Lee M. Kochems, 'The North American Berdache,' *Current Anthropology*, 24.4 (1983): 443–56.

70. For a detailed treatment see Richard C. Trexler, *Sex and Conquest: Gendered Violence, Political Order, and the European Conquest of the Americas* (Ithaca, N.Y.: Cornell University Press, 1995), esp. 134–7.

71. Diego de Landa, *Yucatan Before and After the Conquest* (1566), trans. William Gates (Mineola NY: Dover Publications, 1978), 52.

72. Stuart B. Schwartz and Frank Salomon, 'South American indigenous societies (colonial era),' in *The Cambridge History of the Native Peoples of the Americas*, vol. III, part 2, ed. Frank Salomon and Stuart B. Schwartz (Cambridge: Cambridge University Press, 2000), 472.

73. 'Narrative of Alvar Nuñez Cabeça de Vaca,' in *Original Narratives in Early American History: Early Spanish Explorers in the Southern United States, 1528–1543*, ed. J. Franklin Jameson (New York: Barnes and Noble, 1907), esp. paras 34, 77, 86, 104, 105 (burdens born by women and old men), 154 (*berdaches*), 174 (diplomacy), 182, 188 and 192.

74. Sigal, *From Moon Goddesses to Virgins*, 191–2.

75. Susan Migden Socolow, 'Spanish captives in Indian Societies: cultural contact along the Argentine frontier, 1600–1835,' *Hispanic American Historical Review*, 72.1 (1992), 89.

76. For the *criolo* effect see Weber, *Bárbaros*, 45–6.

77. Laws of Burgos (Spain) XVIII (1512–1513). Repr. in Charles Gibson (ed.), *The Spanish Tradition in America* (New York: Harper & Row, 1968), 71.

78. Weber, *Bárbaros*, 238.

79. See the excellent meditation on Tekawitha's life in Nancy Shoemaker, 'Kateri Tekawitha's tortuous path to sainthood,' in *Negotiators of Change: Historical Perspectives on Native American Women*, ed. Nancy Shoemaker (New York: Routledge, 1995), 49–71.

80. Quoted in Shoemaker, 'Kateri Tekawitha', 54, 69n20.

81. Shoemaker, 'Kateri Tekawitha', 54. Alter among others reported that whipping was applied to captives and slaves by north-eastern natives. See discussion of the Alter captivity above.

82. Shoemaker, 'Kateri Tekawitha', 60.

83. *Jesuit Relations*, ed. Reuben Gold Thwaites (Cleveland, Oh.: Burrows Brothers, 1899) 40: 143, 44: 45, 52: 177.

84. James E. Seaver, *A Narrative of the Life of Mrs. Mary Jemison* (1823) (Syracuse, N.Y.: Syracuse University Press, 1990), 23.

85. Foster, *The Captors' Narrative*, chs 1–2.

86. See Cotton Mather, 'A Narrative of Hannah Swarton Containing Wonderful passages Relating to her Captivity and Deliverance', in *Puritans Among the Indians: Accounts of Captivity and Redemption, 1676–1724*, ed. Alden T. Vaughan and Edward W. Clark (Cambridge, Mass.: Harvard University Press, 1981), 154.

87. John Smith, *Travels and Works of Captain John Smith, President of Virginia and Admiral of New England 1580–1631*, 2 vols, ed. Edward Arber and A. G. Bradley (Edinburgh: John Grant, 1910), 2: 400–01.

88. For the Turkish captivity see John Smith, *The True Travels* (Glasgow: McElhose, 1907), 2: 142–58.

89. 'J.C.B' ['Jolicoeur' Charles Bonin?], *Travels in New France* (c. 1757), ed. Sylvester K. Stevens et al. (Harrisburg: Pennsylvania Historical Commission, 1941), 100.

90. See Roland Viau, *Femmes de personne: Sexes, genres, et pouvoirs en Iroquoisie ancienne* (Montreal: Boréal, 2000), 176.

91. Thwaites, *Jesuit Relations*, v. 44: 45, v. 52: 177.

92. Emma Lewis Coleman, *New England Captives Carried to Canada* (Portland, Maine: Southworth Press, 1925), 2: 292–3.

93. See Henry T. Finck's commentary of the anthropologist Stephen Powers's landmark work *Tribes of California* (1877). Finck, *Primitive Love and Love-Stories* (New York: Charles Scribner's Sons, 1899), 264. More perspective on Finck's analytic framework can be found in the review of *Primitive Love* by Walter Goodnow Everett in the *American Historical Review*, 6.1 (1900), 108–10.

94. See, for example, Daniel K. Richter, *The Ordeal of the Longhouse: The Peoples of the Iroquois League in the Era of European Colonization* (Chapel Hill: University of North Carolina Press, 1994), 62.

95. Kathleen M. Brown, 'The Anglo-Algonqian Gender Frontier', in *American Indians*, ed. Kathleen Shoemaker (Wiley, 2001), 48–62.

96. The Reverend John Williams of Deerfield, Massachusetts.

97. Henry Clay Alder, *A History of Jonathan Alder: His Captivity and Life with the Indians* (c. 1850), transcr. Doyle H. Davison, ed. Larry L. Nelson (Akron, Oh.: University of Akron Press, 2002), 47.

98. For example, the work of 'squaws and boys' among the Shawnees is related by Alder, *A History of Jonathan Alder*, 51.

99. Alder, *A History of Jonathan Alder*, 47.

100. Alder, *A History of Jonathan Alder*, 47.

101. Alice N. Nash, 'The Abiding Frontier: Family, Gender, and Religion in Wabanaki History, 1600–1800' (PhD dissertation, Columbia University, 1997), 266–7.

102. See Thomas Brown, 'A plain narrative of the uncommon sufferings and remarkable deliverances of Thomas Brown,' (c. 1760) in *Captured by the Indians: 15 First Hand Accounts, 1750–1780*, ed. Frederick Drimmer (New York: Dover, 1985), 62–8.

103. See Kathleen Brown, *Good Wives, Nasty Wenches and Anxious Patriarchs: Gender, Race, and Power in Colonial Virginia* (Chapel Hill: University of North Carolina Press, 1996), 68.

104. Arthur Twining Hadley, *Economies: An Account of the Relations between Private Property and Public Welfare* (New York: Ayer, 1972), 27.

105. William Bartram, *William Bartram on the Southeastern Indians* (1791), ed. Gregory H. Weselkov and Kathryn E. Holland Braun (Lincoln: University of Nebraska Press, 2002), 58.
106. For the best comprehensive history of the Deerfield raid see Evan Haefeli and Kevin Sweeney, *Captors and Captives: The 1704 French and Indian Raid on Deerfield* (Amherst: University of Massachusetts Press, 2003). For the cultural impact of the Eunice Williams captivity in particular see John Demos, *The Unredeemed Captive: A Family Story from Early America* (New York: Knopf, 1993). My own *The Captors' Narrative* discusses the unheralded role of French and native women captors as well as English apostate women playing similar roles in orchestrating the fallout from the Deerfield and other similar raids, together with the counter-efforts of Puritan New Englanders to mute and distort the role of women captors.
107. Allan Gallay, *The Indian Slave Trade: The Rise of the English Empire in the American South, 1670–1717* (New Haven, Conn.: Yale University Press, 2002), 311.
108. See Theda Perdue, *Cherokee Women: Gender and Cultural Change, 1700–1835* (Lincoln: University of Nebraska Press, 1999), 69–70.

Chapter 3   Gender, Mastery and Empire: White Servitude in New Worlds

1. Anonymous, *Memoirs of an Unfortunate Young Nobleman, Return'd from Thirteen Years Slavery in America* (London, 1743), reprint (Garland, 1975), 89.
2. Throughout the text the author-narrator seems to believe that two counties of Delaware – Newcastle and Sussex – are located in Pennsylvania.
3. *Memoirs of an Unfortunate Young Nobleman*, 78.
4. *Memoirs of an Unfortunate Young Nobleman*, 62–3.
5. *Memoirs of an Unfortunate Young Nobleman*, 89.
6. *Memoirs of an Unfortunate Young Nobleman*, 92.
7. *Memoirs of an Unfortunate Young Nobleman*, 126.
8. *Memoirs of an Unfortunate Young Nobleman*, 130.
9. *Memoirs of an Unfortunate Young Nobleman*, 63.
10. *Memoirs of an Unfortunate Young Nobleman*, 124.
11. Kate Fawver, 'Women's economies in the Chesapeake: the organization of labor in plantation society', Paper for the Program for Early American Economy and Society, 1 October 2004, 12.
12. Fawver, 'Women's economies in the Chesapeake', 9–10.
13. Carole Shammas, *A History of Household Government in America* (Charlottesville: University Press of Virginia, 2002), 33–4.
14. Fawver, 'Women's economies in the Chesapeake', 15.
15. Hilary McD. Beckles, *Centering Women: Gender Discourses in Caribbean Slave Society* (Princeton NJ: Markus Wiener, 1999), 63. See also Foster, 'Women slave owners', 316.
16. Fawver, 'Women's economies in the Chesapeake', 16–17.
17. Cecily Jones, 'Contesting the boundaries of gender, race, and sexuality in Barbadian plantation society', *Women's History Review* 12 (2003), 218–19. The Bush quote is Barbara Bush, 'White "ladies," coloured "favourites" and black "wenches": some considerations on sex, race and class factors in social relations in white creole society in the Caribbean', *Slavery and Abolition*, 2,

248. The quote from Crow is Francis Crow to Giles Firmin, 7 March 1686/7, *Jamaican Historical Review*, 3 (1959), 54, as quoted in Richard Dunn, *Sugar and Slaves: The Rise of the Planter Class in the English West Indies* (New York: W.W. Norton, 1973), 285.

18. See generally Eleanor Gower, 'Indentured and Convict Runaways in Pennsylvania, c.1730–76', BA dissertation, Cambridge University, 2008.

19. See the case of Henry Justice as related in Gwenda Morgan and Peter Rushton, *Eighteenth-Century Criminal Transportation: The Formation of the Criminal Atlantic* (London: Palgrave Macmillan, 2004), 72–8.

20. See Cissie C. Fairchilds, *Domestic Enemies: Servants and their Masters in Old Regime France* (Baltimore, Md.: Johns Hopkins University Press, 1984), 183.

21. Fairchilds, *Domestic Enemies*. 182.

22. Sarah C. Maza, *Servants and Masters in Eighteenth-Century France: The Uses of Loyalty* (Princeton, N.J.: Princeton University Press, 1983), 187.

23. For *hommes de chambre* in the French context see Jan Noel, 'New France: les femmes favoriseés', *Atlantis*, 6.2 (1981), 82.

24. For the complete Batson Narrative see James L. Rayner et al., *The Complete New-gate Calendar* (London: Navarre Society, 1926), 181–202.

25. *The Vain Prodigal Life and Tragical Penitent Death of Thomas Hellier* (London, for Sam. Crouch, 1680), 5–6.

26. Hellier, 11.

27. Hellier, 11.

28. Hellier, 12.

29. For a concise description of this process see Betty Wood, *Slavery in Colonial America, 1619–1776* (Lanham, Md.: Rowman & Littlefield, 2005), 10–19.

30. Hellier, 25.

31. Hellier, 25–6.

32. Critics were harsh on Howard. See for example, Giles Jacob, *Poetical Register, or the Lives and Characters of the English Dramatick Poets* (1719), 141–2.

33. See, for example, Carol F. Karlsen, *The Devil in the Shape of a Woman: Witchcraft in Colonial New England* (New York: W.W. Norton, 1998), 136; for the dramatic/cultural representations of this phenomenon see Frances Elizabeth Dolan, *Dangerous Familiars: Representations of Domestic Crime in England, 1550–1700* (Ithaca, N.Y.: Cornell University Press, 1994), esp. 216–18.

34. Shammas, *A History of Household Government in America*, 30–2.

35. See the discussion for example in Kathleen Brown, *Good Wives, Nasty Wenches and Anxious Patriarchs: Gender, Race, and Power in Colonial Virginia* (Chapel Hill: University of North Carolina Press, 1996), 80–8.

36. A similar dynamic existed with the '*filles de roi*' (sponsored young female immigrants) in late seventeenth-century colonial French Canada.

37. George Alsop, *A Character of the Province of Maryland* (1666), ed. Newton D. Mereness (Cleveland, Oh.: Burrows Brothers, 1902), 60.

38. Foster, *The Captors' Narrative*, 32–54.

39. For this European phenomenon see generally for example Steven R. Smith, 'The ideal and reality: apprentice–master relations in seventeenth-century London', *History of Education Quarterly*, 21.4 (1981), 449–59.

40. See, for example, Paul Boyer and Stephen Nissenbaum, *Salem Possessed: The Social Origins of Witchcraft*, (1973) (Cambridge, Mass.: Harvard University Press, 1996), 193–4.

41. *Archives of Maryland* 57 (Proceedings of the Provincial Court of Maryland, 1666–1670).

42. See the account of Robert Hendron in the family record kept by Jay McAfree. Thanks to McAfee for posting this manuscript at http://genforum.genealogy.com/hendren/messages/407.html

43. Laurel Thatcher Ulrich, *Good Wives: Image and Reality in the Lives of Women in Northern New England, 1650–1750* (New York: Vintage, 1982), 95.

44. Sarah Lauderdale Graham, *House and Street: The Domestic World of Servants and Masters in Nineteenth-Century Rio de Janeiro* (Austin: University of Texas Press, 1992), 93.

45. Eliza Lucas to Miss Bartlett, April 1742 (precise date missing), reprinted in *The Letterbook of Eliza Lucas Pinckney, 1739–1762*, ed. Elise Pinckney (1972) (Columbia, S.C.: University of South Carolina Press, 1997), 34.

46. Grey's study is the most rigorous, contextualised view of Lucas's life stages currently in the literature. See Rose Grey, 'Eliza Lucas Pinckney and Imperial Daughterhood in Colonial South Carolina,' BA dissertation, Cambridge University Faculty of History, 2009.

47. LOC letters, Charles Coatsworth Pinckney Collection, Container 1, Library of Congress, Washington DC.

48. Grey, 'Eliza Lucas Pinckney', 41–9.

49. *Virginia Magazine of History and Biography*, 20 (1912), 375, 377.

50. Herbert S. Klein and Francisco Vida Luna, *Slavery and the Economy of Sao Paulo, 1750–1850* (Stanford, Calif.: Stanford University Press, 2003), 115.

51. *Greffe* of Gaudron de Chevremont (notary), 24 March 1738, Archives Nationales de Québec-Montréal.

52. For this discussion see Foster, *The Captors' Narrative*, esp. 42–3.

53. Foster, *The Captors' Narrative*, 146–7.

54. Terri L. Snyder, '"As if there was not master or woman in the land": Gender, Dependency and Household Violence in Virginia, 1646–1720', in *Over the Threshold: Intimate Violence in Early America*, ed. Christine Daniels and Michael V. Kennedy (New York: Routledge, 1999), 219–36. See especially York County Deeds, Orders, and Wills, 6:77, 82.

55. For Ashael Batten's wives see Lyon G. Tyler, 'Grammar and Mattey Practice and Model School', *William and Mary College Quarterly Historical Magazine*, 4.1 (1895), note 1.

56. Sommerville, *Sex and Subjection*, 68.

57. 'An Act Concerning Servants and Slaves,' Laws of Virginia, October 1705 4th Anne KLIX 3.447, title VII.

58. Terri L. Snyder, Review of Carla Anzilotti, *In the Affairs of the World: Women, Patriarchy, and Power in Colonial South Carolina*, in *William and Mary Quarterly*, 3rd ser, 60.1 , f.p.

59. Gwenda Morgan and Peter Rushton, 'Visible bodies: power, subordination, and identity in the eighteenth-century Atlantic world,' *Journal of Social History*, 39.1 (2005), 16.

60. Italics as appearing in the original. See the *Pennsylvania Gazette*, 11 April 1751.

61. Original source: Plymouth Court Records 2:73. See Jillian Galle, 'Servants and masters in the Plymouth Colony,' Plymouth Colony Archive Project, 1998–2000. www.people.viginia.edu/~jfd3a/Plymouth/Galle1.html, 11.

62. Raphael Semmes, *Crime and Punishment in Early Maryland* (Baltimore, Md.: Johns Hopkins University Press, 1938), 102.

63. Karl Frederick Geiser, 'Redemptioners and indentured servants in the colony and commonwealth of Pennsylvania,' *Supplement to the Yale Review*, 10.2 (1901), 93.

64. T. B. Macaulay, *The History of England from the Accession of James II*, vol I, (Philadelphia, Pa.: Porter and Coates, 1866), 459–61. For the language of 'slavery' used in reference to the Monmouth rebels see Ruth Paley, 'Imperial politics and English law: the many contexts of Somerset', *Law and History Review*, 24.3, fall 2006, n6.

65. Carteret County North Carolina Minutes 1723–47, 33c.

66. John Harrower, *The Journal of John Harrower*, ed. E. M. Riley (Williamsburg, Va., 1963), 144. Also quoted in David Hackett Fischer, *Albion's Seed: Four British Folkways in America* (New York: Oxford University Press, 1989), 303.

67. Carter G. Woodson, *Free Negro Heads of Families in 1830* (Washington, D.C.: Association for the Study of Negro Life and History, 1925), vii.

68. Woodson, *Free Negro Heads of Families*, 7. My thanks here to Lydia Johansen, for exploring the legal implications of this case.

69. Kathleen Brown, *Good Wives, Nasty Wenches, and Anxious Patriarchs*, 193–4.

70. William Byrd, *The Secret Diary of William Byrd of Westover, 1709–1712*, ed. Louis B. Wright and Marion Tinling (Richmond: Dietz Press, 1941), entry for 8 February 1709, 2. The editors note that the term 'servants' in Byrd's diary might refer to white indentured servants and/or African slaves. Some have interpreted Byrd's 'dance' as sexual intercourse with another. Although these episodes are clearly sexual, Byrd is usually forthcoming in identifying those he interacts with. The 'dances' by contrast strongly suggest solitary activity.

71. *The Secret Diary of William Byrd*, entries for 20–21 October 1711. The phrase 'woman hunts' is used to describe Byrd's nocturnal activities by D. H. Fischer. See *Albion's Seed*, 301.

72. Sharon Block, 'Lines of color, sex, and service: comparative sexual coercion in early America,' in *Sex, Love, Race: Crossing Boundaries in North American History*, ed. Martha Hodes (New York: New York University Press, 1999), 141. Block makes the further point that such a prosecution against the master of black slaves at that time would not have been possible.

73. Pennsylvania Correctional Industries, 'A historical overview of inmate labour in Pennsylvania' (official publication).

74. The prohibition against non-whites owning 'Christian [white] servants' appears twice in Virginia statutes. For the first mention in 1670 see October 1670 22nd Charles II Act V 1670 2:280. For the 1705 update, which expands the specific types of non-whites barred from such ownership, see October 1705 4th Anne Chap KLIX 3.447 Section XI.

75. Laws of Virginia, October 1705 4th Anne Chap KLIX 3.447 Section XVIII.

76. *Essex County (Virginia) Orders*, 1754–63, 80. See case of William Jones (master) and Margaret Irwin (servant) [Richmond, Essex, and Orange Counties, Virginia]. Margaret Jones, born say 1680, was the mother of Ann Jones who was indentured to Ann Fenner (daughter of John Fenner) for 11 years by Richmond county court on 2 May 1705. She may have been identical to Margaret, late servant to John Belfield, now living at John Fenner's, who was presented by the Richmond county court on 4 October 1705 for bearing a 'molatto bastard'. She was called Margaret Chiswick in court on 5 December 1705 when she acknowledged she had a 'mulatto ... begat by a Negro' [Orders 1704–08. 57, 61, 93, 97, 101] She may have been the ancestor of William born say 1715, a 'mulatto' who owned a white servant woman named Margaret Irwin. William sold her to Isaac Arnold before 27 March 1755 when the Orange County court ruled that she was a free woman because William had no right to keep or dispose of her [Orders 1754–63, 80].

77. Orlando Patterson, *Slavery and Social Death: A Comparative Study* (Cambridge, Mass.: Harvard University Press, 1981), 178.

78. Patterson, *Slavery and Social Death*, 422n21. Of the many possible examples of visual representations of this phenomenon, see art historian Robert Baldwin's commentary on Hogarth's *Marriage à la Mode IV: La Toilette* (c. 1734), in which he argues that the two male slaves, one waiting on his white English mistress:

> played on stereotypes of unbridled African sexuality which lay at the core of European myths of African savagery since at least the Renaissance. The lecherous African began circulating in mainstream visual culture only in the seventeenth century in comedic Dutch painting, especially in Hogarth's primary mentor, Jan Steen. In Steen's *Marriage Contract of Tobit and Tobias*, a male servant grins at the bride and at the real viewer while 'tapping the keg', a Dutch expression equivalent to 'deflowering the bride,'
>
> Source: Robert Baldwin, 'Actaeon and the allegory of vision in Hogarth's *Marriage à la Mode IV: La Toilette*'.

79. Paley, 'Imperial politics', 5, 8n11.

80. See Chapter 4.

81. The best single account of Walsh is Silvio A. Bedini, *The Life of Benjamin Banneker: The First African American Man of Science*, 2nd edn (Baltimore: Maryland Historical Society, 1999), esp. 9–14.

82. There is no single scholarly history as yet of the 'Moors of Delaware'. For strands of the myth see for example George P. Fisher, 'The So-Called Moors of Delaware', *Milford Herald*, 15 June 1895, reprinted by the Public Archives Commission of Delaware, 1929.

83. See George E. Brooks, Jr, 'The *signare* of Saint-Louis and Gorée: women entrepreneurs in eighteenth-century Senegal,' in *Women in Africa: Studies in Social and Economic Change*, ed. Nancy J. Hafkin and Edna G. Bay (Stanford, Calif.: Stanford University Press, 1976).

84. Jean Baptiste Duvarot as quoted in Fatima Fall, 'The place of women in the museum of Saint-Louis,' in *Museums and Urban Culture in West Africa*, ed. Alexis B. A. Adandé and Emanuel Arinze (Oxford: James Currey, 2002), 147.

85. George E. Brooks, *Eurafricans in Western Africa, Commerce, Social Status, Gender, and Religious Observance from the Sixteenth to the Eighteenth Century* (Athens, Oh.: Ohio University Press, 2003), 212–13.

86. Lillian Ashcroft Eason, '"She hath voluntarily come": a Gambian woman trader in colonial Georgia in the eighteenth century', in *Identity in the Shadow of Slavery*, ed. Paul E. Lovejoy (New York: Continuum, 2000).

87. See Bruce L. Mouser, 'Women slavers of Guinea-Conakry', in *Women and Slavery in Africa*, ed. Claire C. Robertson and Martin A. Klein (Madison: University of Wisconsin Press, 1983), 329–33.

88. Sylvaine A. Diouf, *Fighting the Slave Trade: West African Strategies* (Oxford: James Currey, 2003), xviii.

89. For an excellent and usefully introduced edition of the narrative see Olaudah Equiano, *The Interesting Narrative of the Life of Olaudah Equiano, Written by Himself with Related Documents*, 2nd edn, ed. with an intro. by Robert J. Allison (Boston, Mass.: Bedford/St Martin's, 2007), 62–4.

90. See Diouf, *Fighting the Slave Trade*, xxii n4.

91. Although Newton's exploits are frequently embellished, an excellent short summary of the essential details of his relationship with the Sherbro woman 'P. I.' is found in Carol P. MacCormack, 'Slaves, slave owners, and slave dealers: Sherbro

coast and hinterlands,' in *Women and Slavery in Africa*, ed. Claire C. Robertson and Martin A. Klein (Portsmouth, N.H.: Heinemann, 1997), 283–4.

92. John Newton, *The Works of John Newton*, vol. I (Philadelphia, Pa.: Uriah Hunt, 1839), letter V, 91.

93. John Newton, *Works*, vol. I, letter VI, 92.

Chapter 4   Gender, Mastery and Nation: Race and Slavery in the United States

1. Marston Bates, Philip S. Humphrey, editors, *Charles Darwin: An Anthology* (Edison, N.J.: Transaction, 2009), 90–1.

2. John Thomas James, *Journal of a Tour in Germany, Sweden, Russia, and Poland during the Years 1813 and 1814* (London: John Murray, 1817), 418.

3. Lewis Clarke, 'Narrative of Lewis Clarke', in Lewis Clarke et al., *Interesting Memoirs and Documents Relating to American Slavery, and the Glorious Struggle Now Making for Complete Emancipation* (London, Chapman Brothers, 1846), 11, 16–17, 18.

4. Interview with Henry Wiencek (author of *Slave and Slavery in George Washington's World*), *Common-Place*, 6.4 (July 2006). Available at http://www.historycooperative.org/journals/cp/vol-06/no-04/reading/

5. Peter Bruner, *A Slave's Adventures Toward Freedom* (Oxford, Ohio, n.d.), 33.

6. *The Anti Slavery Examiner*, part 19, chapter IV.

7. Marietta Morrissey, *Slave Women in the New World* (Lawrence: University Press of Kansas, 1989), 149.

8. E. S. Abdy, *Journal of a Residence and Tour in the United States of North America* (London: John Murray, 1835), ch. 16.

9. Robert Walsh, *Notices of Brazil in 1828 and 1829*, 2 vols (London: Frederick Westley, 1830), 2: 323–4.

10. These stories were unearthed and discussed by Mary C. Karasch in the slightly different context of community efforts to curb excessive violence. See Karasch, *Slave Life in Rio de Janeiro, 1808–1850* (Princeton, N.J.: Princeton University Press, 1986), 114.

11. Karasch, *Slave Life in Rio*, 114–15.

12. For the original source see F. Friedrich von Weech, *Reise über England und Portugal nach Brasilian*, 3 vols (Munich, 1831), 2:12–15.

13. Alexander Majoribanks, *Travels in South and North America* (London: Simpkin and Marshall, 5th edn, 1854), 96.

14. Zachary Macaulay, *Negro Slavery* (London: Richard Taylor, 1823).

15. Thanks to the staff of the Clements Library, University of Michigan for publishing an online summary of the Burwell-Guy family papers (1820–59) which include this quote. See www.clements.umich.edu/webguides/b/burwell.html.

16. *Daily Constitutionalist* (Augusta, Ga.) 1 September 1864, p. 1 c. 3.

17. George Pinckard, *Notes from the West Indies*, vol. 3, letter 14, 179.

18. Pinckard, *Notes*, vol. 2, letter 12, 200–01.

19. Catherine Clinton, *The Plantation Mistress: Women's World in the Old South* (New York: Pantheon, 1982), 208.

20. Clinton, *The Plantation Mistress*, 209.

21. Clinton, *The Plantation Mistress*, 209–10.

22. Robert Walsh, *Notices of Brazil in 1828 and 1829*, 2: 323–8, as quoted in Robert Edgar Conrad, *Children of God's Fire: A Documentary History of Slavery in Brazil* (Pennsylvania State University Press, 1994), 49.

23. Kim and Reggie Harris, *Notes to 'Steal Away: Songs of the Underground Railroad'* (sound recording).

24. American Anti Slavery Society, *The Anti-Slavery Examiner, Omnibus*, part 19, ch. 2.

25. See H. Mattison, *Louisa Piquet, The Octaroon: Or, Inside Views of Southern Domestic Life* (New York, privately published, 1861), in Amelia A. Johnson, *Collected Black Women's Narratives* (New York: Oxford University Press, 1988), 58.

26. 'Caroline A. Turner', entry for 'A Kentuckian's story', HS 108 Project, www.bluegrass.kctcs.edu/HIS/108/project1.html

27. Juan Francisco Manzano, *Autobiography of a Slave* (Detroit, Mich.: Wayne State University Press, 1996), 47, 57.

28. Margaret Law Callcott, *Mistress of Riversdale: The Plantation Letters of Rosalie Stier Calvert, 1795–1821* (Baltimore, Md.: Johns Hopkins University Press, 1992), 105.

29. 'Childhood and family reminiscences of Rebecca Jane Foster (Mrs Alexander Campbell Stevenson),' 2. Foster family papers (privately held).

30. Ken Ringle, 'Up through slavery', *Washington Post*, 12 May 2002. See also Foster, 'Women slave owners', 308.

31. See, for example, Arthur Jones, *Pierre Toussaint* (New York: Doubleday, 2003), 141–8.

32. 'Charlotte' and 'William Solomon', entries for 'A Kentuckian's story', HS 108 Project, www.bluegrass.kctcs.edu/HIS/108/project1.html.

33. See Bill Cecil-Fronsman, *Common Whites: Class and Culture in Antebellum North Carolina* (Lawrence: University Press of Kansas, 1992), 67.

34. See Cecily Jones, 'Contesting the boundaries of gender, race, and sexuality in Barbadian plantation society', *Women's History Review*, 12 (2003), 209. Jones perceptively notes that the language of this will asserted a specific form of white mastery while on the surface appearing to be purely the act of a benevolent mistress. For the original source see Jones, 209n41 (Will of Anne Philips, E. M. Shilstone Notebook Library, 9-23-16, Barbados Museum and Historical Society).

35. Kathleen Bruce, 'Slave labor in the Virginia iron industry', *William and Mary Quarterly*, 2nd series, 7.1 (1927), 26.

36. Robert Olwell, *Masters, Slaves, and Subjects: The Culture of Power in the South Carolina Low Country* (Ithaca, N.Y.: Cornell University Press, 1998), 198.

37. Nancy Priscilla Naro, *A Slave's Place, A Master's World: Fashioning Dependency in Rural Brazil* (London: Continuum, 2000), 58.

38. George Pinckard, *Notes from the West Indies* (London: Longman Hurst, 1806), vol. 1, letter 24, February 1796, 283.

39. George Pinckard, *Notes from the West Indies*, vol. 3, letter 7, 71.

40. Pinckard, *Notes*, vol. 3, letter 14, 178.

41. Winthrop Jordan, 1968, 141, as quoted in Marietta Morrissey, *Slave Women in the New World* (Lawrence: University Press of Kansas, 1989), 151.

42. Stephanie M. H. Camp, *Closer to Freedom: Enslaved Women and Everyday Resistance in the Plantation South* (Chapel Hill: University of North Carolina Press, 2004), 132.

43. Edward E. Baptist, '"Cuffy," "fancy maids," and "one eyed men": rape, commodification, and the domestic slave trade in the United States', *American Historical Review*, 106.5 (2001), 3.

44. Baptist, 'Rape, commodification, and the domestic slave trade', 41.

45. Baptist, 'Rape, commodification, and the domestic slave trade', 52.

46. Camp, *Closer to Freedom*, 43.

47. See Joyce Green McDonald, *Women and Race in Early Modern Texts* (Cambridge: Cambridge University Press, 2002), 97n19. McDonald's careful analysis points out that there is more than one version of Stedman's narrative. The unabridged 1790 text contained specific references to race and sex that were later purged. The quote above was among the discarded characterisations of white planters.

48. Trevor Burnard, *Mastery, Tyranny, and Desire: Thomas Thistlewood and his Slaves in the Anglo-Jamaican World* (Chapel Hill: University of North Carolina Press, 2004), 216.

49. Alexis de Tocqueville, *Democracy in America*, 602.

50. Alabama Slavery Code of 1833, S37.

51. See Lester D. Langley, *The Americas in the Age of Revolution, 1750–1850* (New Haven, Conn.: Yale University Press, 1998), 113.

52. Jesse Torrey, *A Portraiture of Domestic Slavery: In the United States* (Philadelphia, Pa.: John Bioren, 1817), 14, 15.

53. Sterling Brown, 'Negro character as seen by white authors' (1933), repr. in *Dark Symphony: Negro Literature in America*, ed. James A. Emanuel and Theodore L. Gross (New York: Free Press, 1968), 159. Thanks to Kathy Davis for the reference. See Davis, 'Lydia Maria Child's "The Quadroons" and "Slavery's Pleasant Homes"' in *The Online Archive of Nineteenth-Century US Women's Writings*.

54. Clarke, 'Narrative of Lewis Clarke', 19.

55. See Wilma A. Dunaway, *Slavery in the American Mountain South* (Cambridge: Cambridge University Press, 2003), 199.

56. George F. Nagle, 'Fugitive slave incidents in Central Pennsylvania', Afrolumens Project (www. afrolumens.org), 8.

57. See especially Drew Gilpin Faust, *Mothers of Invention: Women of the Slaveholding South in the American Civil War* (New York: Vintage, 1996), 62–9.

58. Mrs. A. C. Carmichael, 'Domestic manners and social conditions' (c. 1833) quoted in Hilary McD Beckles, *Centering Woman: Gender Discourses in Caribbean Slave Society* (Princeton, N.J.: Markus Wiener, 1999), 112. Also see Foster, 'Women slave owners', 316.

59. Callcott, *Mistress of Riversdale*, 105.

60. Beckles, *Centering Woman*, 61–2.

61. Dawn Harris, 'Female slaves not women', *Barbados Nation*, 6 June 1999.

62. T. Stephen Whitman, *The Price of Freedom: Slavery and Manumission in Baltimore and Early National Maryland* (University Press of Kentucky, 1997), 109–10.

63. Serena Zabin, 'Women's trading networks and dangerous economies', 2,28 http://www.librarycompany.org/Economics/PDF%20Files/Zabin.pdf.

64. According to historian of gender and slavery in the Caribbean Hilary Beckles, 58 per cent of slave owners in Bridgetown, Barbados were women. They were 'mostly white, though some were also "coloured" and black'. See Beckles, *Centering Woman*, 63.

65. Maria Odila Silva Dias, *Power and Everyday Life: The Lives of Working Women in Nineteenth-Century Brazil* (Cambridge: Polity Press, 1995), 75, 83.

66. Mary C. Karasch, *Slave Life in Rio de Janeiro*, 211.

67. Beckles, *Centering Women*, esp. 26–32.

68. Bernard Moitt, *Women and Slavery in the French Antilles, 1635–1848* (Bloomington and Indianapolis: Indiana University Press, 2001), 13. 15, 105.

69. Neblett papers, University of Texas, Austin, letter 20 March 1864 as quoted in Faust, *Mothers of Invention*, 74.

70. The Neblett case has been discussed most extensively by Faust. See *Mothers of Invention*, esp. 65–70.

71. Harriet Jacobs, *Incidents in the Life of a Slave Girl* (1861) (Mineola, N.Y.: Dover, 2001), 46.

72. Harriet Jacobs, *Incidents in the Life of a Slave Girl*, 33.

73. See James W. Messerschmidt, '"We must protect our southern women": of whiteness, masculinities, and lynching', in *Regulating Difference: Race, Gender, and Punishment in America*, ed. M. Bosworth and J. Flavin (New Brunswick, N.J.: Rutgers University Press, 2005), 80–1.

74. Alan D. Watson, 'Women in colonial North Carolina: overlooked and underestimated', *North Carolina Historical Review*, 58 (1981), 3.

75. See for example Inge Dornan's descriptions of such networks in Dornan, 'Masterful women: colonial women slaveholders in the urban low country', *Journal of American Studies* (UK) (39:2005), esp. 394–5.

76. Larry Koger, *Black Slaveowners: Free Black Slave Masters in South Carolina, 1790–1860* (Jefferson, N.C.: McFarland, 1985), 23.

77. Koger, *Black Slaveowners*, 25–7.

78. Kimberly S. Hanger, *Bounded Lives, Bounded Places: Free Black Society in Colonial New Orleans, 1769–1803* (Durham, N.C.: Duke University Press, 1997), 71–2.

79. Louis Hughes, *Thirty Years a Slave: From Bondage to Freedom, The Autobiography of Louis Hughes* (Montgomery Ala.: NewSouth Books, 2002), 42–3.

80. Clarke, 'Narrative of Lewis Clarke', 24.

81. Douglass, *My Bondage and My Freedom*, 187.

82. 'Born in slavery', *Slave Narratives from the Federal Writer's Project, 1936–38*, Indiana Narratives, vol. V.

Conclusion

1. Judith Vowles, 'Marriage à la russe,' in *Sexuality and the Body in Russian Culture*, ed. Jane T. Costlow, Stephanie Sandler and Judith Vowles (Stanford, Calif.: Stanford University Press, 1998), 70–1.

2. See James Boswell, *The Royal Treasure: Muslim Communities under the Crown of Aragon in the Fourteenth Century* (New Haven, Conn.: Yale University Press, 1977), 347–8.

3. See Olivia Remie Constable, *Trade and Traders in Muslim Spain: The Commercial Realignment of the Iberian Peninsula, 900–1500* (Cambridge: Cambridge University Press, 1996), 207.

4. Anonymous, *The Story of a Slave: A Realistic Revelation of a Social Relation of Slave Times* (Chicago: Wesley Elmore, and Benson, 1894), iv.

5. Anon., *Story of a Slave*, vi.

6. Anon., *Story of a Slave*, 5–7.

7. Clissold, *The Barbary Slaves*, 46.

8. Anon., *Story of a Slave*, 17–18.

9. Anon., *Story of a Slave*, 42–3.

10. Anon., *Story of a Slave*, 52–64.

11. Anon., *Story of a Slave*, v.

12. Anon., *Story of a Slave*, 4.

Bibliography

Primary printed sources (including memoirs and diaries)

Abdy, E. S. *Journal of a Residence and Tour in the United States of North America*. London: John Murray, 1835.

Alabama Slavery Code of 1833, S37.

Alder, Henry Clay. *A History of Jonathan Alder: His Captivity and Life with the Indians* (c. 1850), transcr. Doyle H. Davison, ed. Larry L. Nelson. Akron, Oh.: University of Akron Press, 2002.

Alsop, George. *A Character of the Province of Maryland* (1666), ed. Newton D. Mereness. Cleveland, Oh.: Burrows Brothers, 1902.

An-Nabhani, Taqiuddin. *The Social System in Islam*. New Dehli: Milli Publications, 2001, ch. 7.

Anon. Discourse 30, 'The Venerable Moisej the Hungarian' (c. 1015 AD) in *The Paterik of the Kievan Caves Monastery*, trans. Muriel Heppel (Cambridge, Mass.: Harvard University Press on behalf of the Ukrainian Research Institute of Harvard University, 1989), 162–7.

Anon. 'Life of St Mary the Younger' [10th century AD], trans. Angeliki E. Laiou. In *Holy Women of Byzantium: Ten Saints' Lives in English Translation*, ed. Alice-Mary Talbot (Washington, D.C.: Dumbarton Oaks Research Library and Collection, 1996), 260.

Anon. *Memoirs of an Unfortunate Young Nobleman, Return'd from Thirteen Years Slavery in America* (London, 1743). New York: Garland, 1975.

Anon. 'The Shepherd of Hermas,' c. 3rd century AD. In Carolyn Osiek, *Shepherd of Hermas: A Commentary*. Minneapolis: Augsberg Fortress, 1999.

Anon. *The Vain Prodigal Life and Tragical Penitent Death of Thomas Hellier*. London, for Sam. Crouch, 1680, 5–6.

Anon. *The Story of a Slave: A Realistic Revelation of a Social Relation of Slave Times* (Chicago: Wesley, Elmore, and Benson, 1894).

Archives of Maryland 57 (Proceedings of the Provincial Court of Maryland, 1666–1670).

Babylonian Talmud, Baba Mezi'a 71, notes 22–3.

Babylonian Talmud, Tractate Gittin 70a. Soncino 1961 edition.

Bartram, William. *William Bartram on the Southeastern Indians* (1791), ed. Gregory H. Weselkov and Kathryn E. Holland Braun. Lincoln, Neb.: University of Nebraska Press, 2002.

Batson, James. 'Narrative'. In *The Complete Newgate Calendar*, ed. James L. Rayner et al. London: Navarre Society, 1926; 181–202.

'Born in slavery', *Slave Narratives from the Federal Writer's Project, 1936–38*, Indiana Narratives, vol. V.

Brooks, Francis. *Barbarian Cruelty*. London: I. Saulsbury, 1693.

Brown, Thomas. 'A plain narrative of the uncommon sufferings and remarkable deliverances of Thomas Brown' (c. 1760). In *Captured by the Indians: 15 First Hand Accounts, 1750–1780*, ed. Frederick Drimmer. New York: Dover, 1985.

Bruner, Peter. *A Slave's Adventures Toward Freedom*. Oxford, Oh., n.d.

Byrd, William. *The Secret Diary of William Byrd of Westover, 1709–1712*, ed. Louis B. Wright and Marion Tinling. Richmond, Va.: Dietz Press, 1941.

Cabeça de Vaca, Alvar Nuñez. 'Narrative of Alvar Nuñez Cabeça de Vaca'. In *Original Narratives in Early American History: Early Spanish Explorers in the Southern United States, 1528–1543*, ed. J. Franklin Jameson. New York: Barnes & Noble, 1907.

Calendar of State Papers (Ireland Series) vol. 252: 1969, 1990, 1971, and vol. 253: 2077.

Callcott, Margaret Law. *Mistress of Riversdale: The Plantation Letters of Rosalie Stier Calvert, 1795–1821*. Baltimore, Md.: Johns Hopkins University Press, 1992.

Carmichael, Mrs A. C. 'Domestic manners and social conditions' (c. 1833), quoted in Hilary McD. Beckles, *Centering Woman: Gender Discourses in Caribbean Slave Society* (Princeton, N.J.: Markus Wiener, 1999), 112.

Carteret County North Carolina Minutes 1723–47.

Cervantes, Miguel de. *Don Quixote*. Modern Library Classics edn, trans. Tobias Smollett. New York: Modern Library, 2001.

Chaucer, Geoffrey. Preamble and tale of the Wife of Bath, in *The Canterbury Tales* (14th century), ed. Richard J. Beck. Edinburgh: Oliver and Boyd, 1964.

Chesnut, Mary Boykin. *A Diary from Dixie*, ed. Ben Ames Williams. Cambridge, Mass.: Harvard University Press, 2002.

'Childhood and family reminiscences of Rebecca Jane Foster (Mrs Alexander Campbell Stevenson)'. Foster family papers (privately held).

Clarke, Lewis. 'Narrative of Lewis Clarke'. In Lewis Clarke et al., *Interesting Memoirs and Documents Relating to American Slavery, and the Glorious Struggle Now Making for Complete Emancipation*. London, Chapman Brothers, 1846.

Clement of Alexandria (Titus Flavuis Clemens). *Christ the Educator* (c. 3rd century), trans. Simon P. Wood. New York: Father of the Church, Inc., 1954.

Crow, Francis to Giles Firmin, 7 March 1686/7, *Jamaican Historical Review* 3 (1959), 54, as quoted in Richard Dunn, *Sugar and Slaves: The Rise of the Planter Class in the English West Indies*. New York: W.W. Norton, 1973. 285.

D'Aranda, Emanuel. *The History of Algiers and its Slavery* (1641). English ed. and trans. John Davies of Kidwelly. London: John Starkey, 1666.

Darwin, Charles. *Charles Darwin: An Anthology*, ed. Marston Bates and Philip S. Humphrey. Edison, N.J.: Transaction, 2009.

De Haedo, D. *Topografía e Historia de Argel* (1612). Repr. in Stephen Clissold, *The Barbary Slaves* (Totowa, N.J.: Rowman & Littlefield, 1977), 43.

De Montalvo, Garci Ordoñez. *Las Sergas de Esplandian* (1510). Potomac, MD: Scripta Humanistica, 2001.

De Tassy, Laugier. *Histoire d'Alger*. Amsterdam, 1725.

De Tocqueville, Alexis. *Democracy in America* (1835). New York: Penguin, 2003.

Dio, Cassius. *Rome*. Book 50. Cambridge Mass, Loeb Classical Library, 1917.

Douglass, Frederick. *My Bondage and My Freedom* (1855). New York: Barnes and Noble, 2005.

Essex County (Virginia) Orders, 1704–08; 1754–63.

Equiano, Olaudah. *The Interesting Narrative of the Life of Olaudah Equiano, Written by Himself with Related Documents*, 2nd edn, ed. Robert J. Allison. Boston, Mass.: Bedford/St.Martin's, 2007.

Greffe of Gaudron de Chevremont (notary), 24 March 1738. Archives Nationales de Québec-Montréal.

Harrower, John. *The Journal of John Harrower*, ed. E. M. Riley. Williamsburg, Va., 1963.

Hughes, Louis. *Thirty Years a Slave: From Bondage to Freedom, The Autobiography of Louis Hughes*. Montgomery, Ala.: NewSouth Books, 2002.

Jacob, Giles. *Poetical Register, or the Lives and Characters of the English Dramatick Poets*. London: Bettesworth, Taylor, and Battey 1723.

Jacobs, Harriet. *Incidents in the Life of a Slave Girl* (1861). Mineola, N.Y.: Dover, 2001.

James, John Thomas. *Journal of a Tour in Germany, Sweden, Russia, and Poland during the Years 1813 and 1814*. London: John Murray, 1817.

'J.C.B.' ['Jolicoeur' Charls Bonin?]. *Travels in New France* (c. 1757), ed. Sylvester K. Stevens et al. Harrisburg: Pennsylvania Historical Commission, 1941.

Juvenal. *Satire* 6. In G.G. Ramsey, ed. and trans., *Juvenal and Persius*. London: Heinemann, 1918.

Laws of Burgos (Spain) XVIII (1512–1513). Reproduced in *The Spanish Tradition in America*, ed. Charles Gibson. New York: Harper & Row, 1968.

Laws of Virginia. 'An Act Concerning Servants and Slaves,' October 1705. 4th Anne Chap KLIX 3.447 Section XVIII, title VII.

LOC letters, Charles Coatsworth Pinckney Collection, Container 1, Library of Congress, Washington DC.

L'Olivier, Abbe. *Memoirs of the Life and Adventures of Signor Rozelli, at the Hague*. London: printed for J. Morphew, 1709.

Lucas, Eliza to Miss Bartlett, April 1742. Reprinted in *The Letterbook of Eliza Lucas Pinckney, 1739–1762*, ed. Elise Pinckney (1972). Columbia, S.C.: University of South Carolina Press, 1997.

Macaulay, Zachary. *Negro Slavery*. London: Richard Taylor, 1823.

Majoribanks, Alexander. *Travels in South and North America*. London: Simpkin and Marshall, 5th edn, 1854.

Manzano, Juan Francisco. *Autobiography of a Slave*. Detroit, Mich.: Wayne State University Press, 1996.

Master of Equities Bills of Complaint, 1839:28, Charleston County, South Carolina.

Mather, Cotton. 'A narrative of Hannah Swarton containing wonderful passages relating to her captivity and delverance.' In *Puritans Among the Indians: Accounts of Captivity and Redemption, 1676–1724*, ed. Alden T. Vaughan and Edward W. Clark. Cambridge, Mass.: Harvard University Press, 1981.

Mattison, H. Louisa Piquet, *The Octaroon: Or, Inside Views of Southern Domestic Life* (New York, privately published, 1861). In Amelia A. Johnson, *Collected Black Women's Narratives*. New York: Oxford University Press, 1988.

Mishneh Torah, Book 12 ('Book of Acquisitions'). (c. 12th century). In Isadore Twersky, *The Maimonides Reader*. Springfield, N.J.: Behrman House, 1972.

Motu Proprio, 9 November 1548, in 'Confirmato Statutorum populi Romani super restitutione servorum in Urbe,' in *Statutorum Almae Urbis Romae* (Rome, 1567), repub. in John Francis Maxwell, *Slavery and the Catholic Church* (Chichester: Barry Rose, 1975), 75.

Mouette, Germaine. *Relation de Captivité*. Paris, 1683.

Musonius, Rufus. Discourse XII: 'On sexual indulgence', in Cora Lutz, *The Roman Socrates*. New Haven, Conn.: Yale University Press, 1942.

Newton, John. *The Works of John Newton*. Philadelphia, Pa.: Uriah Hunt, 1839.

Okeley, William. 'Ebenezer; or, a small monument of great mercy, appearing in the miraculous delivery of William Okeley' (1675). In *Piracy, Slavery, and Redemption: Barbary Captivity Narratives from Early Modern England*, ed. Daniel J. Vitkus and Nabil Matar. New York: Columbia University Press, 2001.

Orientius, *Commonitorium*, II, 167–8.

Pinckard, George. *Notes from the West Indies*. London: Longman Hurst, 1806.

Pitts, Joseph. 'A true and faithful account of the religion and manner of the Mohammetans, with an account of the author's being taken captive' (1704). In *Piracy, Slavery, and Redemption: Barbary Captivity Narratives from Early Modern England*, ed. Daniel J. Vitkus and Nabil Matar. New York: Columbia University Press, 2001.

Plutarch. 'Bravery of women', in *Moralia* (vol. III). Loeb Classical Library, 1931.

Plutarch. *Parallel Lives* (Loeb Classic Edition, 1920), 161–2.

Robbins, Archibald. *A Journal Comprising an Account of the Loss of the Brig 'Commerce'*. Hartford, Conn.: Andrus & Judd, 1833.

Seaver, James E. *A Narrative of the Life of Mrs. Mary Jemison* (1823). Syracuse, N.Y.: Syracuse University Press, 1990.

Seneca. *On Anger* III, 29, in *Seneca: Moral and Political Essays*, ed. John M. Cooper and J. F. Procopé (Cambridge: Cambridge University Press, 1995), 1–117.

Smith, John. *Travels and Works of Captain John Smith, President of Virginia and Admiral of New England 1580–1631* (2 vols), ed. Edward Arber and A. G. Bradley. Edinburgh: John Grant, 1910.

Smith, John. *The True Travels*. Glasgow: McElhose, 1907.

Tacitus. *The Agricola and The Germania*, trans. H. Mattingly. London: Penguin Books, 1970.

Thomas, Ella Gertrude Clanton. *The Secret Eye*.

Thwaites, Reuben Gold (ed.) *Jesuit Relations*. Cleveland, Oh.: Burrows Brothers, 1899.

Torrey, Jesse. *A Portraiture of Domestic Slavery: In the United States*. Philadelphia, Pa.: John Bioren, 1817.

Van Struys, Jan Janszoon. *The Voiages and Travels ...* London: for Abel Swalle and Sam Crowch, 1684.

Virginia Magazine of History and Biography 20 (1912), 375, 377.

Visigothic Code, ed. and trans. S. P. Scott. Boston, Mass.: Boston Book Co., 1910. Repr. Fred B. Rothman & Co., 1982.

Von Weech, F. Friedrich. *Reise über England und Portugal nach Brasilian*, 3 vols. Munich, 1831.

Walsh, Robert. *Notices of Brazil in 1828 and 1829*, 2 vols. London: Frederick Westley, 1830.

Warner of Rouen. *Moriuht* (c. 1010), trans. and comm. Christopher J. McDonough. Toronto: Pontifical Institute of Mediaeval Studies, 1995.

Secondary works

Anderson, Ellen M. 'Playing at Muslim and Christian: the construction of gender and the representation of faith in Cervantes' captivity plays'. In *Cervantes: Bulletin of the Cervantes Society of America*, 13.2 (1993).

Baptist, Edward E. ' "Cuffy," "fancy maids," and "one eyed men": rape, commodification, and the domestic slave trade in the United States'. *American Historical Review*, 106.5 (2001).

Beckles, Hilary McD. *Centering Woman: Gender Discourses in Caribbean Slave Society*. Princeton, N.J.: Markus Wiener, 1999.

Bedini, Silvio. *The Life of Bejamin Banneker: The First African American Man of Science*, 2nd edn. Baltimore: Maryland Historical Society, 1999.

Ben-Naeh, Yaron. '"Blond, tall, with honey colored eyes": Jewish ownership of slaves in the Ottoman Empire'. *Jewish History (Netherlands)* 20 (2006).

Block, Sharon. 'Lines of color, sex, and service: comparative sexual coercion in early America'. In *Sex, Love, Race: Crossing Boundaries in North American History*, ed. Martha Hodes. New York: New York University Press, 1999.

Boswell, James. *The Royal Treasure: Muslim Communities under the Crown of Aragon in the Fourteenth Century*. New Haven, Conn.: Yale University Press, 1977.

Boyer, Paul and Nissenbaum, Stephen. *Salem Possessed: The Social Origins of Witchcraft* (1973). Cambridge, Mass.: Harvard University Press, 1996.

Brooks, George E. *Eurafricans in Western Africa, Commerce, Social Status, Gender, and Religious Observance from the Sixteenth to the Eighteenth Century*. Athens, Oh.: Ohio University Press, 2003.

Brooks, George E. 'The *signare* of Saint-Louis and Gorée: women entrepreneurs in eighteenth-century Senegal'. In *Women in Africa: Studies in Social and Economic Change*, ed. Nancy J. Hafkin and Edna G. Bay. Stanford, Calif.: Stanford University Press, 1976.

Brooten, Bernadette J. *Love Between Women: Early Christian Responses to Female Homoeroticism*. Chicago, Ill.: University of Chicago Press, 1996.

Brown, Kathleen M. *Good Wives, Nasty Wenches and Anxious Patriarchs: Gender, Race and Power in Colonial Virginia*. Chapel Hill, N.C.: University of North Carolina Press, 1996.

Bruce, Kathleen. 'Slave labor in the Virginia iron industry'. *William and Mary Quarterly*, 2nd series, 7.1 (1927).

Burnard, Trevor. *Mastery, Tyranny, and Desire: Thomas Thistlewood and his Slaves in the Anglo-Jamaican World*. Chapel Hill, N.C.: University of North Carolina Press, 2004.

Bush, Barbara. 'White "ladies," coloured "favourites" and black "wenches": some considerations on sex, race and class factors in social relations in white creole society in the Caribbean'. *Slavery and Abolition* 2 (1981): 244–62.

Bush, M. L. *Servitude in Modern Times*. Cambridge: Polity, 2000.

Callender, Charles and Kochems, Lee M. 'The North American berdache'. *Current Anthropology*, 24.4 (1983): 443–56.

Camp, Stephanie M. H. *Closer to Freedom: Enslaved Women and Everyday Resistance in the Plantation South*. Chapel Hill, N.C.: University of North Carolina Press, 2004.

Cecil-Fronsman, Bill. *Common Whites: Class and Culture in Antebellum North Carolina*. Lawrence, Kans.: University Press of Kansas, 1992.

Clinton, Catherine. *The Plantation Mistress: Women's World in the Old South*. New York: Pantheon, 1982.

Clissold, Stephen. *The Barbary Slaves*. Totowa, N.J.: Rowman & Littlefield, 1977.

Cobin, David M. 'A brief look at Jewish law of manumission'. *Chicago-Kent Law Review*, 70 (1995).

Coleman, Emma Lewis. *New England Captives Carried to Canada*. Portland, Maine: Southworth Press, 1925.

Colley, Linda. *Captives: Britain, Empire, and the World, 1600–1850*. London: Jonathan Cape, 2002.

Constable, Olivia Remie. *Trade and Traders in Muslim Spain: The Commercial Realignment of the Iberian Peninsula, 900–1500*. Cambridge: Cambridge University Press, 1996.

Davis, David Brion. 'Introduction'. In *A Historical Guide to World Slavery*, ed. S. Drescher and S. L. Engerman. New York: Oxford University Press, 1998.

Davis, Robert C. *Christian Slaves, Muslim Masters: White Slavery in the Mediterranean, the Barbary Coast, and Italy, 1500–1800*. Basingstoke: Palgrave Macmillan, 2003.

De Landa, Diego. *Yucatan Before and After the Conquest* (1566), trans. William Gates. Mineola, NY: Dover Publications, 1978.

Demos, John. *The Unredeemed Captive: A Family Story from Early America*. New York: Knopf, 1993.

Dias, Maria Odila Silva. *Power and Everyday Life: The Lives of Working Women in Nineteenth-Century Brazil*. Cambridge: Polity Press, 1995.

Dillard, Heath. *Daughters of the Reconquest: Women in Castilan Town Society, 1100–1300*. Cambridge: Cambridge University Press, 1984.

Dillon, Sheila and Welch, Katherine E. (eds). *Representations of War in Ancient Rome*. Cambridge: Cambridge University Press, 2006.

Diouf, Sylvaine A. *Fighting the Slave Trade: West African Strategies.* Oxford: James Currey, 2003.

Dolan, Frances Elizabeth. *Dangerous Familiars: Representations of Domestic Crime in England, 1550–1700.* Ithaca, N.Y.: Cornell University Press, 1994.

Dornan, Inge. 'Masterful women: colonial women slaveholders in the urban low country'. *Journal of American Studies* (UK), 39 (2005).

Dunaway, Wilma A. *Slavery in the American Mountain South.* Cambridge: Cambridge University Press, 2003.

Eason, Lillian Ashcroft. '"She hath voluntarily come": a Gambian woman trader in colonial Georgia in the eighteenth century'. In *Identity in the Shadow of Slavery,* ed. Paul E. Lovejoy. New York: Continuum, 2000.

Evans-Grubbs, Judith. '"Marriage more shameful than adultery": slave–mistress relationships, "mixed marriages," and late Roman law'. *Phoenix,* 47 (1993).

Fairchilds, Cissie C. *Domestic Enemies: Servants and their Masters in Old Regime France.* Baltimore, Md.: Johns Hopkins University Press, 1984.

Fall, Fatima. 'The place of women in the museum of Saint-Louis'. In *Museums and Urban Culture in West Africa, ed.* Alexis B. A. Adandé and Emanuel Arinze. Oxford: James Currey, 2002.

Faust, Drew Gilpin. *Mothers of Invention: Women of the Slaveholding South in the American Civil War.* New York: Vintage, 1996.

Fawver, Kate. 'Women's economies in the Chesapeake: the organization of labor in plantation society'. Paper for the Program for Early American Economy and Society, 1 October 2004.

Finck, Henry T. *Primitive Love and Love-Stories.* New York: Charles Scribner's Sons, 1899.

Fischer, David Hackett. *Albion's Seed: Four British Folkways in America.* New York: Oxford University Press, 1989.

Fisher, Geoffrey. *Barbary Legend: War, Trade, and Piracy in North Africa* (1957). Westport, Conn.: Greenwood Press, 1974.

Foster, David William (ed.). *Spanish Writers on Gay and Lesbian Themes: A Bio-Cultural Sourcebook* Westport, Conn.: Greenwood Press, 1999.

Foster, William Henry. 'Perceptions and realities of the Muslim threat to early Stuart England: sources of discontent and disorder'. Unpublished paper, Cornell University, 1995.

Foster, William Henry. *The Captors' Narrative: Catholic Women and their Puritan Men on the Early American Frontier.* Ithaca, N.Y.: Cornell University Press, 2003.

Foster, W. H. 'Women slave owners face their historians: versions of maternalism in Atlantic World slavery', *Patterns of Prejudice,* vol. 41, nos. 3–4, 2007), 303–20.

Friedman, Ellen G. *Spanish Captives in North Africa in the Early Modern Age.* Madison, Wis.: University of Wisconsin Press, 1983.

Gallay, Allan. *The Indian Slave Trade: The Rise of the English Empire in the American South, 1670–1717.* New Haven, Conn.: Yale University Press, 2002.

Geiser, Karl Frederick. 'Redemptioners and indentured servants in the colony and commonwealth of Pennsylvania'. *Supplement to the Yale Review* 10.2 (1901).

Gerber, Haim. 'Social and economic position of women in an Ottoman City, Bursa, 1600–1700'. *International Journal of Middle East Studies,* 12 (1980): 231–44.

Gibbon, Edward. *The History of the Decline and Fall of the Roman Empire,* vol. 7, (London: Bell and Daldy, 1866).

Glancy, Jennifer A. *Slavery in Early Christianity.* New York: Oxford University Press, 2002.

Goodnow, Everett. Review of *Primitive Love* by Henry T. Finck. *American Historical Review,* 6.1 (1900), 108–10.

Goodwin, Godfrey. *The Private World of Ottoman Women* (1997). London: Saqi Books, 2006.

Gower, Eleanor. 'Indentured and convict runaways in Pennsylvania, c.1730–76'. BA dissertation, Cambridge University, 2008.

Graham, Sarah Lauderdale. *House and Street: The Domestic World of Servants and Masters in Nineteenth-Century Rio de Janeiro.* Austin: University of Texas Press, 1992.

Grey, Rose. 'Eliza Lucas Pinckney and imperial daughterhood in colonial South Carolina'. BA dissertation, Cambridge University Faculty of History, 2009.

Grimm, Jacob and Grimm, Wilhem. 'Der Mann im Pflug'. *Deutsche Sagen,* vol. 2 (1818), no. 357.

Hadley, Arthur Twining. *Economies: An Account of the Relations between Private Property and Public Welfare.* New York: Ayer, 1972.

Haefeli, Evan and Kevin Sweeney. *Captors and Captives: The 1704 French and Indian Raid on Deerfield.* Amherst, Mass.: University of Massachusetts Press, 2003.

Hallett, Judith P. 'Female homoeroticism and the denial of Roman reality in Latin literature'. *Yale Journal of Criticism,* 3 (1989): 209–27.

Hanger, Kimberly S. *Bounded Lives, Bounded Places: Free Black Society in Colonial New Orleans, 1769–1803.* Durham, N.C.: Duke University Press, 1997.

Harris, Dawn. 'Female slaves not women'. *Barbados Nation,* 6 June 1999.

Heers, Jacques. *Esclaves et Domestiques au Moyen Age dans la Monde Mediterranéen.* Paris: Fayard, 1981.

Henzer, Catherine. *Jewish Slavery in Antiquity.* Oxford: Oxford University Press, 2005.

Houston, Stephen, Stuart, David and Taube, Karl. *The Memory of Bones: Body, Being, and Experience among the Classic Maya.* Austin, Tex.: University of Texas Press, 2006.

Hoyland, Robert G. *Seeing Islam as Others Saw It: A Survey and Evaluation of Christian, Jewish, and Zoroastrian Writings on Early Islam.* Princeton, N.J.: Darwin Press, 1997.

Jones, Arthur. *Pierre Toussaint.* New York: Doubleday, 2003.

Jones, Cecily. 'Contesting the boundaries of gender, race, and sexuality in Barbadian plantation society'. *Women's History Review,* 12 (2003).

Karasch, Mary C. *Slave Life in Rio de Janeiro, 1808–1850*. Princeton, N.J.: Princeton University Press, 1986.

Karlsen, Carol F. *The Devil in the Shape of a Woman: Witchcraft in Colonial New England*. New York: W.W. Norton, 1998.

Karras, Ruth Mazzo. 'Servitude and sexuality in medieval Iceland'. In *From Sagas to Society: Comparative Approaches to Early Iceland*, ed. Gísli Pálsson. Enfield Lock: Hisarlik Press, 1992.

Klause, John. 'The two occasions of Donne's *Lamentations of Jeremy*'. *Modern Philology*, 90.3 (1993).

Klein, Herbert S. and Vida Luna, Francisco. *Slavery and the Economy of Sao Paulo, 1750–1850*. Stanford, Calif.: Stanford University Press, 2003.

Koch, Bernard. 'Vincent de Paul (Saint)'. In *Catholicisme*, 15.

Koger, Larry. *Black Slaveowners: Free Black Slave Masters in South Carolina, 1790–1860*. Jefferson, N.C.: McFarland, 1985.

Langley, Lester D. *The Americas in the Age of Revolution, 1750–1850*. New Haven, Conn.: Yale University Press, 1998.

Lazreg, Marnia. *The Eloquence of Silence: Algerian Women in Question*. New York: Routledge, 1994.

Lemaire, Gérard-Georges. *The Orient in Western Art*. Cologne: Könemann, 2001.

Lerner, Gerda. *The Creation of Patriarchy*. New York: Oxford University Press, 1986.

Lilja, Saara. *Homosexuality in Republican and Augustan Rome*. Commentationes Humanarum Litterarum 74, Helsinki: Societas Scientiarum Fennica, 1983.

Macaulay, T. B. *The History of England from the Accession of James II*. Philadelphia, Pa.: Porter & Coates, 1866.

MacCormack, Carol. 'Slaves, slave owners, and slave dealers: Sherbro coast and hinterlands'. In *Women and Slavery in Africa*, ed. Claire C. Robertson and Martin A. Klein. Portsmouth, N.H.: Heinemann, 1997.

Martín, Adrienne L. 'Images of deviance in Cervantes's Algiers'. In *Cervantes: Bulletin of the Cervantes Society of America*, 15.2 (1995).

Matar, Nabil. *Turks, Moors, and Englishmen in the Age of Discovery*. New York: Columbia University Press, 1999.

McDonald, Joyce Green. *Women and Race in Early Modern Texts*. Cambridge: Cambridge University Press, 2002.

Messerschmidt, James W. '"We must protect our southern women": of whiteness, masculinities, and lynching'. In *Regulating Difference: Race, Gender, and Punishment in America*, ed. M. Bosworth and J. Flavin. New Brunswick, N.J.: Rutgers University Press, 2005.

Moitt, Bernard. *Women and Slavery in the French Antilles, 1635–1848*. Bloomington and Indianapolis: Indiana University Press, 2001.

Moreau, Marthe. *L'Age d'Or des Religieuses: Monastères féminins de Languedoc méditerranéen au Moyen Age*. Montpellier, France: Presses de Languedoc, 1988, 122–3.

Morgan, Gwenda and Rushton, Peter. *Eighteenth-Century Criminal Transportation: The Formation of the Criminal Atlantic*. London: Palgrave Macmillan, 2004.

Morgan, Gwenda and Rushton, Peter. 'Visible bodies: power, subordination, and identity in the eighteenth-century Atlantic world'. *Journal of Social History*, 39.1 (2005).

Morrissey, Marietta. *Slave Women in the New World*. Lawrence, Kans.: University Press of Kansas, 1989.

Mouser, Bruce L. 'Women slavers of Guinea-Conakry'. In *Women and Slavery in Africa*, ed. Claire C. Robertson and Martin A. Klein. Madison, Wis.: University of Wisconsin Press, 1983.

Naro, Nancy Priscilla. *A Slave's Place, A Master's World: Fashioning Dependency in Rural Brazil*. London: Continuum, 2000.

Nash, Alice. 'The abiding frontier'. PhD dissertation, Columbia University, 1997.

Necipoglu, G. *Architecture, Ceremonial, and Power*. Cambridge, Mass.: Harvard University Press, 1991.

Nieboer, H. J. *Slavery as an Industrial System: Ethnological Researches*. 2nd rev. edn. Philadelphia, Pa.: Free Library of Philadelphia, 1910.

Nirenberg, David. 'Conversion, sex, and segregation: Jews and Christians in Medieval Spain'. *American Historical Review*, 107.4 (October 2002).

Noel, Jan. 'New France: les femmes favoriseés'. *Atlantis*, 6.2 (1981).

Olwell, Robert. *Masters, Slaves, and Subjects: The Culture of Power in the South Carolina Low Country*. Ithaca, N.Y.: Cornell University Press, 1998.

Operé, Fernando. *Historias de la frontera, el cautiverio en la America hispanica*. Buenos Aires: Fondo de Cultura Economica, 2001.

Osiek, Carolyn. 'Vision of Rhoda'. In *Shepherd of Hermas: A Commentary*. Minneapolis: Augsberg Fortress, 1999.

Osiek, Carolyn, and McDonald, Margaret Y. *A Woman's Place: House Churches in Early Christianity*. Minneapolis, Minn.: Fortress Press, 2006.

Paley, Ruth. 'Imperial politics and English law: the many contexts of Somerset'. *Law and History Review*, 24.3 (2006).

Patterson, Orlando. *Slavery and Social Death: A Comparative Study*. Cambridge, Mass.: Harvard University Press, 1981.

Pelteret, David. 'Slave raiding and slave trading in early England'. In *Anglo-Saxon England* 9, ed. Peter Clemoes. Cambridge: Cambridge University Press, 1981.

Perry, Mary Elizabeth. *Crime and Society in Early Modern Seville*. Hanover, N.H.: University Press of New England, 1980.

Pike, Ruth. *Aristocrats and Traders: Sevillian Society in the Sixteenth Century*. Ithaca, N.Y.: Cornell University Press, 1972.

Playfair, Robert Lambert. *The Scourge of Christendom*. London: Smith, Elder & Co, 1884.

Prestel, David K. 'The Tale of Moses the Hungarian: from Egypt to the Land of Promise'. *Slavic and East European Journal*, 42.2 (1998).

Perdue, Theda. *Cherokee Women: Gender and Cultural Change, 1700–1835*. Lincoln, Neb.: University of Nebraska Press, 1999.

Richter, Daniel K. *The Ordeal of the Longhouse: The Peoples of the Iroquois League in the Era of European Colonization*. Chapel Hill, N.C.: University of North Carolina Press, 1994.

Roberts, Hazel Van Dyke. 'Anthony Jansen Van Sallee'. *New York Genealogical and Biographical Society Record* 103.1: 16–28.

Roscoe, Thomas. *Lives of the Kings of England from the Norman Conquest.* Philadephia, Pa.: Lea & Blanchard, 1846.

Salisbury, Neal. *Manitou and Providence: Indians, Europeans, and the Making of New England, 1500–1643.* New York: Oxford University Press, 1982.

Schwartz, Stuart B. and Salomon, Frank. 'South American indigenous societies (colonial era)'. In *The Cambridge History of the Native Peoples of the Americas,* ed. Frank Salomon and Stuart B. Schwartz. Cambridge: Cambridge University Press, 2000.

Semmes, Raphael. *Crime and Punishment in Early Maryland.* Baltimore, Md.: Johns Hopkins University Press, 1938.

Shammas, Carole. *A History of Household Government in America.* Charlottesville, Va.: University Press of Virginia, 2002.

Shaw, Brent D. *Spartacus and the Slave Wars.* Boston, Mass.: Bedford/St Martin's, 2001.

Shoemaker, Nancy. 'Kateri Tekawitha's tortuous path to sainthood'. In *Negotiators of Change: Historical Perspectives on Native American Women,* ed. Nancy Shoemaker. New York: Routledge, 1995.

Sigal, Pete. *From Moon Goddesses to Virgins: The Colonization of Yucatan Maya Sexual Desire.* Austin, Tex.: University of Texas Press, 2000.

Smith, Steven R. 'The ideal and reality: apprentice–master relations in seventeenth-century London'. *History of Education Quarterly,* 21.4 (1981), 449–59.

Snyder, Terri L. '"As if there was not master or woman in the land": gender, dependency, and household violence in Virginia, 1646–1720'. In *Over the Threshold: Intimate Violence in Early America,* ed. Christine Daniels and Michael V. Kennedy. New York: Routledge, 1999, 219–36.

Snyder, Terri L. Review of Carla Anzilotti, *In the Affairs of the World: Women, Patriarchy, and Power in Colonial South Carolina. William and Mary Quarterly,* 3rd ser., 60.1.

Socolow, Susan Migden. 'Spanish captives in Indian Societies: cultural contact along the Argentine frontier, 1600–1835'. *Hispanic American Historical Review,* 72.1 (1992).

Somerville, Margaret R. *Sex and Subjection: Attitudes to Women in Early-Modern Society.* London: Arnold, 1995.

Soyer, François. 'Muslim slaves and freedmen in medieval Portugal'. *Al-Qantara,* 28.2 (2007).

Stuard, Susan Mosher. 'Ancillary evidence for the decline of medieval slavery', *Past and Present,* 149 (November 1995).

Stuard, Susan Mosher. 'Urban domestic slavery in medieval Ragusa'. *Journal of Medieval History,* 9 (1983).

Thornton, Lynn. *Women as Portrayed in Orientalist Painting.* Paris: ACR, 1994.

Toledano, Ehud R. *Slavery and Abolition in the Ottoman Middle East.* Seattle: University of Washington Press, 1998.

Trexler, Richard C. *Dependence in Context in Renaissance Florence*. Binghamton, N.Y.: Medieval and Renaissance Texts and Studies, vol. 111, 1994.

Trexler, Richard C. *Sex and Conquest: Gendered Violence, Political Order, and the European Conquest of the Americas*. Ithaca, N.Y.: Cornell University Press, 1995.

Tyler, Lyon G. 'Grammar and Mattey Practice and Model School'. *William and Mary College Quarterly Historical Magazine* 4.1 (1895): 3–14.

Tyrwhitt, R. St. J. 'Aetius', in *A Dictionary of Early Christian Biography*, ed. Henry Wace and William C. Piercy. London: John Murray, 1911.

Ulrich, Laurel Thatcher. *Good Wives: Image and Reality in the Lives of Women in Northern New England, 1650–1750* (1980). New York: Vintage, 1991.

Usner, Daniel H. Jr, *Indians, Settlers, and Slaves in a Frontier Exchange Economy: The Lower Mississippi Valley Before 1783*. Chapel Hill, N.C.: University of North Carolina Press, 1992.

Verstraete, Beerte C. and Provencal, Vernon. *Same-Sex Desire and Love in Greco-Roman Antiquity and in the Classical Tradition of the West*. New York: Haworth Press, 2006.

Veyne, Paul, Ariès, Phillipe, Duby, Georges and Goldhammer, Arthur. *A History of Private Life, Volume I: From Pagan Rome to Byzantium*, trans. Arthur Goldhammer. Cambridge, Mass.: Harvard University Press, 1987.

Viau, Roland. *Femmes de personne: Sexes, genres, et pouvoirs en Iroquoisie ancienne*. Montreal: Boréal, 2000.

Vidal-Naquet, Pierre. *The Black Hunter: Forms of Thought and Forms of Society in the Greek World*. Baltimore, Md.: Johns Hopkins University Press, n.d.

Vriman, L.C. *Kaapvaart en zeroverij*. Amsterdam: privately published, 1938.

Walzer, Michael et al. (eds). *The Jewish Political Tradition*. (2 vols). New Haven, Conn.: Yale University Press.

Watson, Alan D. 'Women in colonial North Carolina: overlooked and underestimated'. *North Carolina Historical Review*, 58 (1981).

Weber, David J. *Bárbaros*. New Haven: Yale University Press.

Weinbaum, Batya. *Islands of Women and Amazons: Representations and Realities*. Austin. Tex.: University of Texas Press, 2000, 71.

Westermann, William L. *Slave Systems of Greek and Roman Antiquity*. Philadelphia, Pa.: American Philosophical Society, 1955, 17.

White, Richard. *The Middle Ground: Indians, Empires, and Republics in the Great Lakes Region, 1650–1815*. New York: Cambridge University Press, 1991.

Whitman, T. Stephen. *The Price of Freedom: Slavery and Manumission in Baltimore and Early National Maryland*. Lexington: University Press of Kentucky, 1997.

Wood, Betty. *Slavery in Colonial America, 1619–1776*. Lanham, Md.: Rowman & Littlefield, 2005.

Woodson, Carter G. *Free Negro Heads of Families in 1830*. Washington, D.C.: Association for the Study of Negro Life and History, 1925.

Wyke, Maria. *The Roman Mistress: Ancient and Modern Representations*. Oxford: Oxford University Press, 2002.

Yermolenko, Galina. 'Roxolana: the greatest empress of the East'. *The Muslim World*, 9.2 (2005).

Anonymous and attributed newspaper sources

American Anti Slavery Society, *Anti-Slavery Examiner Ominbus*, part 19, chs 2 and 4.

Daily Constitutionalist (Augusta, Ga.), 1 September 1864, p. 1 c. 3.

Holmes, Joseph as interviewed by Ila B Prine, 11 June 1937. *The American Slave* supp. Ser 2, vol. 1: 5–11, 6.

'Recollections of slavery by a runaway slave'. *The Emancipator*, 23 August 1838. ser 1-1308 Davis Library, University of North Carolina, Chapel Hill.

Pennsylvania Gazette, 11 April 1751.

Ringle, Ken. 'Up through slavery'. *Washington Post*, 12 May 2002.

Online and multimedia sources

Baldwin, Robert. 'Actaeon and the allegory of vision in Hogarth's *Marriage à la Mode IV: La Toilette*' [painting c. 1734].

Brown, Sterling. 'Negro character as seen by white authors' (1933), reprinted in *Dark Symphony: Negro Literature in America*, ed. James A. Emanuel and Theodore L. Gross (New York: Free Press, 1968), 159. Thanks to Kathy Davis for the reference. See Davis, 'Lydia Maria Child's "The Quadroons" and "Slavery's Pleasant Homes"' in *The Online Archive of Nineteenth-Century US Women's Writings*.

Bruyneel, Mark (Vrije Universiteit Amsterdam) 'Jan Janszoon van Haalem (seventeenth century)'. http://zeerovery.nl/history/janszoon.htm.

Burwell-Guy family papers (1820–59), Clements Library, University of Michigan. See www.clements.umich.edu/webguides/b/burwell.html.

'Caroline A. Turner', entry for 'A Kentuckian's story', HS 108 Project, www.bluegrass.kctcs.edu/HIS/108/project1.html

'Charlotte' and 'William Solomon', entries for 'A Kentuckian's story', HS 108 Project, www.bluegrass.kctcs.edu/HIS/108/project1.html.

Harris, Kim and Reggie. *Notes to 'Steal Away: Songs of the Underground Railroad'* (sound recording).

Account of Robert Hendron in the family record kept by Jay McAfree. Thanks to McAfee for posting this manuscript at http://genforum.genealogy.com/hendren/messages/407.html

Interview with Henry Wiencek (author of *Slave and Slavery in George Washington's World*), *Common-Place*, 6.4 (July 2006). Available at http://www.historycooperative.org/journals/cp/vol-06/no-04/reading/

Midrash for the Torah Portion Naso, may be viewed at: www.jewishgates.com/file.asp.

MT Avadim 1:2, may be viewed at: www.shamash.or/listarchives/top/top.mishpatim-fullstudy.2002.

Mutahhari, Murtaza. *The Islamic Modest Dress* (Qum, Iran: Dar us Sequafe), repr. and trans. Ahlul Bayt Digital Library Project, ch. 6, para. 30.

Nagle, George F. 'Fugitive slave incidents in Central Pennsylvania', Afrolumens Project (www. afrolumens.org), 8.

Pamphilus, Eusebius. *Church History, Life of Constantine, Oration in Praise of Constantine*, excerpted from *Christian Classics Etherial Library* (Calvin College), 2005. NPNF V2 01.

Pennsylvania Correctional Industries. 'A historical overview of inmate labour in Pennsylvania' (official publication).

Quotations from Henry Philips, Jr, 'History of the Mexicans as told in their paintings', *Proceedings of the American Philosophical Society*, 21:6 (1883), 641. My gratitude to editor Alec Christensen for making this valuable resource available online through famsi.org (Foundation for the Advancement of Mesoamerican Studies).

Plymouth Court Records 2:73. In Galle, Jillian. 'Servants and masters in the Plymouth Colony,' Plymouth Colony Archive Project, 1998–2000. www. people.viginia.edu/~jfd3a/Plymouth/Galle1.html.

Sahih Bukhari (hadith), vol. 3, book 46, nos 713, 719, 735, 736. See the Universty of Southern California's website for the Center for Muslim–Jewish Engagement, http://www.usc.edu/schools/college/crcc/engagement/resources/texts/muslim/hadith/bukhari.

Sayyid Sa'eed Akhtar Rizvi, *Slavery from Islamic and Christian Perspectives*, 2nd edn (Vancouver, BC, Canada: Islamic Educational Foundation, 1987), ch. 4, sect. 1.

Schulchan Aruch, part II, Yoreh De'ah, chapter 21 'Slaves and proselytes,' 267:19 (16th century). May be viewed at www.torah.org/advanced/sculchan-aruch/classes/chapter21.html

Wilson, James Theron. 'Sinespe libertatis: slavery in Hungary under the House of Arpad'. MA thesis, Indiana University, 1998. HTML formatting by Patrick Feaster, Institute of Hungarian Studies at Indiana University: see http://www.indiana.edu/~iuihsl/wilson.htm.

Zabin, Serena. 'Women's Trading Networks and Dangerous Economies'. http://www.librarycompany.org/Economics/PDF%20Files/Zabin.pdf.

Biblical references (all quotations from King James version)

Leviticus 25: 39; Judges 4: 1–5; Exodus 23: 9; Leviticus 24: 22; Numbers 15: 15–16; Exodus 21:20, 26–7; Deuteronomy 22: 25–7; 23:15–16; Leviticus 19: 20–2; Deuteronomy 21: 13. Deuteronomy 22: 25–7; Leviticus 19: 20–2. Exodus 21: 26. Acts of the Apostles 16: 14–15.

Index